LIST OF CONTRIBUTORS

Dr WG Dixon MSc MRCP(UK)
Specialist Registrar in Rheumatology and Clinical Reserch Fellow
ARC Epidemiology Unit and British Society of Rheumatology Biologics
Register
University of Manchester

Dr B Griffiths MD FRCP
Consultant Rheumatologist
Freeman Hospital
Newcastle Upon Tyne

Dr HJ Longhurst MA PhD FRCP FRCPath
Consultant Immunologist and Lead Clinical, Immunopathology and
Clinical Immunology
St Bartholomew's Hospital and the London NHS Trust
London

Dr SA Misbah MSc FRCP FRCPath
Consultant Clinical Immunologist and Honorary Senior Clinical Lecturer in
Immunology
Oxford Radcliffe Hospitals NHS Trust and University of Oxford
Churchill and John Radcliffe Hospitals
Oxford

Dr N Snowden FRCP FRCPath
Consultant Rheumatologist and Clinical Immunologist
North Manchester General Hospital
Manchester

Royal College
of Physicians
Setting higher medical standards

Published by:
Royal College of Physicians of London
11 St. Andrews Place
Regent's Park
London NW1 4LE
United Kingdom

Set and printed by Graphicraft Limited, Hong Kong

First edition published 2001
Reprinted 2004
Second edition published 2008

ISBN: 978-1-86016-275-6 (this book)
ISBN: 978-1-86016-260-2 (set)

Distribution Information:
Jerwood Medical Education Resource Centre
Royal College of Physicians of London
11 St. Andrews Place
Regent's Park
London NW1 4LE
United Kingdom
Tel: +44 (0)207 935 1174 ext 422/490
Fax: +44 (0)207 486 6653
Email: merc@rcplondon.ac.uk
Web: http://www.rcplondon.ac.uk/

CONTENTS

List of contributors iii
Foreword vii
Preface viii
Acknowledgements x
Key features xi

RHEUMATOLOGY AND CLINICAL IMMUNOLOGY

PACES Stations and Acute Scenarios 3

1.1 History-taking 3
1.1.1 Recurrent chest infections 3
1.1.2 Recurrent meningitis 5
1.1.3 Recurrent facial swelling and abdominal pain 7
1.1.4 Recurrent skin abscesses 9
1.1.5 Flushing and skin rash 12
1.1.6 Drug-induced anaphylaxis 14
1.1.7 Arthralgia, purpuric rash and renal impairment 16
1.1.8 Arthralgia and photosensitive rash 19
1.1.9 Cold fingers and difficulty swallowing 23
1.1.10 Dry eyes and fatigue 25
1.1.11 Breathlessness and weakness 27
1.1.12 Low back pain 30
1.1.13 Chronic back pain 32
1.1.14 Recurrent joint pain and stiffness 33
1.1.15 Foot drop and weight loss in a patient with rheumatoid arthritis 35
1.1.16 Fever, myalgia, arthralgia and elevated acute-phase indices 38
1.1.17 Non-rheumatoid pain and stiffness 40
1.1.18 Widespread pain 42

1.2 Clinical examination 44
1.2.1 Hands (general) 44
1.2.2 Non-rheumatoid pain and stiffness: generalised osteoarthritis 45
1.2.3 Rheumatoid arthritis 46
1.2.4 Psoriatic arthritis 47
1.2.5 Systemic sclerosis 49
1.2.6 Chronic tophaceous gout 49
1.2.7 Ankylosing spondylitis 50
1.2.8 Deformity of bone: Paget's disease 51
1.2.9 Marfan's syndrome 51

1.3 Communication skills and ethics 52
1.3.1 Collapse during a restaurant meal 52
1.3.2 Cold fingers and difficulty swallowing 54
1.3.3 Back pain 55
1.3.4 Widespread pain 56
1.3.5 Explain a recommendation to start a disease-modifying antirheumatic drug 57

1.4 Acute scenarios 59
1.4.1 Fulminant septicaemia in an asplenic woman 59
1.4.2 Collapse during a restaurant meal 61
1.4.3 Systemic lupus erythematosus and confusion 64
1.4.4 Acute hot joints 66
1.4.5 A crush fracture 69

Diseases and Treatments 72

2.1 Immunodeficiency 72
2.1.1 Primary antibody deficiency 72
2.1.2 Combined T-cell and B-cell defects 75
2.1.3 Chronic granulomatous disease 77
2.1.4 Cytokine and cytokine-receptor deficiencies 78
2.1.5 Terminal pathway complement deficiency 80
2.1.6 Hyposplenism 81

2.2 Allergy 82
2.2.1 Anaphylaxis 82
2.2.2 Mastocytosis 84
2.2.3 Nut allergy 85
2.2.4 Drug allergy 87

2.3 Rheumatology 88
2.3.1 Carpal tunnel syndrome 88
2.3.2 Osteoarthritis 89
2.3.3 Rheumatoid arthritis 91
2.3.4 Seronegative spondyloarthropathies 94
2.3.5 Idiopathic inflammatory myopathies 98
2.3.6 Crystal arthritis: gout 99
2.3.7 Calcium pyrophosphate deposition disease 101
2.3.8 Fibromyalgia 101

2.4 Autoimmune rheumatic diseases 103
2.4.1 Systemic lupus erythematosus 103
2.4.2 Sjögren's syndrome 105
2.4.3 Systemic sclerosis (scleroderma) 106

2.5 Vasculitides 109
2.5.1 Giant-cell arteritis and polymyalgia rheumatica 109
2.5.2 Wegener's granulomatosis 111
2.5.3 Polyarteritis nodosa 113
2.5.4 Cryoglobulinaemic vasculitis 114
2.5.5 Behçet's disease 115
2.5.6 Takayasu's arteritis 117
2.5.7 Systemic Still's disease 119

CONTENTS

Investigations and Practical Procedures 121

3.1 **Assessment of acute-phase response** 121
  3.1.1 Erythrocyte sedimentation rate 121
  3.1.2 C-reactive protein 121
3.2 **Serological investigation of autoimmune rheumatic disease** 122
  3.2.1 Antibodies to nuclear antigens 122
  3.2.2 Antibodies to double-stranded DNA 123
  3.2.3 Antibodies to extractable nuclear antigens 124
  3.2.4 Rheumatoid factor 125
  3.2.5 Antineutrophil cytoplasmic antibody 125
  3.2.6 Serum complement concentrations 125
3.3 **Suspected immune deficiency in adults** 126
3.4 **Imaging in rheumatological disease** 129
  3.4.1 Plain radiology 129
  3.4.2 Bone densitometry 130
  3.4.3 Magnetic resonance imaging 131
  3.4.4 Nuclear medicine 131
  3.4.5 Ultrasound 132
3.5 **Arthrocentesis** 132
3.6 **Corticosteroid injection techniques** 133
3.7 **Immunoglobulin replacement** 135

Self-assessment 138

4.1 **Self-assessment questions** 138
4.2 **Self-assessment answers** 141

The Medical Masterclass Series 144
Index 160

Since its initial publication in 2001, *Medical Masterclass* has been regarded as a key learning and teaching resource for physicians around the world. The resource was produced in part to meet the vision of the Royal College of Physicians: *'Doctors of the highest quality, serving patients well'*. This vision continues and, along with advances in clinical practice and changes in the format of the MRCP(UK) exam, has justified the publication of this second edition.

The MRCP(UK) is an international examination that seeks to advance the learning of and enhance the training process for physicians worldwide. On passing the exam physicians are recognised as having attained the required knowledge, skills and manner appropriate for training at a specialist level. However, passing the exam is a challenge. The pass rate at each sitting of the written papers is about 40%. Even the most prominent consultants have had to sit each part of the exam more than once in order to pass. With this challenge in mind, the College has produced *Medical Masterclass*, a comprehensive learning resource to help candidates with the preparation that is key to making the grade.

Medical Masterclass has been produced by the Education Department of the College. A work of this size represents a formidable amount of effort by the Editor-in-Chief – Dr John Firth – and his team of editors and authors. I would like to thank our colleagues for this wonderful educational product and wholeheartedly recommend it as an invaluable learning resource for all physicians preparing for their MRCP(UK) examination.

Professor Ian Gilmore MD PRCP
President of the Royal College of Physicians

PREFACE

The second edition of *Medical Masterclass* is produced and published by the Education Department of the Royal College of Physicians of London. It comprises 12 textbooks, a companion interactive website and two CD-ROMs. Its aim is to help doctors in their first few years of training to improve their medical knowledge and skills; and in particular to (a) learn how to deal with patients who are acutely ill, and (b) pass postgraduate examinations, such as the MRCP(UK) or European Diploma in Internal Medicine.

The 12 textbooks are divided as follows: two cover the scientific background to medicine, one is devoted to general clinical skills [including specific guidance on exam technique for PACES, the practical assessment of clinical examination skills that is the final part of the MRCP(UK) exam], one deals with acute medicine and the other eight cover the range of medical specialties.

The core material of each of the medical specialties is dealt with in seven sections:

- Case histories – you are presented with letters of referral commonly received in each specialty and led through the ways in which the patients' histories should be explored, and what should then follow in the way of investigation and/or treatment.

- Physical examination scenarios – these emphasise the logical analysis of physical signs and sensible clinical reasoning: 'having found this, what would you do?'

- Communication and ethical scenarios – what are the difficult issues that commonly arise in each specialty? What do you actually say to the 'frequently asked (but still very difficult) questions?'

- Acute presentations – what are the priorities if you are the doctor seeing the patient in the Emergency Department or the Medical Admissions Unit?

- Diseases and treatments – structured concise notes.

- Investigations and practical procedures – more short and to-the-point notes.

- Self assessment questions – in the form used in the MRCP(UK) Part 1 and Part 2 exams.

The companion website – which is continually updated – enables you to take mock MRCP(UK) Part 1 or Part 2 exams, or to be selective in the questions you tackle (if you want to do ten questions on cardiology, or any other specialty, you can do). For every question you complete you can see how your score compares with that of others who have logged onto the site and attempted it. The two CD-ROMs each contain 30 interactive cases requiring diagnosis and treatment.

I hope that you enjoy using *Medical Masterclass* to learn more about medicine, which – whatever is happening politically to primary care, hospitals and medical career structures – remains a wonderful occupation. It is sometimes intellectually and/or emotionally very challenging, and also sometimes extremely rewarding, particularly when reduced to the essential of a doctor trying to provide best care for a patient.

John Firth DM FRCP
Editor-in-Chief

ACKNOWLEDGEMENTS

Medical Masterclass has been produced by a team. The names of those who have written or edited material are clearly indicated elsewhere, but without the support of many other people it would not exist. Naming names is risky, but those worthy of particular note include: Sir Richard Thompson (College Treasurer) and Mrs Winnie Wade (Director of Education), who steered the project through committees that are traditionally described as labyrinthine, and which certainly seem so to me; and also Arthur Wadsworth (Project Co-ordinator) and Don Liu in the College Education Department office. Don is a veteran of the first edition of *Medical Masterclass*, and it would be fair to say that without his great efforts a second edition might not have seen the light of day.

John Firth DM FRCP
Editor-in-Chief

We have created a range of icon boxes that sit among the text of the various *Medical Masterclass* modules. They are there to help you identify key information and to make learning easier and more enjoyable. Here is a brief explanation:

> Iron-deficiency anaemia with a change in bowel habit in a middle-aged or older patient means colonic malignancy until proved otherwise.

This icon is used to highlight points of particular importance.

> Dietary deficiency is very rarely, if ever, the sole cause of iron-deficiency anaemia.

This icon is used to indicate common or important drug interactions, pitfalls of practical procedures, or when to take symptoms or signs particularly seriously.

RHEUMATOLOGY AND CLINICAL IMMUNOLOGY

Authors:

WG Dixon, B Griffiths, HJ Longhurst, SA Misbah and N Snowden

Editor:

SA Misbah

Editor-in-Chief:

JD Firth

1.1 History-taking

1.1.1 Recurrent chest infections

> ### Letter of referral to immunology outpatient clinic
>
> Dear Doctor,
>
> **Re: Mr Ian Jones, aged 25 years**
>
> This young man, who works as a systems analyst, has been admitted to hospital with pneumonia three times in the last 2 years. He has also had several episodes of sinusitis. His only other symptom is diarrhoea, which might be related to antibiotics that he has had for his chest and sinuses. I wonder if he has some predisposition to infection and would be grateful for your advice.
>
> Yours sincerely,

Introduction

Is this patient immunodeficient?

You must decide whether this man has an underlying immunological problem and, if so, determine what it is.

- If only one site (eg respiratory tract) is affected, then local causes such as a tumour, foreign body or aspiration are most likely, but less common causes such as immune deficiency or ciliary dysfunction should be considered.

- Unusually severe or frequent infections, affecting different body sites, suggest the possibility of an immunodeficiency.

- Bacterial respiratory tract infections are most commonly associated with antibody deficiency, such as common variable immunodeficiency (CVID).

- Primary immunodeficiencies are uncommon but their diagnosis is often delayed for many years, leading to significant avoidable morbidity and mortality. The respiratory tract, gut and skin are the most common sites of infection in antibody deficiency.

> **Warning signs of immune deficiencies**
>
> - Frequent infections: what constitutes abnormally frequent infection will vary according to the patient, but in general more than one hospital admission for infection in a year or more than six courses of antibiotics should trigger an investigation.
> - Invasive infections: the definition of invasive depends on patient and organism factors. Clearly, a brain abscess in the absence of underlying risk factors would be of more concern than a cutaneous abscess.
> - Unusual organisms: pneumococcal pneumonia can occur in healthy people, whereas *Pneumocystis* pneumonia suggests a severe immunodeficiency, usually HIV.
> - Associated features: paradoxically, immunodeficient people are at greater risk of immunological complications such as granulomas, vasculitis or allergic reactions.
> - Family history: many immune deficiencies are inherited, and hence a known family history of immunodeficiency or unexplained infant deaths may be relevant.

History of the presenting problem

What pathogens has he been infected with to date?

Bacterial infections suggest an antibody deficiency. *Giardia* species are a common bowel pathogen. Mild CD4 deficiency may occur in CVID and manifests as recurrent herpes simplex or zoster. Any suggestion of a more severe T-cell defect should prompt you to consider a combined T- and B-cell defect such as hyper-IgM syndrome or a 'leaky' severe combined immunodeficiency (SCID) (see Section 2.1.2). Although not available in PACES, in routine clinical practice you should check the patient's medical record for results of cultures: if pathogens have been isolated, this will help confirm the relative seriousness of the infections and will guide future antimicrobial therapy.

Severity

How long do infections last? How well do they respond to antibiotics?

The need for surgery or excessive time off work is an indicator of severe disease. In antibody-deficient patients infections may be less acute, but are slow to clear. Antibiotic response is often suboptimal unless high doses and longer duration of treatment (typically 2 weeks for an uncomplicated chest infection) are given.

When did the problem start?
CVID is acquired, usually in early adulthood. If your patient has had a significant history of childhood problems, consider a late presentation of X-linked agammaglobulinaemia (XLA) (see Section 2.1.1) or a leaky SCID. Ask the patient specifically about common childhood illnesses.

Consequences of CVID
You need more details about this man's diarrhoea. It may simply be a result of chronic infection or bacterial overgrowth, but coeliac and inflammatory bowel disease-type enterocolitis may also occur. Ask about symptoms of bronchiectasis (see *Respiratory Medicine*, Sections 1.1.3 and 2.4).

Other relevant history

What is his drug history?
Is the patient taking antiepileptics, eg phenytoin or carbamazepine? Is he on treatment for arthritis, eg gold, penicillamine, sulfasalazine or methotrexate? These are reversible causes of hypogammaglobulinaemia.

Features associated with CVID
Does this man have a personal or family history of organ-specific autoimmunity? Ask about the following.

- Anaemia: pernicious anaemia and autoimmune haemolytic anaemia are common in CVID.

- Arthralgia, which is often reactive but may be septic, is caused by *Mycoplasma* spp. as well as by more conventional organisms. In CVID, granulomas may produce a sarcoid-like picture.

 The mouth is a good place to look for signs of immunodeficiency.

- Tonsils (and other lymphoid tissue) are absent in antibody defects due to B-cell developmental abnormalities such as XLA.
- Herpes, candidiasis or hairy oral leucoplakia is suggestive of a combined or T-cell defect.
- Periodontal disease occurs in chronic granulomatous disease and other neutrophil-killing or chemotaxis defects.
- Aphthous ulcers are a non-specific sign of immunodeficiency.

Primary or secondary antibody deficiency?

If this patient has antibody deficiency, is it primary or secondary? In a 25-year-old, once you have scrutinised his drug history, you are unlikely to find additional underlying pathology. You should, however, consider whether he may have intestinal lymphangiectasia, protein-losing enteropathy, severe nephrotic syndrome or a lymphoproliferative condition, all of which can cause secondary antibody deficiency.

Plan for investigation and management
After explaining to the patient that under normal circumstances you would carry out a thorough clinical examination, you would plan in the interim to undertake blood tests and scans to help with the following:

- define the immunological defect;
- diagnose active infections;

- assess structural damage;
- initiate ongoing monitoring;
- give appropriate treatment.

Define the immunological defect
Baseline investigations include FBC, routine chemistry and immunoglobulins, including protein electrophoresis. Secondary causes of low immunoglobulins include lymphoproliferative disease (particularly myeloma), chronic lymphocytic leukaemia or lymphoma. Low albumin suggests the possibility of protein loss from the bowel or renal tract. For further investigations, see Section 3.3.

Diagnose active infections
This man has several potential sites of active infection.

- Respiratory: request sputum microscopy and culture, and a CXR if symptoms suggest active infection.

- Gastrointestinal tract: request repeated stool microscopy and culture. Organise upper gastrointestinal endoscopy including a duodenal biopsy and aspirate looking for *Giardia* spp. and also for bowel changes such as villous atrophy or, rarely, lymphoid interstitial hyperplasia/lymphangiectasia. Consider colonoscopy if inflammatory bowel disease is a possibility.

- Other sites: obtain samples for culture where possible. Remember that serology is likely to be unhelpful.

Assess structural damage and initiate ongoing monitoring
Perform a baseline CXR and CT scan of the chest (Fig. 1) and sinuses. Take a radiograph of arthritic joints. Do baseline and annual lung function tests. Take

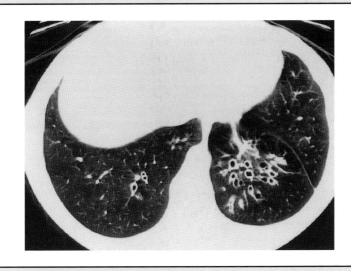

▲ **Fig. 1** CT scan showing the dilated and thickened airways characteristic of bronchiectasis.

blood for baseline liver function and for hepatitis B and C markers if immunoglobulin replacement is contemplated.

Management

You should explain to the patient that the results of blood tests will be reviewed at the next outpatient visit. In the mean time, give appropriate treatment.

- Acute infections require a prolonged course of antibiotics.

- If the patient is shown to have a severe antibody deficiency syndrome, long-term immunoglobulin replacement via the intravenous or subcutaneous route will be required (see Section 3.7). IgG subclass or specific antibody deficiencies can often be managed with prophylactic antibiotics, eg azithromycin 500 mg once daily for 3 days every fortnight.

Further discussion

Consider other causes of a recurrent chest infection, many of which are associated with diarrhoea.

- Common: foreign body, HIV, ciliary dysfunction caused by smoking and cystic fibrosis.
- Uncommon: immotile cilia syndrome and Young's syndrome (obstructive azoospermia and ciliary dysfunction).

Patients with relatively rare conditions such as CVID are unlikely to meet others with the same condition. If the patient has CVID, then offer him contact details of the Primary Immunodeficiency Association (Alliance House, 12 Caxton Street, London SW1H 0QS; telephone 020 7976 7640; website http://www.pia.org.uk), a self-help organisation that provides information and practical support.

1.1.2 Recurrent meningitis

Letter of referral to immunology outpatient clinic

Dear Doctor,

Re: Mr Bill Taylor, aged 20 years

Thank you for seeing this student who has had two episodes of meningococcal meningitis. The first was at the age of 6 years and the second was 3 months ago. He has made a full recovery. I wonder if he has an underlying immunological defect and would be grateful for your opinion.

Yours sincerely,

Introduction

Meningococcal meningitis is a serious infection with significant morbidity and mortality rates (see *Infectious Diseases*, see Section 1.3.11). Your task is to determine whether there is an underlying reason for this man's infection and, if so, to advise on action to prevent a recurrence.

Underlying causes for recurrent meningitis include the following.

- Traumatic or congenital connection with the subarachnoid space causing a cerebrospinal fluid (CSF) leak.

- Deficiency of a component of a terminal pathway of complement (C5, C6, C7 or C8; C9 deficiency is usually asymptomatic), or properdin or factor D in the alternative pathway (see Section 2.1.5 and *Scientific Background to Medicine 1*, Immunology and Immunosuppression – Complement).

- Other immunodeficiencies: the patient's history will almost always reveal associated features.

- Recurrent aseptic meningitis (Mollaret's): some cases are associated with herpes simplex virus infection.

- Behçet's syndrome (see Section 2.5.5).

- Systemic lupus erythematosus (see Section 2.4.1).

History of the presenting problem

In routine clinical practice, ensure that you have enough information to confirm the diagnosis.

- Were meningococci cultured from blood or CSF?

- Were typical features of invasive meningococcal infection present?

Take this opportunity to ensure that appropriate antibiotic prophylaxis was given to your patient and his household contacts after treatment (see *Infectious Diseases*, Sections 1.3.11, 2.1 and 2.3).

Are there any clues to suggest an external connection with the subarachnoid space?

This is the most common cause of recurrent meningitis, but it is uncommon for meningococci to cause infection in this setting and the causative organisms vary (*Streptococcus pneumoniae*, *Haemophilus influenzae*) (Fig. 2).

Ask about the following:

- head injuries, especially fractures involving the base of the skull;

- chronic sinusitis, mastoiditis or inner-ear disease;

- previous brain or pituitary surgery.

Immunological cause

Deficiency of the terminal complement components C5–9 and of the alternative pathway components properdin and factor D are strongly associated with an increased risk of neisserial infection and occasionally *Escherichia coli*. Infection may be recurrent and disseminated, but is often less intense in the presence of complement deficiency.

Other immunodeficiencies are sometimes associated with recurrent meningitis, and so ask the patient about features associated with antibody or cellular deficiencies (see Sections 2.1.1 and 2.1.2).

Other relevant history

Has the patient ever had gonorrhoea? If so, were there complications? Gonorrhoea is a neisserial infection and more likely to be disseminated to the joints or skin in the presence of a terminal complement deficiency.

If the family history suggests X-linked inheritance, properdin deficiency is most likely; autosomal recessive inheritance suggests one of the terminal pathway component deficiencies or, very rarely, factor D deficiency. If the patient has terminal complement or properdin deficiency, he will be asymptomatic and have no physical signs between attacks.

Plan for investigation and management

After explaining to the patient that under normal circumstances you would carry out a thorough clinical examination, you would plan in the interim to investigate as follows.

CSF leak

The investigation of choice is MRI. Increase the diagnostic sensitivity by making sure that the radiologist is fully informed about the clinical picture.

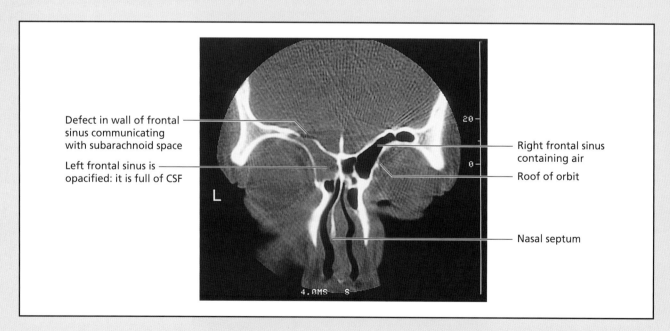

Defect in wall of frontal sinus communicating with subarachnoid space

Left frontal sinus is opacified: it is full of CSF

L

Right frontal sinus containing air

Roof of orbit

Nasal septum

▲**Fig. 2** CT scan of a man who developed meningitis several years after a head injury. A defect in the frontal sinus communicates with the subarachnoid space. The left frontal sinus is opacified because it is full of CSF. (Reproduced with permission from Bannister BA, Begg NT and Gillespie SH. *Infectious Disease*, 2nd edn. Oxford: Blackwell Science, 2000.)

<table>
<tr><td colspan="4">**TABLE 1 INTERPRETATION OF HAEMOLYTIC COMPLEMENT ASSAYS CH50 AND AP50**</td></tr>
</table>

	Classic pathway CH50	
	Normal	**Abnormal**
Alternative pathway AP50		
Normal	No abnormality of complement	C1–4 abnormal
Abnormal	Factor B, D or properdin abnormal	C5–9 abnormal

Complement deficiency

Fresh samples, sent on ice, are required.

- Haemolytic complement assays (CH50 or CH100) measure the ability of the classic complement pathway C1–9 to lyse red cells (Table 1).

- The AP50 (or AP100) measures lysis by the alternative pathway: factor B to C9.

The absence of red cell lysis implies the absence of one of the factors in the assayed pathway. If either of these screening tests is abnormal, each relevant complement component should be measured individually. Occasionally, a non-functional complement component may be present. If no quantitative deficiency is found to account for absent lysis (and you are certain that the CH50 sample was handled correctly), then request functional studies.

Management

You should explain to the patient that the results of blood tests will be reviewed at the next outpatient visit.

Antibiotics Prescribe long-term prophylactic phenoxymethylpenicillin 500 mg twice daily. However, some organisms may be resistant.

Immunisation Conjugated vaccine against *Neisseria meningitidis* type C should be given. You should also consider giving the unconjugated vaccine for types A, C, Y and W-135 in patients with a high risk of exposure. This will give short-term protection. Quadrivalent conjugate vaccines may be available in the future and will give long-term protection. No vaccine is available for type B. Measurements of meningococcal antibody levels can help decide when reimmunisation is necessary, although these may be unreliable. Bear in mind that higher antibody levels may be required for protection in complement-deficient individuals and that disease is often caused by uncommon serotypes not covered by immunisation.

> ⚠ Immunisation will reduce, but not eliminate, the risk of recurrent meningococcal meningitis for this man. For patients with early complement component or C3 deficiency, additional immunisation with Pneumovax (pure pneumococcal polysaccharide), pneumococcal conjugate and *Haemophilus* conjugate vaccines is indicated.

Replacement of missing factor This is not usually practical, because the half-life of circulating complement is extremely short. Infusions of fresh frozen (or commercially available solvent-treated) plasma would be required, with significant expense, inconvenience and some risk to your patient.

CSF leak due to cranial anatomical defects The demonstration of a cranial anatomical defect, either congenital or acquired (following trauma), will require neurosurgical intervention to plug the gap.

Genetic counselling If a complement deficiency is identified, depending on the exact deficit, the CH50 or AP50 may be used for screening of relatives.

1.1.3 Recurrent facial swelling and abdominal pain

Letter of referral to immunology outpatient clinic

Dear Doctor,

Re: Mrs Kathy Leighton, aged 30 years

This woman has had two episodes of angio-oedema. The most recent, which occurred following dental treatment, required overnight hospital admission. She also has recurrent abdominal pain, thought to be due to irritable bowel syndrome. I wonder if she has had an allergic reaction and would be grateful if you could help with establishing an underlying diagnosis.

Yours sincerely,

Introduction

The combination of recurrent angio-oedema and abdominal pain should immediately suggest the possibility of C1 inhibitor deficiency. However, you must differentiate C1 inhibitor deficiency from drug-induced angio-oedema and anaphylaxis. Both C1 inhibitor deficiency and anaphylaxis present with facial and laryngeal oedema, but there are differences in these presentations. This is an important diagnosis to make: both disorders can present as medical emergencies with upper airway obstruction but require very different treatment and prophylaxis.

C1 inhibitor

C1 inhibitor limits activation of the early part of the classic complement cascade, as well as having a regulatory role in other inflammatory pathways. C1 inhibitor deficiency results in activation of the early components C1, C4 and C2, along with release of inflammatory fragments. Other regulatory mechanisms prevent C3 breakdown or further activation of the complement pathway (see *Scientific Background to Medicine 1*, Immunology and Immunosuppression – Complement).

History of the presenting problem

The history is critical in distinguishing between C1 inhibitor deficiency and anaphylaxis.

Are there any features to suggest anaphylaxis?

How soon after the dental work did the reaction occur? How rapidly did the symptoms develop? Anaphylactic reactions usually occur immediately after the allergic stimulus, virtually always within 30 minutes, and the symptoms progress rapidly. Symptoms related to C1 inhibitor deficiency or other forms of angio-oedema usually build up over several hours.

Urticaria, asthma and hypotension caused by generalised vasodilatation do not occur in angio-oedema due to C1 inhibitor deficiency, but they are common features of anaphylaxis (see Section 2.2.1 and *Acute Medicine*, Section 1.2.33).

Is C1 inhibitor deficiency the explanation?

This woman's abdominal pain may be the result of intestinal oedema. This strongly favours a diagnosis of C1 inhibitor deficiency and may be the presenting feature in children. Dermal swellings are common, but urticaria is not associated with this condition.

Precipitating factors
Symptoms following trauma
Even minor trauma such as dental work can precipitate symptoms in someone with C1 inhibitor deficiency. This may be mistaken for allergy to local anaesthetics. Ask about dermal swellings, which often follow minor knocks.

Are there any other triggers causing angio-oedema? Ask about other precipitants of angio-oedema in those with C1 inhibitor deficiency: minor infections, emotional stress and endogenous oestrogens.

Is drug-induced angio-oedema the explanation? Angiotensin-converting enzyme (ACE) inhibitors are a common cause of non-histamine-related angio-oedema. As symptoms do not follow immediately after taking the tablets, the patient may not link the symptoms with the medication. Most people with ACE inhibitor-induced angio-oedema do not have C1 inhibitor deficiency, although it will precipitate attacks in affected people. The following may be other drug-related causes of angio-oedema:

- anaphylactic (IgE-induced mast cell degranulation), eg penicillin allergy;

- anaphylactoid (non-IgE-induced mast cell degranulation), eg radiographic contrast media;

- immune complex mediated, eg blood products.

Do not forget physical factors (cold, pressure and vibration). All these may be associated with urticaria, which effectively excludes the diagnosis of C1 inhibitor deficiency. Idiopathic angio-oedema is common, often associated with urticaria and does not normally require extensive investigation.

Other relevant history
Is there a family history of angio-oedema? C1 inhibitor deficiency may be congenital or acquired.

Congenital
Ask about the patient's family history. Congenital C1 inhibitor deficiency is inherited in an autosomal dominant manner. The onset of symptoms is usually in adolescence. If the diagnosis is confirmed, your patient will need genetic counselling and practical advice on the screening of any potentially affected relatives.

Acquired C1 inhibitor deficiency
Autoantibodies to C1 inhibitor or paraproteins may result in the depletion or functional deficiency of C1 inhibitor. These occur as a result of autoimmune (systemic lupus erythematosus, rheumatoid) or lymphoproliferative disease.

Plan for investigation and management
After explaining to the patient that under normal circumstances you would carry out a thorough clinical examination, you would plan to proceed as follows.

Investigation
Diagnosis of C1 inhibitor deficiency Screen for C1 inhibitor deficiency by checking serum C4 levels (Fig. 3).

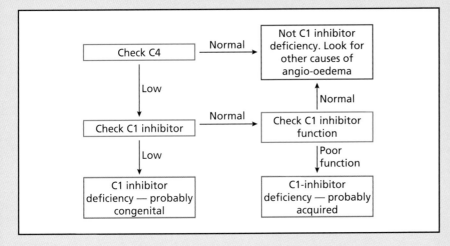

▲**Fig. 3** Algorithm for diagnosis of C1 inhibitor deficiency.

A low C4 level (with normal C3) is a hallmark of both hereditary and functional C1 inhibitor deficiency, even between attacks. Conversely, a normal C4 makes the diagnosis very unlikely.

Associated disease In acquired C1 inhibitor deficiency check the following:

- FBC and film;
- immunoglobulins;
- serum and urine electrophoresis;
- antinuclear antibody;
- rheumatoid factor;
- cryoglobulins.

Management

You should explain to the patient that the results of her blood tests will be reviewed at her next outpatient visit. If a diagnosis of C1 inhibitor deficiency is made, then the principles of management are as follows.

Treatment of acute attacks For severe attacks, give C1 inhibitor concentrate; if this is not available, give fresh frozen plasma. Adrenaline (epinephrine) is likely to be ineffective. For mild attacks,

tranexamic acid can shorten the duration.

Intercurrent prophylaxis For hereditary C1 inhibitor deficiency, either:

- increase production by using modified androgens such as stanozolol or danazol; or
- decrease consumption by giving tranexamic acid.

⚠ Long-term danazol therapy may be associated with hepatocellular adenomas, so monitor the patient's liver function at regular intervals and arrange ultrasonography of the liver every 2 years.

For acquired C1 inhibitor deficiency, treat the underlying cause.

Recommend that the patient wears a Medic-Alert bracelet, and alert her local accident and emergency department so that acute attacks can be appropriately treated.

ACE inhibitor-induced angio-oedema Management involves permanent withdrawal of the drug. Angiotensin II antagonists are tolerated by most patients, but may themselves rarely cause angio-oedema.

Anaphylaxis See Section 2.2.1 and *Acute Medicine*, Section 1.2.33.

Further discussion

Pregnancy and C1 inhibitor deficiency

A patient with this condition needs specific pregnancy advice.

- All androgens should be stopped before conception (to avoid the risk of virilisation).
- Tranexamic acid may be considered after 12 weeks' gestation.
- C1 inhibitor concentrate can be used for acute attacks, and may occasionally be required as twice-weekly prophylaxis.
- Symptoms may improve or worsen during pregnancy.
- Prophylactic C1 inhibitor concentrate should be given for patients undergoing Caesarean section.

Surgical or dental procedures and C1 inhibitor deficiency

- High risk: give C1 inhibitor concentrate preoperatively.
- Low risk: consider high-dose danazol (600 mg once daily) or stanozolol (5 mg once daily) for 6 days before and 3 days after the procedure. Ensure that C1 inhibitor concentrate is available for emergencies; the patient will be at increased risk of attacks for 72 hours after the procedure.

1.1.4 Recurrent skin abscesses

Letter of referral to immunology outpatient clinic

Dear Doctor,

Re: Tom Smith, aged 16 years

Thank you for seeing this boy who has recurrent abscesses on a background of eczema. He has rarely been free of abscesses for the past 2 years, and on three occasions these have required incision and drainage. His father has also suffered from the occasional abscess.

I am concerned that he may have an underlying immunodeficiency and would be grateful for your help in investigating him and formulating an appropriate plan of management.

Yours sincerely,

Introduction

Is this patient likely to be immunodeficient?

Recurrent skin abscesses are common. They are distressing and expensive in time and resources, but are not usually associated with underlying immunodeficiency. However, they may occasionally be the presenting feature of a life-threatening condition such as chronic granulomatous disease (CGD) (Table 2). You must be sure not to miss the occasional serious immunodeficiency, while providing practical advice for controlling the problem to those for whom that diagnosis is excluded. Although your list of differential diagnoses will include CGD and other immunodeficiencies, the most likely explanation for this problem is staphylococcal colonisation.

Chronic granulomatous disease

Phagocytes of patients with CGD cannot efficiently kill organisms that they have engulfed, leading to granuloma or abscess formation and failure to clear the infection.

TABLE 2 DIFFERENTIAL DIAGNOSIS OF RECURRENT SKIN ABSCESSES

Common	Rare
Staphylococcal colonisation	CGD Neutrophil G6PD deficiency (common, but rarely presents with abscesses) Neutrophil MPD deficiency (common, but rarely presents with abscesses) Antibody deficiency Other immune deficiencies: Hyper-Ig E (Job's) syndrome, Wiskott–Aldrich syndrome, combined (antibody/cellular) immune deficiencies

CGD, chronic granulomatous disease; G6PD, glucose 6-phosphate dehydrogenase; Ig, immunolgobin; MPD, myeloperoxidase.

History of the presenting problem

What types of abscesses has he had?

- Location: are they superficial and confined to the skin, or have they affected internal organs? If they have affected the skin only, then staphylococcal colonisation is by far the most likely diagnosis.

- How frequently do they occur?

- Are they large boils, needing surgical drainage, or smaller pustules?

- When did they start? A history of problems going back to childhood or infancy makes a congenital problem more likely.

- Does each abscess respond rapidly to conventional treatment? This makes immunodeficiency less likely.

Other relevant history

Is staphylococcal skin colonisation the explanation?

Ask about chronic skin conditions, particularly eczema (as in this case). Does the patient have diabetes? Both of these common disorders increase the risk of abscesses, usually due to *Staphylococcus*.

Severe eczema causes damage to the protective barrier of the skin and is associated with staphylococcal colonisation. It is also a feature of two primary immunodeficiencies, although both are very rare, especially in adults.

- Hyper-IgE (Job's) syndrome: severe infections, especially skin and chest with pneumatoceles, failure to lose primary dentition, abnormal facies and grossly elevated serum IgE (this is not specific for hyper-IgE syndrome because many patients with atopic eczema have comparable IgE levels).
- Wiskott–Aldrich syndrome: X-linked combined (cellular and antibody) immunodeficiency, with severe infections. Thrombocytopenia with abnormally small platelets on the blood film.

Are there any other features to suggest immunodeficiency?

Ask about the following because the presence of any of these features would make an underlying immune deficiency more likely.

- Has there been associated invasive disease, abscesses of internal organs, chronic periodontitis or persistent lymphadenopathy?

- Does he have inflammatory bowel disease or perineal abscesses?

- Did he have any problems with his BCG immunisation?

- Are there features of other immunodeficiencies (see Section 3.3).

- Has he been infected with unusual organisms? Although not available in PACES, in routine clinical practice you should review the notes and microbiology reports looking for evidence of *Aspergillus*, *Klebsiella*, *Serratia*, *Burkholderia* spp., as well as the more commonplace *Staphylococcus* spp., *E. coli* and *Salmonella* spp.

> Recurrent infections with catalase-positive bacteria and *Aspergillus* spp. are characteristic of serious neutrophil defects such as CGD (Fig. 4).

Family history
Have there been any premature deaths in the family, or unusual infections? CGD is X-linked in 65% of cases, the rest being autosomal recessive. Abscesses resulting from staphylococcal colonisation often affect several members of the household.

Plan for investigation and management
After explaining to the patient that under normal circumstances you would carry out a thorough clinical examination, you would plan in the interim to investigate as follows.

Investigation
Check FBC, immunoglobulins and glucose. Take samples from his abscesses, looking for unusual organisms, and take swabs from

his hairline, nose and perineum to look for *Staphylococcus aureus*.

If the history includes any features of immune deficiency, then further investigation will be necessary to exclude CGD, using specialised tests that require discussion with the laboratory.

- Nitroblue tetrazolium (NBT) slide test: assesses the integrity of the neutrophil respiratory burst, ie nicotinamide adenine dinucleotide phosphate (NADPH) oxidase system. In neutrophil killing defects (CGD, neutrophil G6PD or MPD deficiency), neutrophils fail to reduce the NBT crystals that they have phagocytosed (Fig. 5).

- Neutrophil respiratory burst: may be measured by flow cytometry.

If the NBT screening test suggests a defect:

- check for the absence of individual NADPH subunits;

- if the NADPH system is intact, consider G6PD and MPD deficiency as alternative causes for the defective NBT test.

Management
You should explain to the patient that the results of his blood tests will be reviewed at his next outpatient visit.

No immunological cause is found
Treat eczema (in this case, see *Dermatology*, Section 2.8) and optimise control of diabetes (if relevant) (see *Endocrinology*, Section 2.6). Reduce staphylococcal skin colonisation with at least 2 weeks (often longer) of the following.

- Bath or shower daily using an antiseptic preparation such as povidone-iodine all over the body, including the hair.

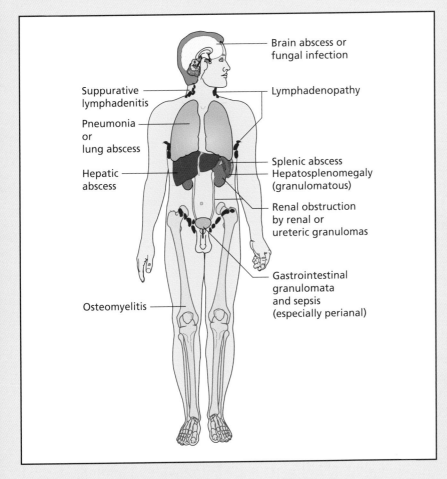

Brain abscess or fungal infection

Lymphadenopathy

Suppurative lymphadenitis

Pneumonia or lung abscess

Hepatic abscess

Splenic abscess
Hepatosplenomegaly (granulomatous)

Renal obstruction by renal or ureteric granulomas

Gastrointestinal granulomata and sepsis (especially perianal)

Osteomyelitis

▲**Fig. 4** Common sites of pathology in CGD.

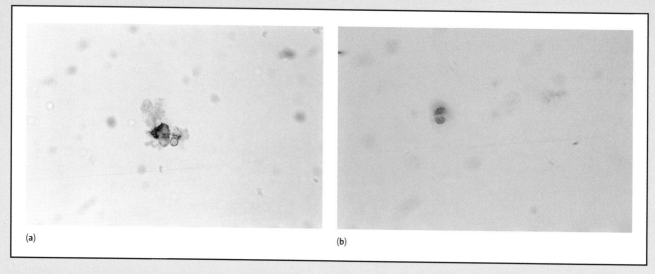

▲ Fig. 5 NBT test: activated neutrophils are tested for their ability to phagocytose and reduce NBT. (a) Reduced NBT is seen as dark-blue crystals. (b) Unstimulated neutrophils, or stimulated neutrophils from patients who have CGD, fail to reduce NBT. Blood from carriers of CGD contains a mixture of normal and abnormal neutrophils.

- Each person in a household should use his or her own towel, which should be changed every day.

- In addition to the above, consider a short course (10 days) of a topical antibiotic, such as Naseptin or (in resistant cases) mupirocin, to the nasal vestibule.

> In cases of staphylococcal carriage, every member of the patient's household should be treated because recolonisation from untreated people will occur.

Chronic granulomatous disease If CGD is the diagnosis, the principles of management are as follows.

- Prescribe prophylactic antibiotics (co-trimoxazole) and antifungal therapy (itraconazole), and give detailed instructions on the personal precautions to take to avoid infection (see Table 3).

- Acute infections: see Section 2.1.3.

- Refer to a specialist with an interest in CGD, who may consider interferon-γ prophylaxis or bone marrow transplantation in difficult cases.

Further discussion

Genetic counselling is important if a diagnosis of CGD is made. Carriers of the condition can be identified by the NBT test, flow cytometric testing (see Fig. 5) and by molecular analysis. Prenatal diagnosis is possible.

1.1.5 Flushing and skin rash

Letter of referral to immunology outpatient clinic

Dear Doctor,

Re: Mrs Jane Brown, aged 45 years

I would be grateful for your help in the investigation and management of this woman who presents with a 3-year history of episodic urticaria. The urticarial episodes occur weekly and are characterised by an intensely itchy rash affecting her trunk and limbs. Over the past year these episodes have been associated with intermittent facial flushing which has been thought to be perimenopausal in

TABLE 3 PREVENTION OF INFECTION IN CGD

Problem	Intervention
Avoid bacterial infection	Keep immunisations up to date Clean all cuts immediately and rinse with antiseptic or hydrogen peroxide (1.5% solution) Use hydrogen peroxide mouthwash after brushing teeth to reduce gingivitis Antibiotic prophylaxis is necessary for dental work
Avoid fungal spores	Avoid hay, wood chips and grass clippings Do not enter barns or caves Do not repot houseplants For cut flowers, use a teaspoon of bleach in the water Avoid newly constructed or renovated buildings until they have been thoroughly cleaned
General	Do not smoke

TABLE 4 DIFFERENTIAL DIAGNOSIS OF FLUSHING

Disorder	Comments and key investigations	Frequency
Physiological/idiopathic	Confined to exposed skin, eg face or neck Sometimes associated with palpitations and syncope No biochemical abnormality	Common
Menopause	Women aged >45 years with menstrual irregularities Males after orchidectomy Gonadotropin levels are unreliable markers of the perimenopause	Common
Carcinoid	Often postprandial flushing associated with diarrhoea and/or wheeze Raised 24-hour urinary 5-HIAA	Rare
Medullary carcinoma of the thyroid	Either sporadic or associated with multiple endocrine neoplasia syndromes Raised serum calcitonin	Rare
Mastocytosis	Flushing associated with urticaria, pruritis and/or diarrhoea Mast cell infiltration on skin/bone marrow biopsy Raised plasma tryptase Raised urinary methylhistamine	Rare
Drugs	Antidepressants, metronidazole (with alcohol) and nicotinic acid	Common

5-HIAA, 5-hydroxyindoleacetic acid.

origin. Clinical examination during an acute episode revealed widespread urticaria.

Both the patient and myself are increasingly frustrated by her urticaria and would value your help in establishing a firm diagnosis.

Yours sincerely,

Introduction

Flushing in a 45-year-old woman could be due to a wide spectrum of disorders, ranging from early menopause to disorders caused by release of endogenous vasoactive mediators (Table 4). In this case, where there is both flushing and urticaria, you need to consider whether her symptoms are triggered by an underlying allergy or if they reflect systemic mastocytosis (SM).

> There are many causes of mild flushing, but the simultaneous occurrence of flushing and urticaria points to mast cell overactivity.

History of the presenting problem

Are there clues in the history to suggest an underlying allergic trigger for her urticaria?

The history is crucial in establishing an allergic trigger. A consistent link with foods, drugs or background atopy should suggest a possible allergy.

Could SM account for her symptoms?

Although flushing in this woman may well reflect the onset of menopause, it would be prudent in the face of intractable symptoms not to ignore the possibility of SM. Ask about the following.

- Frequency of symptoms: completely asymptomatic phases between episodes may occur with either allergy or SM, although the most common rash of SM, urticaria pigmentosa, tends to be fixed.

- Itching: does scratching or mild trauma cause more urticarial lesions to appear (Darier's sign)? This is a characteristic feature of

urticaria pigmentosa (Fig. 6), a localised form of mastocytosis confined to the skin.

- Gastrointestinal symptoms: diarrhoea and abdominal pain. Symptomatic peptic ulcers occur in 50% of patients with SM.

- Palpitations: not uncommon with physiological flushing.

- Constitutional symptoms: prolonged fatigue.

- Is the patient menopausal? Ask about the frequency and duration of her menstrual periods.

Other relevant history

Enquire about exaggerated reactions to drugs that release histamine. This is a frequent feature of mastocytosis and manifests as anaphylactoid reactions associated with the use of mast cell stimulators such as opiates and certain neuromuscular blockers used in anaesthesia.

> ⚠ Beware risk of severe adverse reactions with opioid analgesia and general anaesthesia.

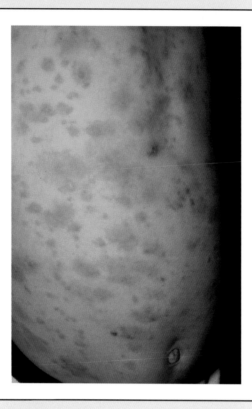

▲**Fig. 6** Pigmented macular lesions of urticaria pigmentosa with urtication. (Courtesy of Dr M. Goodfield, Leeds General Infirmary.)

Plan for investigation and management

After explaining to the patient that under normal circumstances you would carry out a thorough clinical examination, you would plan to investigate as follows.

Investigation

- Allergy: if the history suggests an allergic trigger, perform appropriate skin-prick tests and check allergen-specific IgE. Although food allergy may occasionally cause widespread urticaria in isolation, it would be highly unusual for it to be associated with facial flushing. Nevertheless, should the history incriminate any foods as a consistent trigger, it would be worthwhile performing appropriate skin-prick tests to relevant foods and allergen-specific IgE.

- Mastocytosis: you need to demonstrate mast cell overactivity both histologically and biochemically. Check plasma tryptase, an important mast cell mediator, and plan to proceed to bone marrow examination and/or skin biopsy if the tryptase is elevated.

> Histological demonstration of mast cell hyperplasia in skin and/or bone marrow, combined with biochemical evidence of elevated mast cell mediators, is required to establish a diagnosis of SM. Measurements of mast cell mediators may be normal in mastocytosis confined to the skin.

Management

You should explain to the patient that the results of her blood tests will be reviewed at her next outpatient visit. If targeted skin testing suggests a possible allergenic trigger, give appropriate advice regarding allergen avoidance and ensure that she is taking optimal antihistamine therapy to achieve symptomatic control of urticaria. Use a non-sedating antihistamine such as cetirizine or loratadine.

If mastocytosis is confirmed, the mainstay of management is histamine blockade using a combination of H_1- and H_2-receptor blockers to control cutaneous symptoms and gastric acid production, respectively. In addition to controlling gastric acid production, H_2-receptor blockers such as cimetidine or ranitidine have the added advantage of blocking histamine in the skin, because approximately 20% of cutaneous histamine receptors are of the H_2 class.

Further discussion

Mastocytosis is a myeloproliferative disorder: there are mutations in the c-kit receptor (a tyrosine kinase that functions as the receptor for stem-cell factor, the most important growth factor for mast cells) in most patients with mastocytosis, and there is organ infiltration with mast cells (see Section 2.2.2).

1.1.6 Drug-induced anaphylaxis

Letter of referral to immunology outpatient clinic

Dear Doctor,

Re: Mr Kevin Cook, aged 35 years

Please see this man who presented to the Emergency Department yesterday evening in anaphylactic shock: BP 80/40, severe bronchospasm and widespread urticaria. Fortunately, he responded rapidly to intramuscular adrenaline, and intravenous hydrocortisone and chlorpheniramine.

Five days before admission he had developed pain, redness and swelling in the right foot. His GP suspected cellulitis and gave him flucloxacillin, a drug he had taken in the past without problems. His foot symptoms failed to settle on antibiotics and, with a suspicion of gout, he was prescribed diclofenac. Within a few minutes of taking 50 mg of this drug he developed the first signs of the allergic reaction described above. He had previously been generally well, although in recent months he has had occasional self-limiting attacks of 'nettle rash' with no obvious cause.

I would be grateful for your help in unravelling the cause of this allergic reaction.

Yours sincerely,

Introduction

In principle, nothing could be simpler than prevention of further attacks of drug-induced anaphylaxis: one merely has to identify the offending drug (Table 5) and avoid it. In practice, however, diagnosis and management are complicated by the following.

- Difficulty identifying the triggering drug, particularly where multiple drugs are used before the adverse reaction.

- The pathophysiology of the adverse reaction: these can be

TABLE 5 DRUGS MOST OFTEN ASSOCIATED WITH ANAPHYLAXIS

IgE mediated	Non-IgE mediated
Cephalosporins Penicillins Drugs used in general anaesthesia, especially neuromuscular blocking agents Proteins used as drugs, such as therapeutic antibodies	Radiographic contrast media Aspirin and NSAIDs Angiotensin-converting enzyme inhibitors

classic IgE-mediated type I hypersensitivity reactions or non-IgE-mediated mast cell degranulation (as in the patient described here), where an NSAID has triggered severe mast cell degranulation in a patient with pre-existing mild chronic urticaria and angio-oedema.

- Pattern of cross-reactivity between different drugs, eg type I hypersensitivity to penicillins will often be associated with the potential for similar reactions to cephalosporins.

History of the presenting problem

The history is the main diagnostic tool in the assessment of drug allergy. A painstaking history is therefore essential.

If a patient is acutely unwell, the priority is clearly the recognition and management of the anaphylactic reaction. Little or no history may be available at this stage. It is therefore vital to return to the patient when they have recovered, either on the ward or in the outpatient department (where this PACES scenario is set). Particular attention should be given to the following.

Events immediately preceding and during the reaction The time course of these must be meticulously documented. In clinical practice an account may need to be obtained

from witnesses if the patient's consciousness was impaired, but this will not be available in the PACES examination. However, does the history suggest anaphylaxis or some cause of collapse such as a simple faint, cardiac syncope or epilepsy (see *Acute Medicine*, Section 1.2.8; *Cardiology*, Sections 1.4.1; and *Neurology*, Section 1.1.3)? Not all the components of a full-blown anaphylactic reaction need be present for a diagnosis to be made: it is just as important to identify isolated bronchospasm or severe angio-oedema. Dizziness/presyncope (suggestive of hypotension) in the absence of bronchospasm/swelling/ rashes can occur, but is more suggestive of a cardiac cause. Patients often report gastrointestinal symptoms (diarrhoea and abdominal pain) in addition to classical anaphylactic symptoms.

Previous use of any drugs Drugs taken without problems in the recent past are unlikely to be the cause, but have there been previous reactions to any drugs? Does the patient take any drugs that may trigger anaphylaxis, urticaria or angio-oedema by non-immunological means, such as NSAIDs or angiotensin-converting enzyme inhibitors? And do they use any drugs that may worsen an anaphylactic reaction, especially beta-blockers?

Need the reaction be drug induced? Could this have been triggered by other environmental allergens, eg latex?

Station 2: History Taking   **15**

Other relevant history

- Is there (as in this case) a history suggestive of chronic idiopathic urticaria and angio-odema? Chaotic and unpredictable attacks of urticaria and angio-oedema (often facial/perioral) arise more often at night, with attacks occurring in clusters over time. Such patients are prone to NSAID-induced anaphylaxis and may also occasionally suffer spontaneous anaphylactic attacks (so-called idiopathic anaphylaxis).

- Does the patient have any other medical conditions that may increase the hazards of severe mast cell degranulation, such as unstable asthma or ischaemic heart disease?

> The patient who gives a history of reactions to multiple drugs presents particular difficulties. Multiple drug allergies are extremely rare and most patients who report them have one of the following.
>
> - Idiopathic urticaria and angio-oedema: reactions can be precipitated by some drugs (such as NSAIDs) but also occur spontaneously (when they are often wrongly attributed to outside events).
> - Somatisation disorder: physiological changes caused by stress are perceived as being triggered by external events.

Plan for investigation and management

Explain to the patient that tests are of limited utility in determining the cause of this type of reaction.

Most attempts at investigation will take place in the convalescent stage, often in outpatient departments. Occasionally, in cases of acute illness, if there is uncertainty regarding the cause of an episode of collapse, then

serial measurements of serum mast cell tryptase may be useful.

For some drugs, skin-prick testing and measurement of specific IgE in serum may help to identify the triggering drug. These can be used only for IgE-dependent reactions, and even then they are useful only in a small proportion of cases. Skin testing is difficult because the triggering allergen is often a subtle chemical modification of the administered drug, and hence the use of simple solutions of the drug is likely to lead to false-negative results. It is of most use in the assessment of anaphylaxis associated with β-lactam antibiotics or general anaesthetic drugs, and in the latter case they can be used to pinpoint the likely allergen in a cocktail of administered drugs. The test involves scratching a tiny quantity of a drug into the upper layer of skin: when immediate hypersensitivity is present, an itchy wheal develops at the site of the scratch, which usually disappears within 30 minutes. Very occasional cases of generalised reactions to skin-prick testing have been reported, and treatments need to be on hand if this were to happen. Patients undergoing skin testing should not take antihistamines for 48 hours before the test, as these may cause false-negative results.

The cornerstone of management is avoidance of the suspected drug. Management of acute anaphylactic reactions is described in Sections 1.1.6 and 2.2.1.

> - The drug(s) to be avoided should be clearly recorded on the front of the patient's case notes.
> - The patient should be encouraged to wear a Medic-Alert (or equivalent) necklace or bracelet giving details of the allergy.

1.1.7 Arthralgia, purpuric rash and renal impairment

Letter of referral to rheumatology outpatient clinic

Dear Doctor,

Re: Mrs Deborah Chapman, aged 50 year

Thank you for seeing this woman with a 2-year history of joint pains and an intermittent purpuric rash. On clinical examination the only abnormality is a purpuric rash involving her calves and thighs. The results of initial investigations show negative antinuclear antibody and a normal FBC, but impaired renal function with a plasma creatinine of 170 µmol/L (normal range 50–120).

I would value your help in establishing the underlying diagnosis and planning her further management.

Yours sincerely,

Introduction

The differential diagnoses for this constellation of clinical problems encompass lupus and the systemic vasculitides (Table 6). Lupus is effectively excluded by the negative antinuclear antibody. Of the vasculitides, type II mixed cryoglobulinaemia would fit her clinical problems well and should be considered the prime working diagnosis. Other small-vessel vasculitides such as Wegener's granulomatosis and microscopic polyangiitis (MPA) may also present in this manner.

TABLE 6 DIFFERENTIAL DIAGNOSIS OF ARTHRALGIA, PURPURIC RASH AND RENAL IMPAIRMENT

Disorder	Key investigation
Lupus	Antinuclear antibody
Mixed cryoglobulinaemia	Cryoglobulins, C3, C4 and rheumatoid factor
Wegener's granulomatosis and MPA	ANCA and tissue biopsy
Rheumatoid vasculitis	Clinically apparent because it develops on a background of severe rheumatoid disease
Henoch–Schönlein purpura	Rare in this age group and with such a long history: tissue biopsy (skin, kidney) showing IgA deposition would make the diagnosis

ANCA, antineutrophil cytoplasmic antibody; C3, C4, complement factors 3 and 4; MPA, microscopic polyangiitis.

History of the presenting problem

Skin rash

Since a purpuric rash on the legs on a background of renal impairment and joint pains suggests a multisystem disorder such as cryoglobulinaemic vasculitis, you should characterise the rash bearing in mind the diagnoses listed in Table 6.

- Clarify distribution of the rash and any relationship to cold: a purpuric rash affecting the lower limbs is present in >90% of patients with mixed cryoglobulinaemia (Fig. 7).

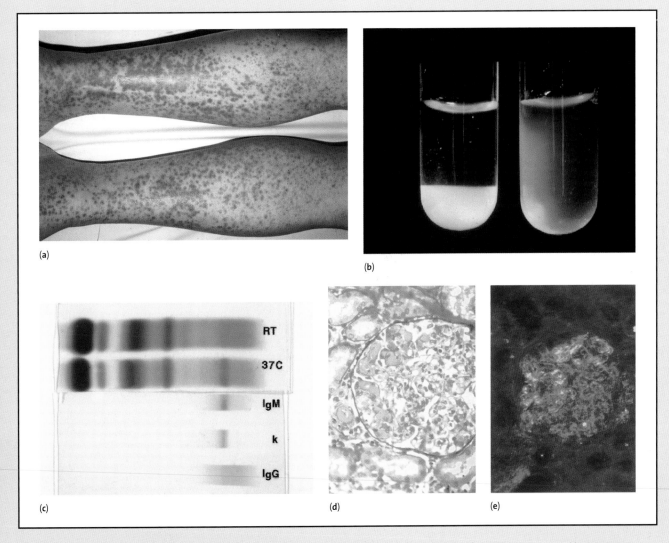

(a)

(b)

(c)

(d)

(e)

▲**Fig. 7** Clinical and laboratory manifestations of mixed cryoglobulinaemia in a patient with hepatitis C infection. (**a**) Palpable purpura caused by cutaneous vasculitis. (**b**) Stored serum showing cryoprecipitate after 24-hour incubation at 4°C (left), and redissolving on heating to 37°C (right). (**c**) Zone electrophoresis of serum collected at 37°C shows the redissolved cryoprecipitate as a discrete band in the γ region, which on immunofixation is shown to be composed of monoclonal IgM κ and polyclonal IgG. Note the absence of γ band in sample collected at room temperature (RT). (**d**) Renal biopsy showing eosinophilic glomerular deposits of cryoglobulin (pseudothrombi), corresponding to IgG deposits (**e**) on immunofluorescence. (Reproduced with permission from Maricic MJ. Winners of the 1992 ACR Slide Competition and future plans for the Clinical Silde Collection on the rheumatic diseases. The ACR Audiovisual Aids Subcomittee. *Arthritis Rheum.* 1992; 35: 1106–7.)

- Ask about leg ulcers, which are a feature of severe cutaneous vasculitis.

- Has there been poor circulation in the hands, feet and nose? Ask about Raynaud's phenomenon: although this is a common feature of cryoglobulinaemia reflecting peripheral vascular obstruction due to cryoglobulins, it also occurs frequently in lupus and scleroderma. In all these conditions, patients may describe episodic symptoms on a background of permanently cold hands.

Joint pains

Ask about the following.

- Onset and course of pain: arthralgia associated with early morning stiffness may occur in most of the disorders listed in Table 6, but is particularly pronounced in patients with rheumatoid vasculitis.

- Distribution and symmetry: symmetrical arthralgia affecting the hands, knees, ankles and elbows is common in mixed cryoglobulinaemia, but rarely progresses to frank arthritis.

Renal impairment

The degree of renal impairment noted in this patient at presentation will not directly produce any symptoms, but is it a new finding related to her acute presentation or does she have unrelated chronic renal failure (stage 3 chronic kidney disease)? Enquire about previous history of any renal problems including urinary tract infection, urinary stones, haematuria, tests of the urine for medicals or when pregnant, hypertension, family history of renal disorder and previous blood tests to measure renal function.

Rapidly progressive glomerulonephritis, which can cause advanced renal failure, may occur

as part of the ANCA-associated vasculitides, but in this case the length of the history suggests a more slowly evolving disorder such as mixed cryoglobulinaemia. Glomerulonephritis occurs in about 50% of cases of mixed cryoglobulinaemia (Fig. 7) but remains asymptomatic in the early stages: oedema and hypertension are common manifestations of advanced renal disease.

Are there features to suggest any of the alternative diagnoses listed in Table 6? Ask directly about the following.

- Problems with the nose (bleeding and/or discharge) and ears (deafness and/or discharge), which would suggest Wegener's granulomatosis.

- Is there anything to support the diagnosis of lupus, eg pleurisy, pericarditis or photosensitive rash (see Section 1.1.8).

Other relevant history

Aside from a rapid screen of past medical history and a functional enquiry, ask about Sjögren's syndrome, lupus and rheumatoid

arthritis because cryoglobulinaemic vasculitis can occur as a complication of any of these disorders.

> Enquire about exposure to blood products because hepatitis C virus (HCV) infection now accounts for about 70% of cases of mixed cryoglobulinaemia.

Plan for investigation and management

After explaining to the patient that under normal circumstances you would carry out a thorough clinical examination to confirm the findings in the referral letter, you would plan to perform the following blood and urine tests to arrive at a diagnosis.

Immunological tests

Cryoglobulins The key to detecting cryoglobulins is meticulous attention to detail. Collect a clotted sample of blood at 37°C and transport immediately and at the same temperature to the immunology laboratory. Once a cryoglobulin has been detected (see Fig. 7), it is essential to characterise the type in view of the different disease associations (Table 7).

TABLE 7 CLASSIFICATION OF CRYOGLOBULINS

Type	Composition	Disease associations
I	Composed entirely of monoclonal immunoglobulin, usually IgM or IgG	Waldenström's macroglobulinaemia Myeloma Lymphoproliferative disease
II	Monoclonal IgM rheumatoid factor plus polyclonal IgG	Infections, particularly HCV Autoimmune Lupus Sjögren's syndrome Rheumatoid arthritis A minority of cases are labelled 'idiopathic' (mixed essential cryoglobulinaemia)
III	Polyclonal IgM rheumatoid factor plus polyclonal IgG	

Types II and III cryoglobulins have overlapping disease associations.
HCV, hepatitis C virus.

Serum C3 and C4 Like any immune complex, mixed cryoglobulins activate the classic complement pathway; hence C4, but not C3, is reduced in their presence.

> 🔑 A markedly low C4 occurs in about 90% of patients with mixed cryoglobulinaemia as a result of classic pathway activation.

Rheumatoid factor Check the rheumatoid factor because it forms an integral part of mixed cryoglobulins.

> 🔑
> • The IgM component of mixed cryoglobulins exhibits strong rheumatoid factor activity, which together with the low C4 is an important clue pointing to mixed cryoglobulinaemia.
> • In contrast, Wegener's granulomatosis and MPA are characterised by normal or elevated complement levels as part of the acute-phase response.

Antineutrophil cytoplasmic antibodies Check ANCAs in view of the possibility of Wegener's granulomatosis/MPA.

Other tests

- Urine: dipstick for proteinuria and haematuria; microscopy of sediment for red cell casts as evidence of active glomerulonephritis.

- Renal function: to determine whether this has changed since referral.

- Liver function: in view of the strong association between HCV and mixed cryoglobulinaemia.

- Viral serology, especially HCV. If negative, proceed to polymerase chain reaction analysis of cryoprecipitate for HCV RNA.

- CXR: this may show changes compatible with Wegener's granulomatosis; lung involvement is unusual in mixed cryoglobulinaemia.

Explain to the patient that the results of any investigations will be reviewed at the next outpatient visit. It would also be appropriate to briefly discuss the need for a renal biopsy to confirm the diagnosis of cryoglobulinaemic vasculitis and rule out other causes of renal dysfunction, eg drug-related interstitial nephritis. The glomerulonephritis in mixed cryoglobulinaemia has distinctive features, being characterised by marked deposition of immunoglobulin and complement (see Fig. 7). In contrast, a pauci-immune glomerulonephritis (little or no complement or immunoglobulin deposited in the glomeruli) would favour ANCA-positive systemic vasculitis.

Further discussion

Symptoms in mixed cryoglobulinaemia are the result of a combination of immune complex-induced vasculitis and vascular obstruction by cryoglobulin. Most cases (60–80%) of cryoglobulinaemic vasculitis associated with a mixed cryoglobulin are now known to be driven by HCV infection. Prior to the 1990s these cases were categorised under the term 'mixed essential cryoglobulinaemia'. Although the role of HCV in causing liver infection is plausible, its role in driving a monoclonal population of plasma cells is less clear. Recent evidence suggests that HCV may do this by using CD81 (a cell-surface glycoprotein found on both lymphocytes and hepatocytes) as a receptor to gain entry into these cells. See Section 2.5.4 for discussion of management.

1.1.8 Arthralgia and photosensitive rash

> ### Letter of referral to rheumatology outpatient clinic
>
> Dear Doctor,
>
> **Re: Miss Chloe Taylor, aged 22 years**
>
> I would value your opinion on this nurse who presents with a 6-month history of joint pains and a facial rash. The rash is intermittently present and appears to be predominantly associated with outdoor activities. Clinical examination is essentially normal, but she is particularly concerned about the possibility of systemic lupus erythematosus (SLE) because her mother had cutaneous lupus diagnosed 5 years ago. Is SLE the diagnosis in this case?
>
> Yours sincerely,

Introduction

The combination of joint pains and a facial rash (Fig. 8) in a young woman certainly raises the possibility of SLE, more so in the presence of a family history of lupus, as in this case. However, although SLE should be the main diagnosis under consideration, you should be aware of other disorders that present with joint pains and a rash.

- Viral infection, eg parvovirus, may mimic SLE.

- Dermatomyositis: this may present with arthralgia and a

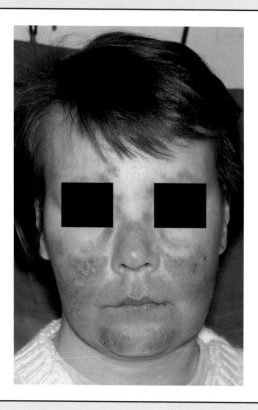

▲ Fig. 8 Patchy facial erythema with scarring and marked eyebrow involvement in a patient with SLE. (Courtesy of Dr M. Goodfield, Leeds General Infirmary.)

• Morning stiffness? This is a non-specific feature of any inflammatory joint disorder.

> Joint involvement occurs in 90% of patients with lupus and is characterised by a symmetrical, distal and non-erosive arthritis. Frank deforming arthritis is rare and occurs in a small minority of patients.

Rash

Ask about the distribution of the rash. Does it predominantly affect sun-exposed areas of the body? Does sunlight precipitate or aggravate the rash? Skin manifestations of lupus may occur either on their own [discoid lupus erythematosus (Fig. 9) and subacute cutaneous lupus erythematosus] or in association with systemic disease. In subacute cutaneous lupus erythematosus a photosensitive malar rash affecting the bridge of the nose and the cheeks is characteristic (Fig. 10). Photosensitivity is a characteristic feature of the skin rash of lupus, which is probably due to the induction of keratinocyte apoptosis by ultraviolet light and the consequent exposure of lupus autoantigens to the immune system.

Other relevant history

Since SLE is a multisystem disease, ask about the following pointers to the diagnosis and activity of lupus:

• hair loss;

• livedo reticularis;

• Raynaud's phenomenon;

• mouth ulcers (Fig. 11);

• chest or abdominal pain (serositis) and dyspnoea;

• headaches;

• seizures;

photosensitive rash in the 'V' of the neck and upper trunk.

• Lyme disease and rheumatic fever: characterised by distinctive skin rashes that appear in association with arthralgia and systemic disease; they should not cause difficulties in differential diagnosis.

• Psoriatic arthritis.

Note that photosensitivity is not a feature of viral infection, Lyme disease, rheumatic fever and psoriatic arthritis. Each of these disorders has characteristic features that enable it to be distinguished from SLE on clinical grounds. Proceed to serology in cases of diagnostic doubt.

History of the presenting problem

Is SLE the explanation? The aim must be to clarify the presenting symptoms, and also to ask relevant questions regarding involvement of other organ systems.

Joint pains

Ask about the following.

• Onset and course of the pain: non-specific joint pains associated with early morning stiffness may occur with any inflammatory disorder and will not help in differentiating between lupus, parvoviral infection and psoriatic arthritis.

• Distribution and symmetry: is it proximal or distal? An asymmetrical distal arthropathy may occur with both lupus and psoriatic arthritis, but is distinguished by characteristic distal interphalangeal joint involvement accompanied by skin changes in psoriasis. Large joint involvement tends to occur more frequently in psoriatic arthropathy.

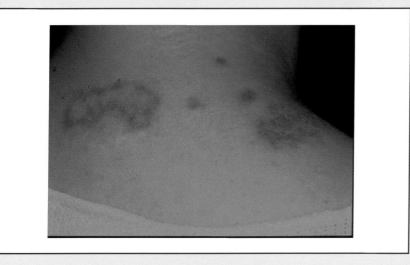

▲ **Fig. 9** Rash of discoid lupus in a patient with isolated cutaneous lupus.

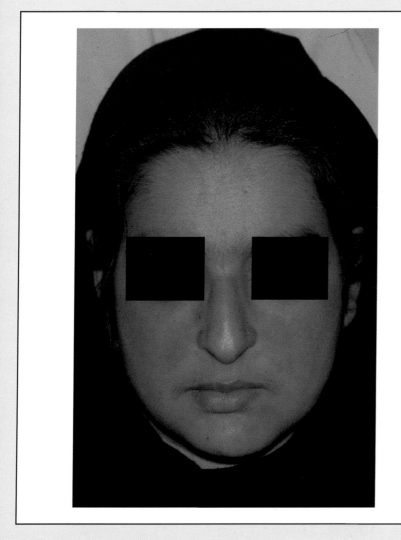

▲ **Fig. 10** Photosensitive malar rash in a patient with systemic lupus.

- drug history to exclude the possibility of drug-induced lupus – more than 80 drugs have been reported to trigger lupus, with common culprits being sulfasalazine, hydralazine and minocycline.

Plan for investigation and management

After explaining to the patient that under normal circumstances you would carry out a thorough clinical examination to confirm the findings in the referral letter, you would plan to perform the following tests.

Immunological investigations
Antibodies to nuclear antigens
As SLE is the main diagnosis under consideration, the patient's antinuclear antibody (ANA) status is crucial.

Using human epithelial cells as a substrate:
- ANA positivity (titre >1:80) occurs in >99% of patients with untreated SLE;
- negative ANA effectively excludes systemic lupus.

As a positive ANA can occur in a variety of other disorders, it is important to characterise its specificity, ie is it directed against double-stranded DNA and/or other extractable nuclear antigens (ENA; individual specificities known as Ro, La, Sm and ribonucleoprotein)?

Antibodies to DNA and ENA are specific for lupus or lupus overlap disorders and occur in 30–90% of patients.

Serum complement levels Check C3 and C4 levels. Patients with lupus may be hypocomplementaemic as

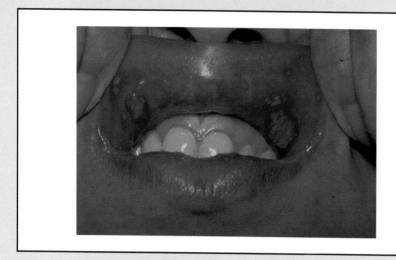

▲ Fig. 11 Mouth ulcers in a patient with active lupus.

a result of active disease and/or possession of one or more C4 null alleles.

Antiphospholipid antibodies

Check for anticardiolipin antibodies and lupus anticoagulant. These antibodies occur in 30% of lupus patients and act as markers for thrombosis (Fig. 12).

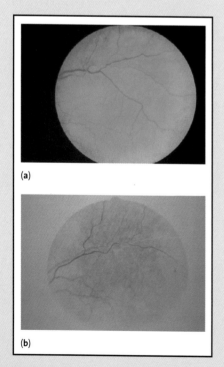

(a)

(b)

▲ Fig. 12 **(a)** Branch retinal artery occlusion in a patient with SLE and the antiphospholipid syndrome; the defect is more pronounced in the subtraction angiogram **(b)**.

Other tests

Check the following.

- Urine: dipstick to check for proteinuria and haematuria. If there is proteinuria, quantitate by estimating urinary albumin/creatinine ratio; if there is haematuria, microscopy of sediment for red cell casts as evidence of active glomerulonephritis.

- Renal function.

- Liver function.

- FBC: looking for cytopenia.

- C-reactive protein: marker of inflammation/infection. This is often normal in active uncomplicated lupus despite elevated erythrocyte sedimentation rate or plasma viscosity.

It would be worthwhile pointing out that further investigations may be required should the diagnosis of lupus be confirmed. If renal function is significantly impaired and/or there is an active urinary sediment, then it is likely that a renal biopsy will be required to determine prognosis and guide treatment decisions. Skin biopsies are seldom performed in the assessment of SLE, although the demonstration of a 'lupus band' is useful in the diagnosis of cutaneous lupus erythematosus (Fig. 13).

Further discussion

Given the multisystem nature of the disease, the American College of Rheumatology have drawn up a list of criteria to help in the diagnosis of SLE. Although these are helpful for research and disease classification, it is important to recognise that rigid adherence to them in clinical practice may, on occasions, lead to the delayed diagnosis of lupus.

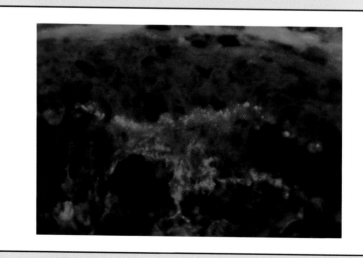

▲ Fig. 13 Granular IgG deposits at the dermoepidermal junction (lupus band). (Courtesy of Dr W. Merchant, Leeds General Infirmary.)

American College of Rheumatology criteria for the diagnosis of SLE

- Malar rash.
- Discoid rash.
- Photosensitivity.
- Oral ulcers.
- Non-erosive arthritis.
- Serositis (pleuritis/pericarditis).
- Renal disease (persistent proteinuria/casts).
- Neurological disorder (seizures/psychosis).
- Haemolytic anaemia/leucopenia/thrombocytopenia.
- Antinuclear antibody.
- Antibodies to double-stranded DNA/anti-ENA/antiphospholipid antibodies.

To establish a diagnosis of SLE, four or more criteria are required serially or simultaneously during any period of observation.

If this patient is shown to have lupus, it would be worthwhile excluding primary complement deficiency in view of the positive family history. Homozygous deficiency of early complement components (C1q, C1r and C1s, C4 and C2) is strongly associated with the development of SLE. See Section 2.4.1 for discussion on management.

1.1.9 Cold fingers and difficulty swallowing

Letter of referral to rheumatology outpatient clinic

Dear Doctor,

Re: Mrs Hannah Adams, aged 50 years

Thank you for seeing this woman who describes a 9-month history of cold painful fingers. She has some mild swallowing difficulties that have started recently, but is otherwise well. She has no past medical history of note. Please would you advise as to whether she requires any further investigation or ongoing follow-up?

Yours sincerely,

Introduction

It is important to clarify both these symptoms, because cold fingers mean different things to different people and the meaning of difficulty in swallowing can range from occasional benign choking to true dysphagia. The following are key questions to consider.

- Are her cold fingers a result of Raynaud's phenomenon and, if so, is it primary or secondary (see Table 8)?

- If the diagnosis is scleroderma, the commonest of the connective tissue diseases associated with Raynaud's, is it limited cutaneous systemic sclerosis (LCSS) or diffuse cutaneous systemic sclerosis (DCSS)?

- Is there evidence of internal organ involvement?

Causes of secondary Raynaud's phenomenon

- Connective tissue diseases: scleroderma, SLE, rheumatoid arthritis (RA) and inflammatory myositis.
- Occlusive arterial disease: thoracic outlet syndrome, atherosclerosis/embolism and thromboangiitis obliterans.
- Occupational: vibrating tools.
- Drugs/toxins: ergotamine, beta-blockers and polyvinyl chloride (PVC).
- Intravascular coagulation or aggregation: cryoglobulinaemia, cold agglutinin disease and polycythaemia rubra vera.

History of the presenting problem

Are the cold fingers caused by Raynaud's phenomenon? Consider the following, which also help to distinguish primary from secondary causes.

- Is there a colour change? Well-demarcated pallor, then cyanosis and then rubor (white → blue → red) are the typical triphasic colour changes of Raynaud's phenomenon, although many patients will describe only biphasic changes.

Characteristics	Primary Raynaud's phenomenon	Secondary Raynaud's phenomenon
Age (average) (years)	Teenage	>50
Sex	Female	Female
Tissue damage	Absent	Digital ulcers and gangrene
Symmetry	Symmetrical attacks	Can have asymmetrical attacks
Nail-fold microscopy	Negative	Positive
Antinuclear antibody	Negative	Positive
Associated disease	No associated disease	Scleroderma, SLE and lupus overlap

TABLE 8 COMPARISON OF PRIMARY AND SECONDARY RAYNAUD'S PHENOMENON

SLE, systemic lupus erythematosus.

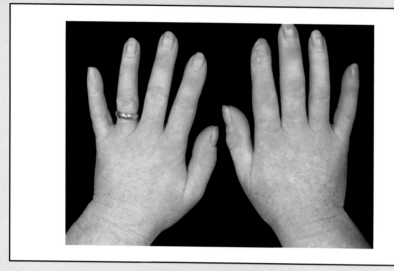

▲**Fig. 14** Finger pallor during an attack of Raynaud's phenomenon.

- What are the precipitating factors? Raynaud's phenomenon is usually provoked by exposure to cold and emotional stress and is terminated by rewarming, although it may abate spontaneously.

- Where? Usually in the fingers (Fig. 14), but other areas affected are toes and ears.

- How bad and for how long?

- Is the problem associated with trophic changes/ulcers in the fingers?

Obstruction of major arteries

Consider obstruction of major upper arm arteries (atherosclerosis, thrombosis and embolism), which may mimic Raynaud's phenomenon.

- Colour changes may be similar to those in Raynaud's.
- Symptoms are more likely to be unilateral.
- Arm claudication is characteristic.
- There will be low BP and reduced peripheral pulses in the affected arm.
- Arteriography demonstrates the arterial lesion.

Explore the history of dysphagia (see *Gastroenterology and Hepatology*, Section 1.1.2).

Other relevant history
Does the patient have one of the causes of secondary Raynaud's phenomenon? Consider the following.

Systemic sclerosis
This is clearly the most likely diagnosis in this case, so pursue symptoms commonly seen in this condition.

- Skin: sclerodactyly, digital ulceration, calcinosis and telangiectasia.

- Gastrointestinal: dysphagia, indigestion/heartburn, weight loss and faecal incontinence.

- Respiratory: shortness of breath, which may reflect lung fibrosis or pulmonary hypertension.

Also note that cranial neuropathies, in particular facial pain secondary to trigeminal neuralgia, are rarely seen.

If the patient has systemic sclerosis (SS), ask about the timing of Raynaud's in relation to sclerodactyly: Raynaud's can precede skin changes by many years in LCSS.

Other connective tissue disorders
Ask about arthralgia/arthritis, photosensitivity, rashes, alopecia and proximal muscle weakness; also enquire regarding any family history of connective tissue diseases.

Other issues

- Drug history: beta-blockers, anti-migraine compounds and cytotoxics can exacerbate Raynaud's.

- Occupation, eg use of vibrating tools and exposure to PVC/organic solvents.

- Smoking: an obvious risk factor for obstructive arterial disease.

Plan for investigation and management
After explaining to the patient that under normal circumstances you would carry out a thorough clinical examination to confirm the findings in the referral letter, you would plan to perform the following tests.

Diagnosis/prognosis

- Antinuclear antibodies: typically negative in primary Raynaud's phenomenon; anti-centromere is associated with limited SS, anti-topoisomerase/anti-Scl-70 are present in diffuse SS.

- Inflammatory markers: erythrocyte sedimentation rate and C-reactive protein are usually normal in primary Raynaud's phenomenon, but may be elevated in secondary Raynaud's phenomenon if there is tissue inflammation/damage.

- Radiology: CXR to look for basal fibrosis, followed by high-resolution CT of the chest

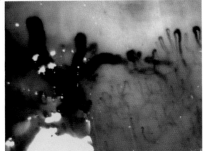

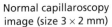
Normal capillaroscopy image (size 3 × 2 mm)

Dilated capillary structure to the grade of mega-capillary.

▲**Fig. 15** Abnormal nail-fold capillary morphology characterised by dilatation and loss of capillaries, depicted on microscopy with normal appearances for comparison. (Courtesy of Dr John Allen, Freeman Hospital.)

if this is present. Use cervical rib views if hand/arm symptoms are unilateral.

- Nail-fold capillary microscopy: useful in differentiating primary from secondary Raynaud's phenomenon. Abnormal nail-fold capillary morphology depicting dilatation and drop-out (Fig. 15) indicates secondary disease and predicts the presence, or future development, of autoimmune rheumatic disease (see Section 2.4).

- Cold challenge test: abnormal rewarming is seen in SS but is unusual in primary Raynaud's.

Assessment of organ damage

- FBC: patients with secondary Raynaud's phenomenon may be anaemic as a result of the chronic disease itself, gastrointestinal blood loss and/or malabsorption.

- Urine dipstick for protein and blood (with estimation of urinary albumin/creatinine ratio and urine microscopy for casts if positive) and estimation of renal function: abnormalities would not be expected in primary Raynaud's phenomenon and would suggest renal problems related to a secondary disorder.

Even though 5% of the general population have Raynaud's phenomenon, only a minority eventually develop an associated connective tissue disease. The following are the frequencies of Raynaud's phenomenon in those with autoimmune rheumatic disease:

- scleroderma 95%;
- SLE 20%;
- Sjögren's syndrome 20%;
- myositis 20%;
- RA 5%.

Other tests that might be considered, depending on clinical findings and the outcome of initial tests, include echocardiography to assess right-sided heart pressures (pulmonary hypertension occurs in LCSS) and pulmonary function tests (to look for interstitial lung disease associated with SS).

Management

For any patient with troublesome Raynaud's phenomenon, it will be appropriate to consider the following.

- General measures: patient education; advise patients to keep their hands warm.

- Smoking cessation: this should be strongly encouraged.

- Vasodilators, eg nifedipine.

- Careful control of BP.

No other treatment is required for most patients with primary Raynaud's and regular follow-up in hospital is generally not needed. Some causes of secondary Raynaud's may be amenable to specific treatment, but unfortunately options for patients with SS (as likely in this case) are limited (see Section 2.4.3).

Further discussion

Absence of signs or symptoms of connective tissue diseases in a patient with late-onset Raynaud's does not mean the Raynaud's is primary. The presence of abnormal nail-fold microscopy or positive autoantibodies is strongly predictive of an associated connective tissue disease. Raynaud's may precede other symptoms by many years in cases of LCSS.

LCSS and DCSS are differentiated clinically according to the extent of skin involvement (cut-off at elbows and knees). A common misconception is that in LCSS there is no internal organ involvement, which is not true: although less common than in DCSS, there can be very serious internal complications such as pulmonary artery hypertension.

1.1.10 Dry eyes and fatigue

Letter of referral to rheumatology outpatient clinic

Dear Doctor,

Re: Mrs Beth Stokes, aged 53 years

Thank you for seeing this woman who has had dry eyes for over 6 months. It is uncomfortable and appears to be interfering with her work. She is also troubled by facial swelling, increasing fatigue, breathlessness and pain in her hands. On examination it seems as though her parotid glands are enlarged, but I cannot convince myself of any other physical signs.

Please can you see her and advise regarding appropriate investigation and management.

Yours sincerely,

Introduction

Dry eyes are caused by insufficient tear production. Possible causes include the following.

- Ageing, especially postmenopausal women.

- Medication: diuretics, anticholinergics, antihistamines, beta-blockers and the oral contraceptive pill.

- Sjögren's syndrome: primary or secondary.

- Damage to the eyes/eyelids.

- Blepharitis.

- Idiopathic.

In this case, the associated fatigue and facial swelling caused by enlarged parotid glands point towards Sjögren's syndrome, with arthralgia suggesting a secondary cause of this.

History of the presenting problem

Assess the severity of the patient's sicca symptoms by asking the following questions.

- Do you feel a gritty sensation in your eyes?

- Do you have sore eyes or difficulty in wearing contact lenses?

- Do you have difficulty in trying to eat dry foods (cracker sign)?

- Do you need to take liquids to aid swallowing?

- Do you wake up at night with a dry mouth and have to take sips of water?

Consider other causes of parotid swelling (Table 9), although it would be uncommon for the other disorders listed in this table to cause sicca symptoms.

Once the diagnosis of Sjögren's seems likely, establish whether this is primary or secondary (ie associated with an established connective tissue disease). The presence of hand pain in this case should lead you to ask questions directed towards rheumatoid arthritis (see Section 1.1.14), a common association of Sjögren's syndrome. Enquire about disease manifestations beyond the dry eyes and mouth, which can be divided into exocrine and non-exocrine (Table 10).

Other relevant history

Dental caries is increased in Sjögren's, so ask the patient

TABLE 9 CAUSES OF BILATERAL PAROTID ENLARGEMENT

Disorder	Comments
Viral infection (mumps, EBV, coxsackievirus A, CMV, HIV)	Usually acute in onset on a background of systemic ill-health
Sarcoidosis	Occurs on a background of systemic disease
Sjögren's syndrome	Positive ANA, rheumatoid factor and antibodies to Ro and La
Miscellaneous group: diabetes, hyperlipidaemia, alcohol abuse, acromegaly and chronic renal failure	Other clues to primary diagnosis usually present

ANA, antinuclear antibodies; CMV, cytomegalovirus; EBV, Epstein–Barr virus.

TABLE 10 MANIFESTATIONS OF SJÖGREN'S SYNDROME

Exocrine	
Eyes	Dry
Mouth/upper respiratory tract	Dry, hoarseness and oral candidiasis
Gastrointestinal	Dysphagia (can also be secondary to dysmotility)
Pancreas	Rarely clinically apparent
Vagina	Dyspareunia/vaginal dryness
Non-exocrine	
Musculoskeletal	Arthralgia, arthritis and myalgia (60–70% of cases)
Skin	Raynaud's (in ~20–40% of cases of primary Sjögren's) Purpura (mixed cryoglobulinaemia) Vasculitis (5–10% of cases)
Lungs	Interstitial pneumonitis (10–20% of cases) NB Suspect lymphoma if CXR shows hilar/mediastinal lymphadenopathy
Renal	Interstitial nephritis May rarely present as distal renal tubular acidosis with renal colic and hypokalaemic muscle weakness
Neurological	Peripheral neuropathy (secondary to vasculitis)

---

questions regarding dental health and frequency of dental appointments.

The impact of ocular and oral dryness on quality of life is often underestimated. It has an effect on social interactions, particularly as meal times are a focal point for socialising.

Plan for investigation and management

To confirm Sjögren's syndrome

- Schirmer's test to obtain objective evidence of reduced tear secretion: insert a small strip of filter paper under the patient's lower eyelid. Wetting of <5 mm in 5 minutes is considered pathological.

- Check ANA and antibodies to Ro and La antigens: these are present in 40–90% of patients with Sjögren's syndrome.

Biopsy of minor salivary glands can reveal histological evidence of focal lymphocytic infiltrates, but is rarely required because of the ease of detecting antibodies to Ro and La.

Other investigations

Keratoconjunctivitis sicca, a consequence of reduced tear production, is diagnosed using rose bengal staining of the cornea. Severity of xerostomia can be assessed using salivary gland scintigraphy and sialometry, but these investigations are rarely performed in routine practice.

Other autoimmune and inflammatory markers:

- rheumatoid factor is positive in 90% of cases of Sjögren's syndrome;

- C3 and C4 levels are usually normal;

- erythrocyte sedimentation rate is usually elevated (a direct consequence of polyclonal

hypergammaglobulinaemia) but C-reactive protein is often normal.

Check thyroid function in view of the strong association between Sjögren's syndrome and hypothyroidism.

Other tests are performed as clinically indicated, eg in light of the breathlessness in this case, pulmonary function tests and/or high-resolution CT may be warranted depending on the findings of clinical examination. Also consider investigations specific to rheumatoid arthritis if it is suspected following history and examination (see Section 1.1.14).

Management

Therapy for Sjögren's syndrome is limited to symptomatic relief and limitation of the damaging local effects of the sicca complex using the following:

- artificial tears, sugar-free candies and chewing gum;

- meticulous dental hygiene;

- avoidance of diuretics and anticholinergic agents that worsen sicca symptoms.

Immunosuppressive therapy is of little value in uncomplicated Sjögren's syndrome.

1.1.11 Breathlessness and weakness

Letter of referral to rheumatology outpatient clinic

Dear Doctor,

Mrs Brenda Wilde, aged 35 years

Please see this woman who presents with a 6-week history of breathlessness, aching thighs

and shoulders, and insidiously progressive weakness. She now finds it difficult to climb stairs or rise from a low chair. Her previous medical history is unremarkable.

Yours sincerely,

Introduction

The history raises an immediate suspicion of a proximal myopathy. This should trigger a hierarchy of diagnostic questions. Is the weakness real, or could the primary problem be pain rather than weakness? Weakness is usually more prominent than pain in primary muscle disease. Is this true proximal weakness, or could there be another cause of symmetrical leg weakness (eg spinal cord pathology).

If a myopathic pattern of weakness is present, consider the diagnoses listed in Table 11. If dermatomyositis (DM) or polymyositis (PM) is likely, consider a search for associated malignancy. Also, remember to be alert for non-muscular manifestations of connective tissue disease.

In suspected myosis think about:

- alternative causes of weakness;
- malignancy;
- changes in other systems, especially the lungs.

History of the presenting problem

Muscular/neurological

Gain a picture of the pattern of symptoms and their rate of progression. Ask the patient about the following.

TABLE 11 CAUSES OF PROXIMAL MUSCLE WEAKNESS DEVELOPING OVER A FEW WEEKS

Disorder type	Disorder	Comments
Inflammatory (idiopathic)	PM/DM	DM associated with heliotrope rash affecting eyelids and Gottron's papules (Fig.16) Other features of autoimmune rheumatic disorder 25% of cases associated with malignancy
	Polymyalgia rheumatica	>55 years only Weakness secondary to pain General malaise Anaemia of chronic disorder Raised inflammatory markers No other organ involvement Negative serological tests
Endocrine/metabolic	Cushing's syndrome	Look for associated features of steroid excess Exogenous steroids are a very common cause of proximal myopathy
	Thyrotoxicosis	Look for associated features Check thyroid function tests
	Osteomalacia	Rare in this age group, when the problem is likely to be the result of malabsorption
	Diabetes mellitus	Diabetic amyotrophy affects the quadriceps, causing pain and weakness Usually asymmetrical Does not affect shoulder girdle
Other	Myasthenia gravis	Critical clinical feature is fatiguability
	Carcinomatous neuromyopathy	Usually found in patients with known malignancy, but can be a presenting feature
	Trichinella spiralis	Acquired from eating improperly cooked pork Weakness caused by muscular pain is a feature of the larval migration stage

DM, dermatomyositis; PM, polymyositis.

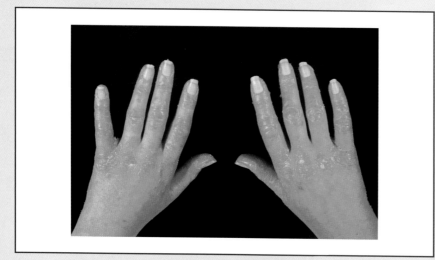

▲ **Fig. 16** Scaly patches (known as Gottron's papules) on the dorsal surface of the hands in dermatomyositis.

- When did the weakness start? A very long history might suggest an inherited muscle dystrophy presenting in an adult. Although the history is said to be of 6 weeks' duration, could it be longer than this? A year ago, could she walk as far and as fast as other people? Has she ever been able to do this?

- What are the functional consequences of the weakness? Can she get up stairs at all and, if so, how does she do it? Can she brush her hair? Is there anything to suggest defective control of swallowing or the upper airway? Has she choked when drinking?

- Is pain a prominent feature? If it is, this might indicate osteomalacia or fibromyalgia.

- Does the history suggest a rapid onset of fatigue with repeated movement, possibly as a result of myasthenia (see *Neurology*, Section 2.2.5)?

- Has the patient had headaches? This woman is too young but, in an older patient, have there been headaches that might indicate temporal arteritis/polymyalgia rheumatica?

- Are there any other neurological symptoms, particularly sensory changes, that would suggest a non-myopathic cause?

Other systems

Ask specifically about the breathlessness. Is exercise limited by weakness of the legs or by the breathing? Breathing difficulty could be caused by myopathy of the respiratory muscles or be associated with lung disease (alveolitis).

If information does not emerge spontaneously, pursue the following, which may give important clues about a systemic disorder. Think about the conditions listed in Table 11 as you do so.

- General: weight loss or weight gain, and preference for hot or cold weather. These could be clues to malignancy, Cushing's syndrome or thyrotoxicosis.

- Skin: has there been a rash, especially a photosensitive rash, which might be found in both systemic lupus erythematosus and DM?

- Joints: has there been any pain or swelling?

- Hands: does the woman have Raynaud's phenomenon?

- Eyes and mouth: has she had any problems with gritty eyes or a dry mouth? These might indicate Sjögren's syndrome (see Section 1.1.10).

- Respiratory: has there been pleuritic pain or haemoptysis?

- Gastrointestinal: have there been any new symptoms?

- Pregnancy history: multiple fetal losses might indicate the presence of an antiphospholipid antibody.

- Previous vascular or thromboembolic disease: this also might indicate the presence of an antiphospholipid antibody.

Plan for investigation and management

After explaining to the patient that under normal circumstances you would carry out a thorough clinical examination to look for evidence of disorders that may be responsible for her symptoms, you would plan to carry out the following blood and muscle tests to arrive at a diagnosis. It would be prudent to warn the patient at this stage that you may wish to proceed to muscle biopsy.

Investigations

The diagnosis may be clear from the history and examination, in which case investigations should be appropriately tailored; otherwise, the following issues need to be addressed.

Muscle disease The following investigations should be considered.

- Creatine kinase (CK) estimation is the most useful marker of muscle damage, but remember that myopathies may occur with a normal CK, and that CK may be raised in the absence of muscle disease (eg after heavy exercise).

- Other enzymes (eg aspartate transaminase and alanine transaminase) may be raised, leading to the potential for confusion with liver disease if myopathy is not initially suspected.

- Electromyography provides useful evidence to confirm myopathy and to exclude denervation as a cause of weakness.

- Muscle biopsy remains the only tool for definitive differential diagnosis of myopathy.

- MRI is useful in patchy myositis to identify a site for biopsy.

Identifying the underlying cause
The extent of investigation for malignancy is determined by clinical suspicion and the patient's age. A minimal screen would be a CXR and abdominal and pelvic ultrasonography. Endocrinological investigation (for steroid excess and vitamin D studies) should be considered, depending on the clinical picture.

Are immunological markers of inflammatory myositis present? Consider appropriate tests in suspected lupus and other connective tissue disease (see Sections 1.1.8 and 3.2). Antibodies to Jo-1 (histidyl-tRNA synthetase) occur in 30–50% of patients with DM and PM, and act as a marker for interstitial lung disease.

> **Antibodies to Jo-1**
>
> Antibodies to Jo-1 identify a distinct group of patients with inflammatory myositis, designated the anti-synthetase syndrome (myositis, fever, interstitial lung disease, Raynaud's phenomenon and symmetrical non-erosive arthritis).

Management

You should explain to the patient that the results of blood and muscle tests will be reviewed at an urgent follow-up visit. It would be sensible to warn her that she may require hospital admission for the initiation of immunosuppressive treatment if the diagnosis turns out to be inflammatory myositis.

Beware of respiratory failure in patients severely affected by PM/DM. Swallowing and the airway may be compromised with the risk of aspiration. Any patient with severe muscular weakness will require physiotherapy to minimise wasting and prevent contractures. Management otherwise depends on the cause. Treatment of inflammatory muscle disease is with corticosteroids and immunosuppressants, eg methotrexate or azathioprine.

Further discussion

Be alert to the possibility that DM may present as a paraneoplastic manifestation of underlying malignancy such as carcinoma of the ovaries, gastrointestinal tract, lung or breast and non-Hodgkin's lymphoma.

1.1.12 Low back pain

Letter of referral to rheumatology outpatient clinic

Dear Doctor

Re: Mr Manny Vass, aged 35 years

Thank you for seeing this man who has recently had to stop work as a plasterer because of low back pain. His symptoms began in his early twenties and have progressed to a near-constant pain. He has recently developed a sharp shooting pain down his right leg. His sleep is now disturbed and he is increasingly depressed and frustrated. I suspect his back pain is mechanical in origin but would value your opinion.

Yours sincerely,

Introduction

Most low back pain is mechanical in nature, requiring little or no investigation. However, a few patients have serious, progressive pathology that needs rapid access to appropriate investigations and management. When considering

TABLE 12 DIFFERENTIAL DIAGNOSIS OF LOW BACK PAIN

Category	Disease process
Mechanical (common)	Facet joint arthropathy
	Degenerative disc disease
	Vertebral fractures
Inflammatory	Ankylosing spondylitis
	Sacroiliitis
Infiltrative	Malignancy
	Infection (osteomyelitis, discitis or abscess)
Radicular	Foramenal stenosis
	Herniated intervertebral disc
Metabolic	Paget's disease
	Osteomalacia
Referred	Intra-abdominal pathology, eg aneurysm, ovarian cysts and endometriosis

back pain, try to categorise the differential diagnosis into the following major groups: mechanical, metabolic, inflammatory, referred and infiltrative (Table 12). Note that patients may have more than one disease process going on simultaneously.

These categories may be differentiated by some of the features listed in Table 13.

History of the presenting problem

- What was the progression of his symptoms? The natural history of mechanical back pain, the commonest cause of low back pain, is initially short infrequent episodes of disabling pain, usually of sudden onset, interspersed with episodes of good health. The episodes become more frequent over time and ultimately the patient may develop constant chronic low back pain, often with superimposed exacerbations.

- When did it start? Mechanical low back pain usually starts between the ages of 20 and 40. New-onset back pain over the age of 55 is a 'red flag' symptom (see below).

- What is the character of the leg pain? Sharp lancinating pain

suggests direct nerve root involvement, eg a herniated intervertebral disc, whereas pain referred from other lumbar-innervated structures tends to be more dull and aching.

- What is the distribution of the leg pain? Is there any associated altered sensation/loss of sensation/weakness? Are there exacerbating/alleviating factors?

Nerve roots are commonly compressed in spinal pathology. Unilateral nerve root compression is indicated by referred pain with a radicular distribution, lower limb dermatomal sensory disturbance or lower limb motor disturbance. Peripheral nerve compression, such as entrapment of the sciatic nerve in the piriformis fossa, can give similar symptoms. Features of nerve root lesions are shown in Fig. 17 and Table 14.

Neuropathic pain that is made worse with exertion is typical of spinal claudication. This may be differentiated from true intermittent claudication by the association of back pain or by the pattern of resolution with spinal claudication. In some cases, simply resting can be insufficient to alleviate the pain,

TABLE 13 FEATURES OF MECHANICAL, INFLAMMATORY AND INFILTRATIVE CAUSES OF LOW BACK PAIN

	Mechanical	Inflammatory	Infiltrative
Onset	Episodic. Acute becoming chronic	Subacute	Insidious. May be a sudden onset if there is a pathological fracture
Site	Diffuse	Diffuse. May be localised to sacroiliac joints or referred to buttocks or back of thighs	Focal, though muscle spasm may lead to diffuse pain
Exacerbating factors	Variable. Often related to increasing forces, eg lifting or bending	Worse with inactivity and at night	Worse at night; can prevent sleep
Alleviating factors	Rest	Exercise	
Morning stiffness	Mild	Severe (>1 hour)	None
Systemic features	None	Peripheral arthritis, iritis, colitis and psoriasis	Fever, weight loss and change in bowel habit

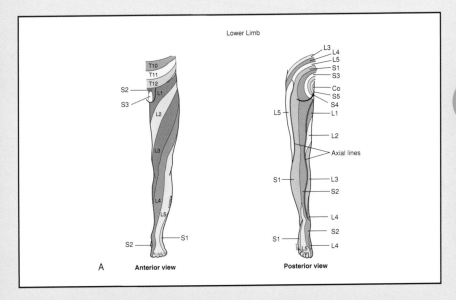

▲**Fig. 17** Lower limb dermatomes and peripheral nerves.

TABLE 14 FEATURES OF NERVE ROOT LESIONS

Nerve root	Weakness	Reflex
L2	Hip flexion and abduction	
L3	Knee extension	Knee
L4	Knee extension and ankle dorsiflexion	Knee
L5	Knee flexion, great toe dorsiflexion and foot inversion	
S1	Knee flexion, ankle plantarflexion and foot eversion	Ankle

although it may be eased by sitting or lying with the hips and knees flexed. Pain exacerbated by raising a straight leg suggests sciatic nerve root irritation (L4–S1), and pain exacerbated by hip extension suggests femoral nerve root involvement (L2–4).

Other relevant history

It is important to explore the suggestion of psychosocial distress in the referral letter. Psychosocial 'yellow flags' indicate barriers to recovery and a poor prognosis.

Psychosocial 'yellow flags'

- Past or present depression.
- Tendency to somatise.
- Belief that serious disease is present and the prognosis is poor.
- Secondary gain from the 'sick role', including ongoing litigation.
- Tendency to view problems in a catastrophic fashion.

Plan for investigation and management

Investigation

Investigation is unlikely to be helpful in this patient. Plain radiographs may even cause iatrogenic harm by revealing incidental radiological features of doubtful clinical significance, which often reinforce the patient's belief that they have a serious and irreversible problem with their back. However, on occasions, patients may find negative investigations reassuring.

Therapeutic options and pain management

In chronic low back pain, exercise and a multidisciplinary

pain management approach are beneficial in improving pain and function. Analgesics, NSAIDs, back schools, behavioural therapy, massage and trigger point injections may all provide some benefit. Other treatments are of unproven benefit. Drugs such as amitriptyline or gabapentin may be of benefit for neuropathic pain.

1.1.13 Chronic back pain

Letter of referral to rheumatology outpatient clinic

Dear Doctor,

Re: Mrs Tina Forbes, aged 68 years

This woman has had chronic low back pain for over 25 years, but recently the pain has affected the thoracic spine and become more severe, leading to poor sleep. She is very worried and is losing weight. She is a heavy smoker and has a history of long-standing chronic obstructive airways disease and glaucoma.

Is anything serious going on, or does she simply require better analgesia?

Yours sincerely,

Introduction

The GP's referral letter describes four definite 'red flags', suggesting a probable sinister cause of her back pain and indicating that she requires rapid investigation and/or treatment of a potentially serious underlying condition.

'Red flags' in chronic back pain

- Age <20 or >55.
- Non-mechanical pain (capsular pattern).
- History of malignancy, steroids, HIV or other significant past history.
- Systemic symptoms such as weight loss.
- Progressive neurological deficit, eg saddle anaesthesia, sphincteric disturbance and other motor or sensory deficits.
- Structural deformity.
- Persistent night pain.
- Thoracic pain.

The differential diagnoses to explore in this case are:

- infiltrative cause, eg malignancy or infection;
- osteoporosis and vertebral fracture (steroid use is likely given the history of long-standing chronic obstructive airways disease);
- worsening of chronic low back pain.

History of the presenting problem

What is the nature of the pain? How did it start and how has it progressed?

Pain from infiltrative lesions is severe, often prevents sleep and is not eased by movement. Pain from vertebral fractures may also be severe. The two may be differentiated by the onset: osteoporotic vertebral fractures begin acutely, sometimes precipitated by lifting something heavy; infiltrative lesions start more insidiously. The pain from osteoporotic fractures improves slowly over months, whereas infiltrative lesions tend to progress into a more serious problem.

Is there any neurological involvement? If so, is it progressive and how fast is the progression?

Progressive neurological symptoms are suggestive of a worsening or expanding lesion and require urgent investigation. Ask specifically about both power and sensation in the legs, and also about the function of the bladder and bowels.

Cauda equina syndrome (altered perineal sensation with or without bowel or bladder paralysis) is a neurosurgical emergency.

Other relevant history

Are there associated symptoms suggestive of the underlying cause?

Malignancy

Quantify the weight loss. Are there symptoms of a primary on systems review? In this case, be particularly aware of lung cancer (as the patient has a strong smoking history). Is there bony pain at any other sites? Are there any symptoms of hypercalcaemia?

Infection

Is it a fever/systemic illness? Note any past history of serious infections, particularly tuberculosis.

Osteoporosis

Has she used steroids for her chronic obstructive pulmonary disease, and does she have any other of the following osteoporotic risk factors:

- female gender;
- increasing age;
- ethnicity (white or Asian);

- positive family history;

- sex hormone deficiency, including early menopause, late puberty and nulliparity;

- past history of low-trauma fracture;

- slender build;

- drugs, eg steroids;

- endocrine disorders, eg hyperthyroidism and hyperparathyroidism;

- neoplasia, eg multiple myeloma;

- gastrointestinal disorders, eg coeliac disease;

- rheumatic diseases, eg rheumatoid arthritis and ankylosing spondylitis;

- smoking;

- excessive alcohol consumption;

- low calcium intake;

- poor weight-bearing exercise.

The referral letter states that the patient is worried: try to find out why. Is it the severity of the pain, is she concerned about what might be causing it or does she have other worries? A detailed discussion of such matters would be the preserve of Station 4 in PACES, but some acknowledgement of these concerns would be appropriate and necessary in Station 2 as it would clearly be required when taking a history in routine clinical practice.

Plan for investigation and management

Explain to the patient that although she has had back pain for a long time, it is a concern to you that the nature of the back pain has changed and that the severity is such that she is not able to get a good night's

sleep. Because of this, you need to perform some investigations.

If you suspect cord compression or a cauda equina syndrome, then arrange admission for an urgent MRI scan and neurosurgical opinion. If there are no symptoms or signs to suggest these conditions, then tests to be organised include the following.

- Plain radiology: lumbar spine and chest radiographs.

- Blood tests: FBC, renal function, liver and bone profiles, inflammatory markers and blood cultures.

- Further imaging: discuss these with radiological colleagues. MRI is excellent for imaging discs, bone marrow, neural tissue, spinal canal, ligaments and paraspinal tissues. CT is good for spinal stenosis, bone tumours and fractures, and osteophytes.

If after the investigations listed above it seems likely that there has been an osteoporotic fracture, then arrange a dual-energy X-ray absorptiometry bone density scan.

Further discussion

The challenge in assessing patients with back pain is to sort the wood from the trees using clinical acumen. Very few patients, as is likely in this case, have a serious progressive pathology that requires rapid access to the appropriate investigations and management. Most patients have mechanical back pain and require little or no investigation: they are best served by a rehabilitative approach with minimal medical intervention.

1.1.14 Recurrent joint pain and stiffness

Letter of referral to rheumatology outpatient clinic

Dear Doctor,

Re: Mr Bobby Williams, aged 42 years

Thank you for seeing this self-employed labourer who has recently stopped work because of pains in his hands and shoulders. He also has pains in his feet. He feels constantly tired and stiff, particularly in the mornings. His father had recent hip surgery for osteoarthritis and he is worried he may also have the same condition, although I am concerned he may have rheumatoid arthritis.

Please will you see him and advise regarding probable diagnosis and appropriate management.

Yours sincerely,

Introduction

When considering polyarthralgia (pain in multiple joints), firstly consider inflammatory versus non-inflammatory arthropathies.

- Inflammatory joint disease is associated with pain, swelling, tenderness and stiffness. Early morning stiffness of more than 60 minutes is usual in severe active rheumatoid arthritis (RA). Tiredness, lethargy and feeling generally unwell are features of active disease.

- Non-inflammatory arthritis can also be seen after inactivity, but it lasts for only a few minutes. It is not associated with significant morning stiffness. The pain of non-inflammatory arthritis tends to get worse with increased use of the affected joint.

The differential diagnosis can then be narrowed down according to the distribution of involved sites and associated disease characteristics.

Inflammatory joint disease

- RA.
- Seronegative spondyloarthropathies, eg psoriatic arthritis, reactive arthritis and enteropathic arthritis.
- Polymyalgia rheumatica: in older patients.
- Crystal arthritis, eg gout.
- Connective tissue diseases, eg systemic lupus erythematosus (SLE).

Non-inflammatory/mechanical arthritis

- Osteoarthritis (OA).
- Fibromyalgia/chronic widespread pain.
- Soft-tissue rheumatism.

History of the presenting problem

You will clearly want to explore the duration, site and character of the pain, but note the following particularly.

- Do the symptoms change with movement? Non-inflammatory conditions will tend to get worse, whereas patients with inflammatory conditions may say that things improve as they get 'warmed up'.

- Are they stiff in the mornings and how long does it last? As stated above, prolonged early morning stiffness is typical in RA, but not in OA.

- What is the pattern of joint involvement? Is it monoarticular, oligoarticular or polyarticular? Additive or migratory? RA often presents in an additive polyarticular symmetrical distribution. The commonest sites of initial joint involvement are the metacarpophalangeal joints, wrists, proximal interphalangeal joints and metatarsophalangeal joints. See Section 1.2.1 for further discussion.

- How fast did it come on? Most cases of RA develop insidiously over weeks or months.

- Are there any extra-articular manifestations of RA, such as subcutaneous rheumatoid nodules and secondary Sjögrens syndrome? Has the patient had any respiratory or neurological problems that might be caused by RA or another connective tissue disease?

Different patterns of onset of RA

- Acute polyarthritis.
- Subacute insidious polyarthritis.
- Polymyalgic presentation, particularly in elderly people: it is important to differentiate this from polymyalgia rheumatica (see Section 2.5.1).
- Acute monoarthritis (rare, see Section 1.4.4).

Explore the differential diagnoses for an inflammatory arthritis: bear in mind the conditions listed in the Key point box above as you enquire about specific areas.

- Eyes: inflammatory eye disease and dry eyes.

- Skin: psoriasis, other rashes, Raynaud's phenomenon and sclerodactyly.

- Gastrointestinal: inflammatory bowel disease.

- Infection: recent diarrhoea or urethritis.

- Drug history: what analgesia has been tried so far? Has the patient taken any drugs that might have precipitated the problem, eg diuretics causing gout or drug-induced SLE (minocycline).

Other relevant history

It is important to explore the functional limitations caused by the arthritis, and the impact of these limitations on the particular patient. Ask 'Can you wash and dress yourself without any difficulty? Can you walk up and down stairs without any difficulty?' Also enquire about examples of daily tasks that the patient struggles or needs help with (and what help is available to them). Ask the patient what effect the arthritis is having on his job (a severe arthritic condition is likely to have a devastating impact on a self-employed labourer) and on his finances, home life and relationships.

As always, it is sensible to ask (both in PACES and in routine clinical practice) if the patient has any specific issues that you have not already addressed.

Plan for investigation and management

Explain to the patient that his story is in keeping with an inflammatory arthritis, such as RA. You plan to examine him and then request some tests to support your diagnosis. Explain that if the investigations support your clinical suspicions, then it is likely that he will need to start long-term medication (see Section 1.3.5).

> The diagnosis of RA is based on a collection of features rather than a specific pathognomonic abnormality.

Diagnosis

- Rheumatoid factor: this is positive in 70% of cases of RA and usually negative in OA, but remember that around 5% of a healthy general population are rheumatoid factor positive. Seronegative arthropathies are rheumatoid factor negative by definition.

- Inflammatory markers: erythrocyte sedimentation rate and C-reactive protein are expected to be high in inflammatory arthritis but normal in OA.

- Plain radiology: changes in RA (marginal erosions) are most commonly seen in the hands, wrists and feet. However, radiographs may be normal in the early stages of the disease.

- Arthrocentesis: examination of the patient's synovial fluid may be useful in selected cases in order to differentiate RA from non-inflammatory arthritis and crystal arthritis (see Section 3.5).

Damage/prognosis

- Significant erosive disease within the first year of symptoms is a predictor of a poor prognosis. Serial radiographs of the affected joints provide a useful clue to disease progression and response to treatment (see Section 2.3.3).

- Renal and liver function tests: likely to be normal, but important to establish a pretreatment baseline.

Complications

FBC may show anaemia of chronic disease.

Management

The principles of management are based on the following:

- preservation of function and maintenance of the patient's normal lifestyle if at all possible (using physiotherapy, occupational therapy, podiatry and social support);

- patient education regarding their chronic disease;

- relief of symptoms via simple analgesia, NSAIDs and intra-articular steroids;

- prevention of structural damage and deformity using disease-modifying antirheumatic drugs (DMARDs) and anti-tumour necrosis factor therapy;

- surgical correction of severe structural damage.

The patient's next review should be within a few weeks as it is important to start DMARDs early if they are required.

Further discussion

Never forget to treat pain, starting with simple analgesia. Current management strategies for RA involve early aggressive treatment with one or more DMARDs. Failure of DMARDs may lead on to biological agents.

RA is a chronic disease: some patients (~10%) go into clinical remission, but the remainder often suffer progressive disability. RA is associated with a two-fold increased standardised mortality rate, with increased mortality from cardiovascular, malignant and infectious causes.

1.1.15 Foot drop and weight loss in a patient with rheumatoid arthritis

Letter of referral to rheumatology outpatient clinic

Dear Doctor,

Re: Mr Michael Jennings, aged 63 years

Thank you for seeing this man urgently. He has been under the care of the rheumatology unit for more than 15 years with severe seropositive rheumatoid arthritis, treated with intramuscular gold and 7.5 mg prednisolone daily. His arthritis seems to have been inactive recently, but over the last 4 months he has been non-specifically unwell and has lost more than 10 kg in weight. He has been extensively investigated by the gastroenterologists (investigations include upper and lower gastrointestinal endoscopy, CXR and abdominal ultrasound), but no underlying cause has been found.

I saw him yesterday when he had developed profound weakness of dorsiflexion of the left foot, which makes it difficult for him to walk. I am concerned and puzzled. Please can you see him and advise?

Yours sincerely,

Introduction

The onset of foot drop in a patient with seropositive rheumatoid arthritis (RA) is very suggestive of systemic rheumatoid vasculitis. The development of localised tissue damage due to vasculitis is often

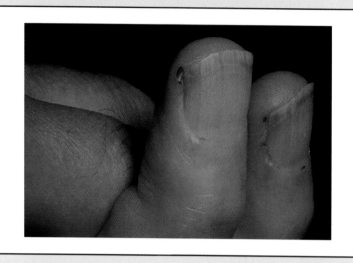

▲**Fig. 18** Nail-fold digital infarcts in rheumatoid vasculitis. (Reproduced with permission from Dieppe PA, Kirwan J and Cooper C. *Arthritis and Rheumatism in Practice*. London: Gower Medical Publishing, 1991.)

preceded by a period of non-specific ill-health, with features such as weight loss and fever. Patients who are ultimately found to have vasculitis are often extensively investigated for malignancy and infections such as tuberculosis. This is entirely appropriate because vasculitis tends to occur in people who have long-standing and severe RA (ie in older patients who tend to have a background of corticosteroid use) and in smokers. The articular disease is often quiescent at the onset of vasculitis.

History of the presenting problem

Although the clinical picture is highly suggestive of rheumatoid vasculitis, do not exclude the possibility that the systemic ill-health might be due to malignancy or tuberculosis.

Take a detailed history of the recent ill-health, along with a full systems

review: are there any relevant chest or gastrointestinal symptoms? This man has been seen by the gastroenterologists, but it would be unwise in routine clinical practice or in PACES to fail to ask about any recent symptoms: something may have developed since his gastroenterological investigations were completed. Whilst being alert to possible other causes of chest and abdominal symptoms, do not forget that chest symptoms may be due to rheumatoid disease (pleural disease and pulmonary fibrosis) and gastrointestinal symptoms may be due to gut vasculitis (abdominal pain and bloody diarrhoea).

When exploring the history remember the following.

- Do not exclude the possibility that the foot drop might reflect more mundane pathology such as a lumbar disc prolapse: does the patient have any history of back pain? See Sections 1.1.12 and 1.1.13).

Consider systemic rheumatoid vasculitis in RA in the presence of:

- persistent fever, fatigue and unexplained weight loss (95% of cases);
- painful red eye (scleritis and 'corneal melt' syndrome);
- nail-fold infarcts, splinter haemorrhages, chronic leg and sacral ulcers, and digital gangrene (Figs 18–20);
- mononeuritis multiplex (50% of cases);
- glomerulonephritis (<5% of cases).

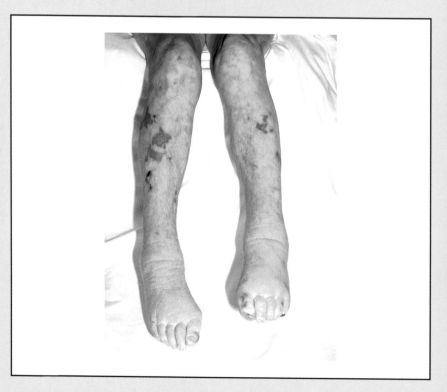

▲**Fig. 19** Vasculitic skin rash in RA.

▲**Fig. 20** Digital gangrene in polyarteritis nodosa.

- Ask specifically about the features of rheumatoid vasculitis detailed in the Key point box above: painful red eyes, leg ulcers, digital ischaemia and other skin lesions.

- Assess the pattern of onset and the severity of the foot drop. Ask about patchy alteration in sensation and focal weakness that might suggest a more widespread mononeuritis multiplex: this can progress very quickly in vasculitis.

Other relevant history
Obtain an overview of the patient's arthritis: its duration, severity, treatment and any resultant disability. Is the patient a smoker? This is a risk factor for vasculitis.

Immunosuppressive treatment and high-dose steroids are likely to be required. Are there any features present which might make this difficult, eg high levels of comorbidity, recurrent infection or a history of tuberculosis?

Plan for investigation and management
After explaining to the patient that under normal circumstances you would carry out a thorough clinical examination to verify the physical

signs noted in the referral letter as well as any new signs, you would need to carry out blood/urine tests and tests of nerve function to confirm your suspicion that he has rheumatoid vasculitis. If he had not previously been investigated by the gastroenterologists, you would also need to recommend some general investigations for other causes of weight loss, such as imaging of the chest, abdomen and bowels. In this case, however, you would simply want to review all investigations that have been performed.

The aim of investigation should be to assess the activity of the vasculitic process and the degree of tissue damage due to vasculitis and, if possible, to obtain histological confirmation of vasculitis. However, this is not always possible in rheumatoid vasculitis, which is often a clinical diagnosis.

- Acute-phase indices: both C-reactive protein and erythrocyte sedimentation rate are invariably raised with active disease.

- Rheumatoid factor: likely to be positive in patients with systemic rheumatoid vasculitis, but does not correlate with the severity of vasculitis.

- Dipstick urine for proteinuria and haematuria: if positive, perform microscopy for red cell casts. Check renal function: could this man have rheumatoid renal vasculitis, which is rare but possible?

- Electrophysiological studies: document the extent and type of neuropathy. The presence of mononeuritis multiplex in a non-diabetic patient with raised inflammatory markers is virtually pathognomonic of vasculitis (although do not forget leprosy as a rare cause).

- Tissue biopsy: obtain histological evidence of vasculitis if possible. Sural nerve biopsy can be useful in the diagnosis of mononeuritis multiplex if you have access to both an individual experienced in biopsy and a skilled neuropathologist. Alternatively, biopsy of tender muscle or purpuric skin lesions may be informative.

Management
After an urgent review of the investigations it is likely that the patient will need to be hospitalised to commence treatment with powerful immunosuppressive drugs and high-dose corticosteroids to prevent severe tissue damage (see Section 2.3.3). This form of treatment is usually effective and well tolerated, but does bring a significant risk of infection due to immune suppression. Review the potential side effects of corticosteroids, including the need for prophylaxis against bone loss: is the patient already taking a bisphosphonate? Has bone densitometry been performed already?

Further discussion
Although many of the features of rheumatoid vasculitis may also

TABLE 15 COMPARISON OF SYSTEMIC RHEUMATOID VASCULITIS AND PAN

Feature	Systemic rheumatoid vasculitis	PAN
Joints	Almost always occurs on a background of seropositive, nodular RA	Arthralgia in 50%. Frank non-deforming arthritis in 20%
Skin, purpura and digital infarcts	Seen in both conditions	Seen in both conditions
Mononeuritis multiplex	Seen in both conditions	Seen in both conditions
Glomerulonephritis	<5% of cases	Rare in classic PAN
Angiography	Not useful	Diagnostically useful investigation revealing aneurysms of visceral arteries
Hepatitis B surface antigen	No association	Positive in 20%
Complement (C3 and C4)	Normal or ↓	Normal or ↓
ANCA	p-ANCA in 10–20%	Negative in classic PAN

ANCA, antineutrophil cytoplasmic antibody; PAN, polyarteritis nodosa; RA, rheumatoid arthritis.

occur in other systemic vasculitides such as polyarteritis nodosa (PAN), in practice there is little difficulty in differentiating between the two (Table 15).

1.1.16 Fever, myalgia, arthralgia and elevated acute-phase indices

Letter of referral to rheumatology outpatient clinic

Dear Doctor,

Re: Mr Frank Marsden, aged 50 years

This man has a 4-month history of episodic pyrexia, myalgia, arthralgia and loss of weight. Further questioning has revealed a history of testicular pain and a recent history of postprandial abdominal pain. On examination he has palpable purpura (Fig. 21). The results of initial investigations are as follows: neutrophils 11×10^9/L (normal range 2–7), erythrocyte sedimentation rate 110 mm/hour, C-reactive protein 80 mg/L (normal <6), antinuclear antibody negative, antineutrophil cytoplasmic antibody negative, rheumatoid factor negative, serum immunoglobulins and C3 and C4 levels normal, and CXR normal.

I am unsure of the diagnosis but am concerned by his general malaise and would be grateful if you could advise on further investigations, his diagnosis and management.

Yours sincerely,

Introduction

Persistent episodic fever, systemic symptoms and a marked acute-phase response in a middle-aged patient may be caused by a wide range of disorders (Table 16). Of the vasculitides, Wegener's granulomatosis and microscopic polyangiitis (MPA) are rendered unlikely (but not excluded) by the negative antineutrophil cytoplasmic antibody (ANCA), and the negative antinuclear antibody effectively excludes lupus. Polyarteritis nodosa (PAN) remains a diagnostic possibility (see Table 15) and is compatible with the clinical presentation and results of initial investigations.

Polyarteritis nodosa

The American College of Rheumatology criteria for the classification of PAN are given below. PAN should be considered as a diagnosis if a patient has at least three of these criteria:

- weight loss;
- livedo reticularis;
- testicular pain or tenderness;
- myalgia;
- mononeuropathy or polyneuropathy;
- diastolic BP >90 mmHg;
- renal impairment;
- hepatitis B antigenaemia (particularly in Oriental patients, who have a high background prevalence of hepatitis B);
- arteriographic abnormality (aneurysms and arterial occlusion);
- biopsy of small or medium-sized artery containing polymorphs.

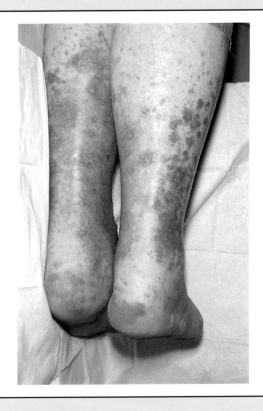

▲ **Fig. 21** Necrotic purpuric rash in PAN.

TABLE 16 DIFFERENTIAL DIAGNOSIS OF PERSISTENT FEVER (>2 WEEKS), SYSTEMIC SYMPTOMS AND A MARKED APR IN AN ADULT WHO IS NOT IMMUNOSUPPRESSED

Type of disorder	Comment
Infection	Bacterial: • Subacute bacterial endocarditis and TB are the most likely • Consider liver abscess Viral: • Infection with EBV and CMV can be persistent Other: • Consider malaria in anyone who might have been exposed to it • Consider wider differential in anyone who has been to the tropics or who is immunosuppressed for any reason
Inflammatory disorders	Autoimmune rheumatic disorders: • Lupus and lupus overlap disorders • Adult-onset Still's disease • Rheumatoid arthritis Other: • Sarcoidosis • Vasculitis – MPA, Wegener's granulomatosis and PAN • Drug fever
Malignancies	Haematological – lymphoma Renal
Other	A very few cases will be factitious

CMV, cytomegalovirus; EBV, Epstein–Barr virus; PAN, polyarteritis nodosa; MPA, microscopic polyangiitis; TB, tuberculosis.

History of the presenting problem

Is PAN the likely diagnosis?
Clarify the nature of the following.

- Pyrexia and systemic symptoms.

- Abdominal pain: recurrent postprandial central abdominal pain may indicate critical bowel ischaemia ('mesenteric claudication').

Also ask about the following.

- Skin rash: is this compatible with cutaneous vasculitis? Is there a history to suggest critical digital ischaemia, such as digital gangrene (see Fig. 20)?

- Has he had numbness, paraesthesiae or muscle weakness that might indicate mononeuritis multiplex?

Is there a history of exposure to recreational drugs?
Exposure to recreational drugs, particularly in a younger patient (eg cocaine-induced vasculitis), may mimic PAN.

Other diagnoses
Consider the diagnostic possibilities listed in Table 16 when taking the history: are there any leads to one or other of these conditions? Dental extraction 4 months previously might have led to endocarditis, masked by two courses of antibiotics given for fever, etc. Haematuria might indicate hypernephroma.

Other relevant history
Is there a history of tuberculosis exposure, cardiac abnormality, risk factor for endocarditis, travel abroad, blood transfusion or a known malignancy? Ask about hepatitis B infection because hepatitis B surface antigenaemia is a feature of 10–20% of cases of

PAN and may affect management (see below).

Plan for investigation and management

After explaining to the patient that under normal circumstances you would carry out a thorough clinical examination to verify the physical signs noted in the referral letter and look for new signs, you would plan to carry out the following blood tests, special scans and possibly tissue biopsy to arrive at a diagnosis. It would be sensible to warn the patient regarding the likely need to perform visceral angiography and sural nerve biopsy in order to make a definitive diagnosis.

Investigation

PAN seems the most likely diagnosis on clinical grounds. The following investigations are useful in establishing this and/or excluding other conditions listed in Table 16.

- FBC: neutrophilia is expected, and occasionally eosinophilia.

- Check acute-phase markers: both C-reactive protein and erythrocyte sedimentation rate will be elevated and reflect disease activity.

- Electrolytes, renal, liver and bone function tests.

- Autoimmune/vasculitic serology: already performed in this case.

- Hepatitis B status.

- Blood cultures: several.

- Urine dipstick looking for proteinuria and/or haematuria. If positive, proceed to microscopy for casts and estimation of albumin/creatinine ratio (urinary).

- Echocardiogram: if normal and there is high suspicion of

endocarditis, consider a transoesophageal study.

- CT scan of the chest, abdomen and pelvis looking in particular for lymphadenopathy and at the kidneys.

- Visceral angiography for evidence of aneurysms and arterial occlusion (Fig. 72).

- Tissue biopsy: consider sural nerve biopsy in patients with neuropathy and skin biopsy in patients with cutaneous features; 'blind' muscle biopsy may also be informative.

Other investigations may be indicated depending on clinical suspicion, eg thick film for malaria.

Management

If the diagnosis of PAN is confirmed, immunosuppressive therapy with steroids and cyclophosphamide will be required for treatment of severe cases. Patients with disease confined to the skin may respond to steroids alone. Where PAN is associated with hepatitis B infection, antiviral treatment using a combination of vidarabine/lamivudine and interferon alfa is often helpful.

Further discussion

The rarity of PAN has contributed to difficulties in differentiating it from MPA, an ANCA-associated predominantly small-vessel vasculitis (also see Section 2.5.3).

PAN versus MPA

In a patient with systemic vasculitis, the following features favour MPA rather than PAN:

- glomerulonephritis;
- ANCA positivity;
- normal visceral angiography.

1.1.17 Non-rheumatoid pain and stiffness

Letter of referral to rheumatology outpatient clinic

Dear Doctor,

Re: Mr Alexander Jacobs, aged 55 years

This mechanic has been complaining of increasing widespread pain over the last year, particularly affecting his hands, knees and lower back. He is having some functional difficulty at work because of his hand problems and has noticed bony lumps developing over his finger joints.

I suspect that he is developing early osteoarthritis, but would be grateful for your views. Am I missing something else?

Yours sincerely,

Introduction

The first thing to establish in cases of polyarthralgia is whether the symptoms sound inflammatory or non-inflammatory (see Section 1.1.14 for relevant discussion).

History of the presenting problem

What is the location of the pain?

Primary osteoarthritis (OA), like rheumatoid arthritis, has a tendency to affect certain joints more than others (Table 17). Involvement of the thumb carpometacarpal joints, with pain on opening jars or wringing out cloths, is highly suggestive.

What is the pattern of the pain?

The pain of OA tends to get worse with movement and better with rest.

TABLE 17 LIKELIHOOD OF INVOLVEMENT OF PARTICULAR JOINTS IN PRIMARY OA	
Joints typically involved	**Joints typically not involved**
Distal interphalangeal joints	Metacarpophalangeal joints
Proximal interphalangeal joints	Wrists
First carpometacarpal joints	Elbows
Acromioclavicular joints	Shoulders
Hips	Ankles
Knees	Second to fifth metatarsophalangeal joints
First metatarsophalangeal joints	
Facet joints	

Is there any joint stiffness? There may be morning stiffness, although it is less severe and prolonged than in inflammatory arthritides, and inactivity-associated stiffness (or gelling) is common, particularly in the knees.

Have your joints changed shape?
Bony swellings over the distal and proximal interphalangeal joints are typical in nodal OA, sometimes with palmar and/or lateral deviation of the distal phalanx. Severe knee OA may be associated with valgus or varus deformities.

Have you noticed your joints creaking, crunching or grinding?
Crepitus is a common feature of OA, most commonly experienced in the knees.

Other relevant history
If there is OA in an atypical joint distribution, consider secondary causes (see Section 2.3.2).

Ask about family history (this is often strongly related in cases of generalised nodal OA) and previous trauma. The patient's occupation may be relevant; also note obesity, a risk factor for OA of the knee.

What are the functional limitations secondary to the arthritis? How well is the patient able to continue his job? Are there options for alternative employment? Are there financial implications? Explore psychological factors associated with function and chronic pain.

Plan for investigation and management
Explain that his story and pattern of joint involvement is suggestive of OA, and that you plan some tests to confirm this diagnosis.

Plain radiography
In OA (Fig. 22), these reveal the following:

- loss of joint space;

- sclerotic bone on either side of the joint;

- bony spurs (osteophytes) at the joint margin.

Less frequently they may show:

- cystic changes in subchondral bone;

- chondrocalcinosis, suggesting calcium pyrophosphate disease.

Synovial fluid analysis
If a joint is swollen, then joint aspiration may reveal characteristic features of OA: fluid from a non-inflammatory arthropathy is typically clear, straw-coloured and viscous, and aspiration also helps to exclude sepsis and crystal arthritides.

Blood tests
These are not often necessary, but a normal C-reactive protein and/or erythrocyte sedimentation rate help exclude an inflammatory arthritis. Ferritin, serum iron and total iron-binding capacity should be checked if haemochromatosis is suspected (see Section 2.3.2).

Management
The management of OA should be based around the following.

- Education: the patient should understand that the goal of treatment is pain relief and maintenance of function but not alteration to the natural history.

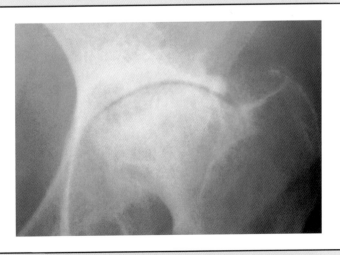

▲ **Fig. 22** Radiograph showing severe OA of the hip, with loss of joint space, subchondral sclerosis and osteophyte formation. (Courtesy of Dr M. Pattrick.)

- Reducing pain and stiffness: analgesia (oral and topical); intra-articular therapy (steroids and viscosupplementation); paraffin-wax baths for hands; superficial heat packs; insoles to improve foot posture and hydrotherapy.

- Maintaining muscle strength, fitness and joint mobility.

- Supporting unstable joints, eg wearing a knee brace.

- Minimising disability using walking aids, splints and tools; also managing psychological distress.

- Surgery: arthroplasty and osteotomy.

1.1.18 Widespread pain

Letter of referral to rheumatology outpatient clinic

Dear Doctor,

Re: Mrs Wendy Hawkins, aged 38 years

Please see this woman with a 4-year history of widespread musculoskeletal pain, fatigue and tiredness. She is now unable to work and is becoming increasingly dependent on her family. She spends much of her day in bed and is now asking for the provision of a wheelchair. She has seen several physicians and orthopaedic surgeons over the last few years, but extensive investigation has shown no evidence of any serious neurological or musculoskeletal disease. She appears low in mood and angry to me, but denies that she is depressed and has declined a trial of antidepressant treatment.

Am I missing any serious organic condition here? How can we best help her?

Yours sincerely,

Introduction

Widespread pain and fatigue have many causes. The case description given here points strongly towards the syndrome known as fibromyalgia, but diagnostic thoughts should be cast wider than this, particularly if 'red flag' features are present. Fibromyalgia is discussd in more detail in Section 1.3.4.

'Red flag' features in widespread pain

- Onset age >50 years.
- Recent onset and progressive history.
- Weight loss.
- Previous history of malignancy or immunosuppression.
- Focal versus diffuse pain.
- Fever.
- Any abnormal physical signs other than tenderness.
- Abnormal blood tests.

History of the presenting problem

Although it seems very likely that this woman has fibromyalgia, it would be wrong to assume this immediately without the benefit of a full systems enquiry. Are any 'red flag' features present? Also remember that fibromyalgia is not an exclusive diagnosis: fibromyalgic pain may (and often does) coexist with other rheumatological causes of pain such as rheumatoid arthritis, osteoarthritis and mechanical spinal pain.

Pain

Document the pattern of pain and its progression over time. Pain in fibromyalgia is very widespread but usually predominantly axial rather than peripheral, and typically inexorable but rarely progressive (Fig. 23). At presentation most patients have had widespread pain for many months, if not years. The patient will usually feel that 'everything hurts', but will usually identify the muscles rather than the joints as the main sites of pain. Descriptions of the pain will often lead rapidly onto other non-pain symptoms, especially fatigue and

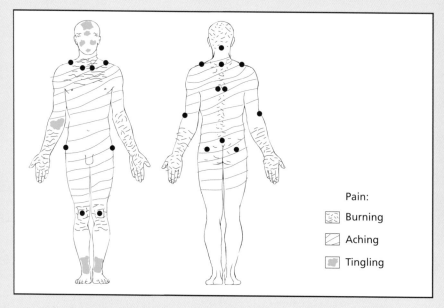

▲**Fig. 23** Pain diagram showing classic tender points (filled circles) in fibromyalgia plus patient's own illustration of site and nature of pain.

low mood. Numbness and other sensory disturbances are often described, but these are usually flitting in site, transient in duration and have no obvious neuroanatomical correlates.

Fatigue

Ask what the patient means by fatigue. Is this localised muscle weakness (raising suspicions of neurological disease) or, typical of fibromyalgia, a more generalised feeling of tiredness or lack of energy ('tired all the time')? In fibromyalgia this is often associated with other cognitive symptoms such as difficulty concentrating and a feeling of 'muzzy-headedness'. Other neurological symptoms may be present, particularly flitting paraesthesia.

Disability

Gain a picture of the patient's degree of disability and the impact on her life. High degrees of disability are usually reported, but this often relates to fatigue and poor stamina rather than difficulty performing any specific activities. What is the patient's current exercise capacity?

Depression and related conditions

Ask about sleep patterns and sleep disturbance: is sleep refreshing? Poor-quality, unrefreshing sleep is virtually universal. Is there evidence of depression currently? Note that other cognitive symptoms may occur and are often associated with depression. Is there a history of other functional syndromes (see Key box below)? Has the patient had any previous psychiatric illness?

> A review of the past medical history (and in routine clinical practice of the case notes, plus discussion with the GP) may be particularly helpful. Look for the following:
>
> - irritable bowel syndrome;
> - chronic fatigue syndrome/myalgic encephalopathy;
> - unexplained breathlessness or chest pain;
> - unexplained gynaecological symptoms;
> - unexplained headache or dizziness;
> - multiple 'allergies' in the absence of objective evidence.

> Most patients with fibromyalgia will give an immediate impression of distress and depression; this in itself is striking and significant. The psychological state of patients with most illnesses depends heavily on their personality and coping strategies: a patient with rheumatoid disease can be cheerful, stoical, anxious or depressed, but a patient with fibromyalgia will invariably be weary and sad. Despite this unhappiness, the patient usually appears physically well.

Plan for investigation and management

After explaining to the patient that under normal circumstances you would carry out a thorough clinical examination, you will need to carry out a few investigations to exclude diseases that can present in this way.

Investigation

This requires a balance between the need to exclude serious pathology and the harm that may be caused by over-investigation. Patients with fibromyalgia (and other functional syndromes) will often have undergone repeated episodes of negative investigation. This process strongly reinforces a belief that their symptoms have a serious physical cause, which would be identified if only the right tests were done. However, as further negative investigations are performed, patients come to feel that the doctor does not believe that their symptoms are real ('you think it's all in my mind'). This results in the doctor–patient relationship deteriorating, and the patient may move on to repeat the process elsewhere. It is therefore more helpful to try to make a postive diagnosis of fibromyalgia at an early stage based on the clinical picture, rather than a negative diagnosis of exclusion after negative investigation.

The need for investigation should be determined by the degree of clinical suspicion that the diagnosis is not fibromyalgia. Pay attention to the 'red flag' features listed above. Unfortunately, however, investigation is often driven by insecurity, lack of experience and a fear of 'missing something'.

It is very important that the rationale for investigation be explained to the patient. If you feel that the results are likely to be negative, say so and explain why. A minimalist approach to investigation might include the following:

- FBC;

- renal, bone and liver biochemistry, and blood glucose;

- creatine kinase;

- thyroid function;

- acute-phase markers (C-reactive protein and erythrocyte sedimentation rate);

- myeloma screen in patients >50 years;

- antinuclear antibodies;

- CXR, especially in smokers.

Management

Further explanation of the diagnosis and management plan is discussed in Section 1.3.4.

1.2 Clinical examination

1.2.1 Hands (general)

Instruction

This man has pain and stiffness in his joints. Please examine his hands.

All hand examinations should follow a routine structure, as with all other systems. Each disease involving the hands will have specific findings for each subheading of the structure.

General features

Although occasionally limited to the hands, musculoskeletal diseases are often more widespread, affecting other joints or organs. The patient's attitude or posture, and the environment around him (walking aids, orthotics and medication), will give you clues as to what you might expect to find when examining his hands. In routine clinical practice, the gait will also provide you with information as the patient walks into the consulting room.

Hand examination

A quick look at the hands and the pattern of joint involvement will often give a 'spot diagnosis', targeting what else to look for on closer examination.

Figures 24–28 show the five main hand diagnoses likely to be seen (including systemic sclerosis). Look systematically for the following features.

Skin and subcutaneous tissues

- Texture (waxy and thin/bruised).

- Rashes.

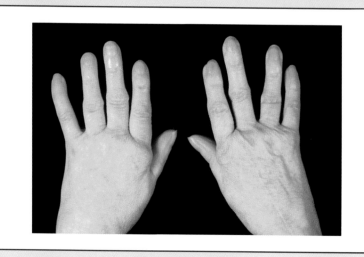

▲ **Fig. 24** Typical rheumatoid hands.

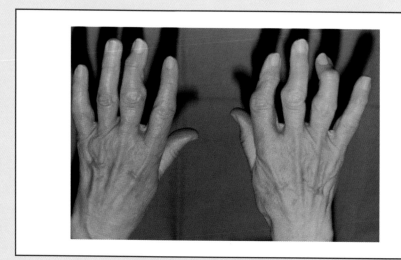

▲ **Fig. 25** Classic nodal osteoarthritis.

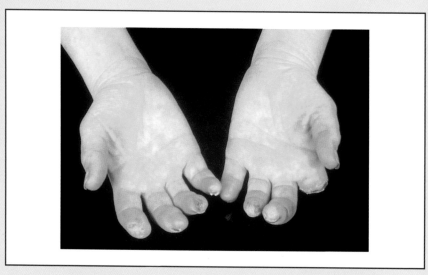

▲ **Fig. 26** Severe digital ischaemia leading to multiple auto-amputations in a patient with diffuse cutaneous systemic sclerosis.

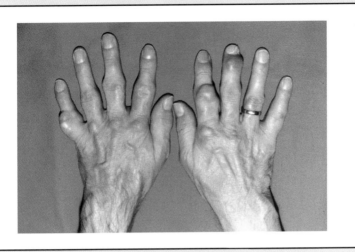

▲ **Fig. 27** Tophaceous gout in the hands of an elderly woman on diuretics.

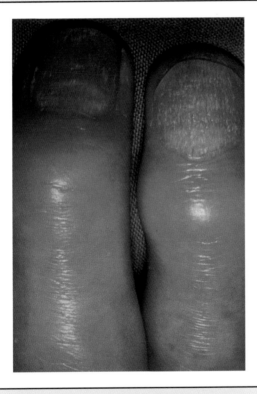

▲ **Fig. 28** Distal interphalangeal joint and nail involvement in psoriatic arthropathy. (Courtesy of Dr M. Pattrick.)

- Digital ulcers and fissuring.
- Scars.
- Subcutaneous lumps: nodules/tophi/calcinosis.

Nails

- Nail disease, eg pitting and onycholysis.
- Nail-fold infarcts.

- Capillary loops.

Muscles and tendons

- Wasting.
- Rupture.

Joints

Look, feel and move only after ensuring there is no pain.

Pattern of joints involved (Table 18)
Look for the following:

- metacarpophalangeal, proximal interphalangeal, distal interphalangeal or first carpometacarpal involvement;
- 'row' or 'ray' distribution.

Deformity Look for symmetry, subluxation and angulation.

Swelling Look for the following:

- inflammatory/non-inflammatory (firm or soft, tenderness);
- site, origin and extent of swelling.

Function Check the patient's ability to make a fist and to perform a power grip and pinch grip.

Sensation

- Evidence of carpal tunnel syndrome, ulnar neuropathy, peripheral neuropathy or cervical spine disease.

If asked to do so by the examiner, be prepared to examine other sites or systems relevant to the case.

1.2.2 Non-rheumatoid pain and stiffness: generalised osteoarthritis

Instruction

This woman is having difficulty opening jars. Please examine her hands.

General features

Look for the following.

- Signs of other joint involvement, eg varus/valgus knee deformities, knee brace, knee effusion, quadriceps wasting or any scars of joint replacement surgery.
- Does she have any walking aids or splints (particularly carpometacarpal)?

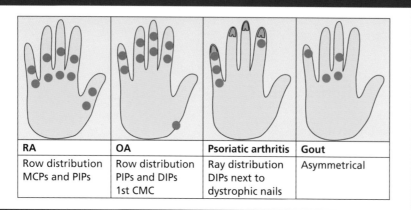

TABLE 18 PATTERN OF JOINT INVOLVEMENT IN VARIOUS CONDITIONS AFFECTING THE HANDS

RA	OA	Psoriatic arthritis	Gout
Row distribution MCPs and PIPs	Row distribution PIPs and DIPs 1st CMC	Ray distribution DIPs next to dystrophic nails	Asymmetrical

- If you have the opportunity to see her walk, then does she have a Trendelenberg (waddling) gait?

Hand examination

Look systematically for the following features.

Skin and subcutaneous tissues

- Depigmentation from intra-articular steroid injections to first carpometacarpal joints.

Joints

Pattern of joints involved Look for evidence of distal interphalangeal, proximal interphalangeal or first carpometacarpal joint involvement.

Deformity Look for evidence of:

- palmar and/or lateral deviation of distal phalanx;

- squaring of the thumb.

Swelling Look for the following.

- Firm bony swelling limited to joints: Heberden's nodes in distal interphalangeal joints; Bouchard's nodes in proximal interphalangeal joints.

- Early nodes may be tender, but are usually pain-free once established.

Function The patient's ability to make a fist may be impaired. Power grip may also be reduced.

If given the opportunity to examine other joints, use the GALS (gait, arms, legs and spine) system (see *Clinical Skills*, Clinical Skills for PACES – Station 5) and concentrate on sites likely to be involved with osteoarthritis:

- knees (deformity, effusion and crepitus);

- hips;

- acromioclavicular;

- first metatarsophalangeal.

Further discussion

Consider examining for secondary causes of non-inflammatory degenerative arthropathies (see Section 2.3.2), especially if there is evidence of osteoarthritis in atypical joints.

1.2.3 Rheumatoid arthritis

Instruction

This woman has widespread pain, swelling and morning stiffness. Please examine her hands.

General features

Note the following.

- Is the patient wearing any aids: soft collar, wrist splints or orthotic shoes?

- Is there scleritis, episcleritis or nodular eye disease?

- Is there generalised or focal muscle wasting?

- Is there evidence of chronic steroid use: thin skin, bruising and kyphosis?

- What other joints appear affected from the end of the bed: is there fixed flexion of the elbows, knee swelling or foot deformities?

Look around the patient's chair or bed for walking aids, soft collar and orthotic shoes (and if the shoes are off, look for insoles). Also look for a sputum pot.

Hand examination

Look systematically for the following features.

Skin and subcutaneous tissues

- Rheumatoid nodules.

- Thin fragile skin, reflecting long-term steroid use.

- Surgical scars: metacarpophalangeal joint replacement, Darrach's procedure (removal of ulnar styloid) and/or extensor tendon repair, wrist fusion, carpal tunnel release.

Nails

- Nail-fold vasculitis (see Fig. 18).

Muscles/tendons

- Thenar eminence wasting: carpal tunnel syndrome.

- Tenosynovitis.

- Tendon rupture (inability to extend fingers).

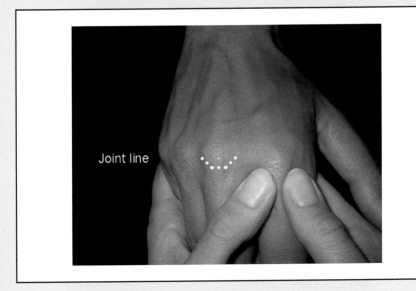

▲**Fig. 29** Surface markings and examination of the metacarpophalangeal joint.

- Tendon 'bowstring' (secondary to wrist subluxation).

Joints
Pattern of joints involved Assess metacarpophalangeals, proximal interphalangeals and wrists.

Deformity Usually symmetrical (Fig. 24). Look for presence of:

- metacarpophalangeal subluxation;

- ulnar deviation;

- swan-neck, boutonnière and Z-deformity of the thumb.

Swelling Is the disease active or not? The presence of tenderness and swelling would indicate that it is, so be careful to ensure that the patient is not in pain when palpating joints: look at the face at all times, not just at the hands. Remember where the metacarpophalangeal joint line is, ie distal to metacarpal heads (Fig. 29).

Function The pinch grip is often modified, using lateral border rather than tip of thumb/index finger.

Sensation

- Carpal tunnel syndrome.

If given the opportunity to extend your examination beyond the hand, then look for other affected joints and for the extra-articular manifestations of rheumatoid arthritis (RA) listed below (see also Table 19 and Section 2.3.3):

- nodules;

- vasculitis;

- inflammatory/nodular eye disease;

- lung disease (interstitial lung disease, pleural effusions and bronchiectasis);

- ischaemic heart disease (coronary artery bypass grafting and peripheral vein harvesting);

- anaemia.

Remember to also look for the side effects of treatment:

- steroids (osteoporosis, thin skin/bruising and cushingoid appearance);

- anaemia.

Further discussion
Deformity is a consequence of prolonged active disease. Patients with early disease, or well-controlled disease, may have none of the classic deformities of RA (Fig. 31).

1.2.4 Psoriatic arthritis

Instruction

This woman has difficulty getting washed and dressed. Please examine her hands.

General features
Note the following.

- Is there any psoriasis visible on the scalp or elsewhere?

- Is the patient tanned from psoralen ultraviolet A treatment?

- Are any topical treatments obvious on the skin?

System	Clinical feature
TABLE 19 NON-ARTICULAR MANIFESTATIONS OF RA	
Eye	Episcleritis, scleritis, keratoconjunctivitis sicca and scleromalacia perforans (Fig. 30)
Skin	Rheumatoid nodules, vasculitis (palpable purpura), palmar erythema and pyoderma gangrenosum
Haematological	Anaemia, splenomegaly, Felty's syndrome, lymphadenopathy and cryoglobulinaemia
Respiratory	Pleurisy with effusion, pulmonary fibrosis and Caplan's syndrome
Cardiovascular	Raynaud's phenomenon, pericarditis, myocarditis, cardiac nodules and mitral valve disease
Neurological	Carpal tunnel syndrome, peripheral neuropathy, mononeuritis multiplex and cervical myelopathy

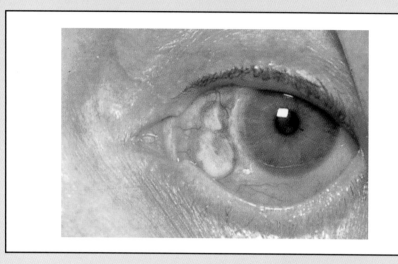

▲ **Fig. 30** Scleromalacia perforans in a patient with seropositive RA. (Reproduced with permission from Dieppe PA, Kirwan J and Cooper C. *Arthritis and Rheumatism in Practice*. London: Gower Medical Publishing, 1991.)

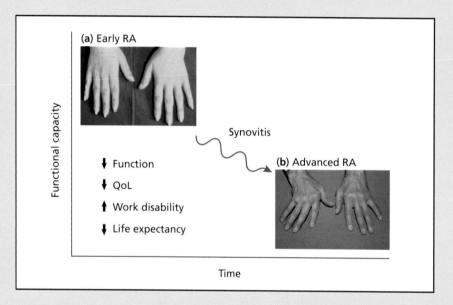

▲ **Fig. 31** (a) Early RA with synovitis but no deformities. (b) Established RA with characteristic deformities.

- Is there suggestion of axial disease when the patient turns or bends?

- Is there ocular inflammation?

- Are functional aids/orthotics in evidence?

Hand examination

Skin and subcutaneous tissues

- Psoriatic plaques: check elbows and scalp/hair-line; if further examination is permitted later in the station, check umbilicus (natal cleft).

Nails

- Pitting.

- Onycholysis.

- Hypergryphosis.

- Dystrophy.

Joints

Pattern of joints involved Look for the following.

- Psoriatic arthritis more commonly affects 'rays' (ie distal interphalangeal, proximal interphalangeal and

metacarpophalangeal joints) of one digit rather than 'rows' (ie all metacarpophalangeal joints).

- Check for the presence of one of the five classical patterns (Moll and Wright classification): (i) distal interphalangeal involvement, (ii) rheumatoid-like pattern, (iii) asymmetrical oligoarthritis, (iv) axial disease, (v) arthritis mutilans.

Deformity Look for:

- rheumatoid-like pattern clinically indistinguishable from rheumatoid arthritis;

- digital telescoping, subluxation and 'flail' joints in arthritis mutilans.

Swelling Check the following.

- Differentiate soft-tissue swelling from firm bony swelling of Heberden's nodes in osteoarthritis.

- Distal interphalangeal swelling of psoriatic arthritis is often associated with nail changes at adjacent nail.

- Tenosynovitis along a digit may present as dactylitis (more common in the feet).

Function A patient's pinch/grip is often weak if the index distal interphalangeal joint is involved. Function is very poor in cases of arthritis mutilans.

Further discussion
Psoriatic arthritis occurs in about 15% of patients with psoriasis, as well as in a significant proportion of patients with Crohn's disease. The latter association is interesting in view of the overlap in genetic control of inflammation in both disorders and the therapeutic benefit of anti-tumour necrosis factor treatment in both psoriatic arthritis and Crohn's disease.

1.2.5 Systemic sclerosis

Instruction

This woman has painful hands, particularly in cold weather. Please examine her hands.

General features

Since her history is highly suggestive of Raynaud's phenomenon, you should aim to differentiate between primary and secondary Raynaud's by looking for evidence of diseases associated with the latter, in particular scleroderma. Check the following.

- Face: telangiectasia, microstomia and 'beaked' nose.

- Respiratory system: is the patient short of breath or cyanosed?

- Gastrointestinal system: is there evidence of long-term intravenous access for parenteral feeding?

- Collateral clues: look around you for gloves (if so, are they heated?), parenteral nutrition bags, and medication (particularly ambulatory iloprost for pulmonary hypertension).

Hand examination

Skin and subcutaneous tissues

Look for the following signs.

- Sclerodactyly: take note of tight, shiny and waxy skin. Assess the extent of its involvement by working from distal phalanges, proximally. If it is limited to distal limbs (ie below elbows and knees), this is suggestive of limited cutaneous systemic sclerosis (LCSS); if the spread is more proximal, it is suggestive of diffuse cutaneous systemic sclerosis (DCSS).

- Digital ischaemia (worse in LCSS): indicated by digital ulceration or digital pitting (healed ulcers) at finger pulps. Also examine distal and proximal interphalangeal joints, looking for signs of infection, ie digital pulp atrophy, gangrene or auto-amputations.

- Raynaud's phenomenon.

- Calcinosis: more prominent in LCSS.

- Telangiectasia.

Nails

- Increased curvature of nails can be seen, secondary to the resorption of distal phalanx.

- Dilated tortuous nail-fold capillaries are suggestive of connective tissue disease as a cause of secondary Raynaud's. These are best appreciated by examination at ×20 magnification using an ophthalmoscope (see Fig. 15), although use of this would not be expected in PACES (indeed most examiners would regard it as eccentric, which would be a bad thing).

Muscles/tendons

The involvement of these is more common in DCSS. Check for friction rubs in active disease and for contractures.

Joints

The problems this patient has with her hands may be associated with inflammatory arthritis.

Function

Find out if the patient has:

- impaired ability to make a fist (assess fingertip to palmar crease distance);

- impaired pinch grip secondary to sclerodactyly and pain of digital ulceration.

Further discussion

It is important to distinguish between primary and secondary Raynaud's to plan further management (see Section 1.1.9 for a discussion of the investigation and management of patients presenting with Raynaud's phenomenon).

1.2.6 Chronic tophaceous gout

Instruction

This man with hypertension has a long history of pains in his hands, knees, ankles and feet. Please examine his hands.

General features

Look for the stigmata of risk factors for gout:

- excess alcohol consumption (ruddy face, palmar erythema and spider naevi);

- psoriasis;

- obesity.

Note any special features of the patient's footwear (eg oversize shoes), incisions over first metatarsophalangeal joints, or if wearing sandals on a cold day.

Hand examination

Skin and subcutaneous tissues

Look particularly for the following.

Subcutaneous tophi This may be confused with rheumatoid nodules, so look for pale, chalky and subcutaneous lumps; also check for signs of discharge of material with toothpaste-like consistency. It is also important to note the sites of tophi in the hands, which can include the following:

- around any finger joints, sometimes extending beyond the joints to resemble dactylitis of psoriatic arthritis or reactive arthritis;

- finger pulps;

- dorsal or palmar side of the hand;

- overlying Heberden's or Bouchard's nodes, particularly in women with gout.

Oedema Acute gout is often accompanied by pitting oedema extending well beyond the involved joint.

Cutaneous exfoliation Can sometimes be seen on resolution of an acute attack.

Joints

Pattern of joints involved Look for evidence of metacarpophalangeal, proximal interphalangeal or distal interphalangeal joint involvement.

Deformity Check for evidence of deformity but note the following:

- there is no characteristic pattern of deformity;

- patients may develop the swan-neck, boutonnière and flexion deformities seen in rheumatoid arthritis.

Swelling In acute gout there is usually marked erythema, the joints feel hot and they are exquisitely tender.

Function This will depend on the extent of disease.

Sensation

Check for wrist involvement or for tophi within flexor tendons of the hand and wrist (rare), which may cause carpal tunnel syndrome.

If you are given the opportunity to extend your examination beyond the hand, then carry out the following.

Elbows

- Olecranon bursae are often chronically swollen and may have acute bursitis.

- Tophi over elbow/within bursae.

Gouty tophi

Next, check gouty tophi at other sites, particularly:

- pinnae of the ears;

- first metatarsophalangeal joints;

- Achilles tendons;

- prepatellar bursae.

Other affected joints

Examine first metatarsophalangeal joints, knees and ankles.

Further discussion

In patients presenting with rheumatoid-like deformities in the hands and no tophi elsewhere, it may be difficult to differentiate between rheumatoid arthritis and gout.

Differentiating gout and rheumatoid arthritis

- Rheumatoid factor: a negative rheumatoid factor and lumps over the elbows usually means the diagnosis is gout because rheumatoid nodules are associated only with seropositive disease.
- Synovial fluid analysis: negatively birefringent needle-shaped crystals indicate gout.
- Radiographs of the hand: erosions are typically periarticular in rheumatoid arthritis but juxta-articular in gout, with overhanging edges (see Section 2.3.6).

Note that serum uric acid does not differentiate the two: it may be normal in gout or elevated in rheumatoid arthritis.

Gout is uncommon in young men and premenopausal women, when it is likely to be due to an enzyme defect in the purine pathway or a renal tubular defect.

The history of hypertension in the question is relevant because of the association between diuretics and gout, particularly thiazide diuretics. Acute gout is commonly seen in medical inpatients after aggressive treatment of left ventricular failure with diuretics. Gout is also associated with dyslipidaemia, the metabolic syndrome and renal impairment.

1.2.7 Ankylosing spondylitis

Instruction

This 35-year-old man has low back pain associated with early morning stiffness that lasts for 2 hours. Please examine his spine.

General features

Some patients with psoriasis will have a spondyloarthropathy, so look for plaques, nail pitting and onycholysis.

Examination of the spine

Follow the general principles of inspection, palpation and movement.

- Take a general overview, particularly looking at the shape of his spine. With the patient standing, inspect from the side and from behind. Does he have kyphosis and loss of lumbar lordosis, the typical features of the 'question-mark' posture of ankylosing spondylitis?

- Assess movement: cervical spine flexion, extension, rotation and lateral flexion. Is there any evidence of fusion?

- Measure the wall to occiput distance: an unaffected individual should be able to put his or her head against the wall. If unable to do so, it may be because of fusion of the cervical spine or a thoracic kyphosis.

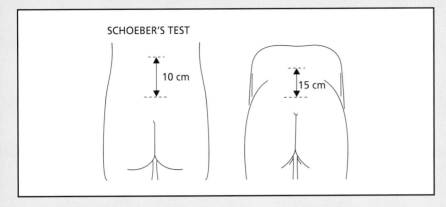

▲ **Fig. 32** Schoeber's test to measure lumbar flexion.

- Assess lumbar flexion: measure the finger to floor distance (ie distance from the tips of the fingers to the floor) if the patient is unable to touch his toes.

- Measure Schoeber's expansion, which is a more accurate way of determining if there is fusion of the lumbar vertebrae (Fig. 32); should be 15–20 cm.

- With the patient sitting on the couch, assess thoracic rotation to see if there is fusion.

- Measure chest expansion using a tape measure placed at approximately the level of the nipples: expansion after inspiration should be ≥3 cm.

If given the opportunity to ask questions or extend your examination beyond the spine, then consider complications in other sites/organ systems:

- iritis;

- psoriasis;

- inflammatory bowel disease;

- peripheral inflammatory arthritis;

- lung apical fibrosis;

- aortitis.

1.2.8 Deformity of bone: Paget's disease

Instruction

This 85-year-old man has pain in his right hip and lower leg. Please examine his lower limbs.

General features

Look at the posture the patient adopts when standing: is there bowing of the tibia consistent with Paget's disease? Examine his gait. Look for enlargement of the skull and a hearing aid.

Examination of lower limbs

- Sit the patient on the couch with his legs straight: again look for any deformity. Is there bowing and/or a fixed flexion deformity?

- Assess the patient's skin temperature. Is this warm due to increased vascularity of active Paget's disease?

- Palpate the knee to look for tenderness and an effusion (patellar tap/bulge sign).

- Assess full flexion and extension of the knee.

- Ask the patient to flex his hip and test for abduction/adduction and internal and external rotation.

Further discussion

Paget's disease is characterised by accelerated bone turnover due to osteoclast-mediated resorption. New bone formation occurs in parallel with resorption, leading to irregular thickening and softening of bones.

Paget's disease is particularly common in the elderly: by the ninth decade, 10% of people are affected. Any bone can be involved, but the most frequent are the pelvis, lumbar spine, femur, thoracic spine, sacrum, skull, tibia and humerus. Pagetic bones are more fragile and can fracture easily. Complications include deafness, cranial nerve involvement, vertebrobasilar insufficiency, nerve root compression, spinal cord lesions, cauda equina syndrome, high-output cardiac failure and osteosarcoma.

Noteworthy laboratory abnormalities include elevated alkaline phosphatase due to high bone turnover. Plain radiographs show increased trabeculation (Fig. 33). An isotope bone scan will show if multiple bones are affected.

Treatment is with bisphosphonates, either intravenous or oral.

1.2.9 Marfan's syndrome

Instruction

This man is 'double jointed'. He has problems with his vision. Please examine his joints.

General features

The instructions suggest immediately that the most likely diagnosis is Marfan's syndrome, so look for the following.

- Is the patient tall and does his arm span look greater than his height? This is common in a patient with Marfan's syndrome.

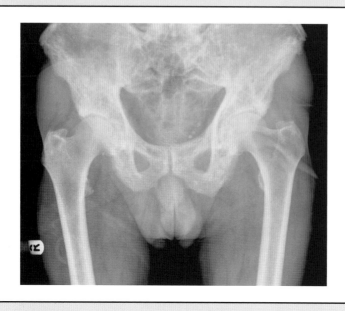

▲ **Fig. 33** Pelvic radiograph showing characteristic trabeculation in a patient with Paget's disease.

- Are his fingers long (arachnodactyly)?

- Does he have pectus excavatum/carinatum or kyphoscoliosis?

Joint examination

To demonstrate hypermobility perform the following manoeuvres.

- Apposition of thumb to flexor aspect of forearm: the ability to do this is abnormal.

- Hyperextend fingers at the metacarpophalangeal joints:

the ability to do this to >90° at the fifth metacarpophalangeal joint is abnormal.

- Hyperextend elbows: beyond 180° is abnormal.

- Hyperextend the knees: beyond 180° is abnormal.

- Pes planus.

- Is the patient able to put his hands flat on the floor with his knees extended?

If given the opportunity to ask questions or extend your

examination, then consider complications in other sites/organ systems:

- high-arched palate;

- lens dislocation (Fig. 34), which occurs in 70% of cases and is usually bilateral;

- cardiac manifestations (mitral valve prolapse and/or aortic incompetence are common).

Further discussion

Marfan's syndrome is an inherited autosomal dominant multisystem disorder of connective tissue caused by mutations in the extracellular matrix protein fibrillin 1. The main burden of the disease predominantly affects the cardiovascular system (mitral valve prolapse and dilated aortic root with risk of dissection), eyes (ectopia lentis and severe myopia) and the skeleton (kyphoscoliosis, pectus deformities, high-arched palate and arachnodactyly).

1.3 Communication skills and ethics

1.3.1 Collapse during a restaurant meal

Scenario
Role: you are a junior doctor working on a general medical ward.
You have admitted a 19-year-old female student following a severe anaphylactic reaction to peanuts. Following emergency treatment she is well. She has no significant past medical history and lives in a university flat

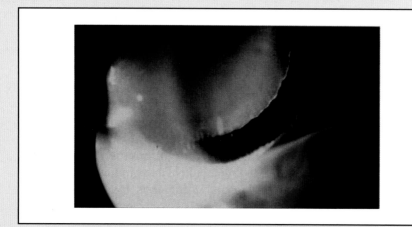

▲ **Fig. 34** Lens dislocation with stretching of zonules in a patient with Marfan's syndrome. (Reproduced with permission from Ho NC, Tran JR and Bektas A. Marfaris syndrome. *Lancet* 2005; 366: 1978–81.)

with two fellow students, one female and one male.

Your task: to explain to the patient the diagnosis of nut allergy as the cause of her anaphylaxis, and avoidance measures and the use of self-injectable adrenaline/epinephrine (eg EpiPen). There is no specialist allergy service in your hospital, but one of the pharmacists would be able to show the patient how to use EpiPen and you would be able to make an outpatient referral to the regional allergy service.

Key issues to explore

It will obviously be appropriate to ask the patient if she has any particular concerns and to address these, but the most important issue that must be tackled is to find out what she understands about her anaphylactic reaction. Understanding is important if she is to feel confident about minimising future risk. Lifestyle issues will be important.

- She will need to know how to minimise the risk of ingesting 'hidden' sources of peanut if eating out.

- She will need to read food labels if buying preprepared food.

- Does she have a partner, flatmates or family? They could be important allies in avoiding peanuts and may be able to assist in an emergency, if given the appropriate information.

Key points to establish

After an appropriate introduction, let the patient know that the purpose of your interview is to discuss what happened so that the chance of it happening in future is minimised.

Say that you will also discuss simple but effective treatment that she can give herself in case of emergency. You must try to give her confidence in her ability to manage the situation.

Explain how to avoid future reactions

Emphasise that she should continue to live a normal life, but that she must take appropriate precautions. Discuss potentially difficult or risky situations: parties, restaurants and choosing peanut-free food when shopping. Allow her time to express her concerns.

Discuss self-management of anaphylaxis

Discuss the need to carry two self-injectable epinephrine devices at all times, the recognition of anaphylaxis and measures which should be taken if it happens again. Be aware that she may be afraid of using injectable epinephrine and encourage her to discuss this. Encourage her to discuss her peanut allergy with her friends, who may be trained in the use of the epinephrine if appropriate, but you should ensure that she gains the confidence to self-inject in an emergency: her friends will not always be with her.

Appropriate responses to likely questions

Patient: why did this happen? I've eaten peanuts lots of times before.

Doctor: that's a good question, and I'm afraid that I don't have a good answer. All I can say is that this often happens: for some reason we don't know, people can become allergic to peanuts, and to other things, and their body starts to react in this dangerous way if they are exposed to them.

Patient: is it just peanuts I'm allergic to?

Doctor: that's another good question and at the moment I can't be sure. Sometimes people who react to peanuts also react to other nuts, so my advice for now is that it's very important that you avoid all nuts. But I will, with your agreement, refer you to the regional allergy service as an outpatient. They will do various tests to find out whether it's just peanuts that you're allergic to, or other nuts as well.

Patient: I couldn't possibly inject myself. How can I? I'm scared of needles.

Doctor: it's natural to feel that way at first, but you can overcome your fear. You will feel safer knowing that you know what to do in an emergency. One of the pharmacists in the hospital can show you how to use a device that does all the work for you: you don't actually see the needle and you can practice using a 'trainer' pen, which doesn't actually inject you. We could also show your flatmates how to use it too, if you wanted that and they were willing to learn.

Patient: how will I know when to use the epinephrine?

Doctor: the epinephrine is only for severe reactions like the one you had today. If you think you may be having an allergic reaction, you should take epinephrine if you feel any throat tightness, wheezing or faintness.

Patient: I'll be too frightened to eat out in a restaurant: what if the same thing happened again?

Doctor: I can understand why you are worried about that, but you can minimise the chances by taking simple measures. Most restaurants are aware of the difficulties faced by people with allergies: some have allergy information on the menus. However, you should always ask the waiter to specifically check with the cook in the kitchen if what you're thinking of ordering contains any nuts at all.

Patient: what about travelling abroad? Should I cancel my holiday?

Doctor: there is no need to cancel your holiday, but be cautious about unfamiliar foods that may contain nuts and always check in restaurants, as I've said before. Make sure that you carry your epinephrine with you and, to avoid difficulties on the plane and at customs, it would be wise to carry a doctor's letter explaining what it is and why you need it. I can write one of these for you.

Patient: what if the epinephrine doesn't work?

Doctor: in any situation where you need to use the epinephrine, an ambulance should also be called. The aim of the epinephrine is to give time for the ambulance to get to you. The epinephrine will work, but if the effect is insufficient or if your symptoms start to come back, you should use your second epinephrine syringe. By that time medical help is likely to be there.

1.3.2 Cold fingers and difficulty swallowing

Scenario

Role: You are a junior doctor in a rheumatology outpatient clinic.

Mrs Hope Adams, aged 50 years, has recently been referred to the outpatient clinic with cold fingers. The clinical suspicion from the initial consultation that she has secondary Raynaud's in association with systemic sclerosis has been supported by

the detection of anti-centromere antibodies in her blood. She tells you that, despite her doctor's concern, the Raynaud's does not trouble her too much and she can control her symptoms by avoiding cold weather and wearing gloves.

Your task: To explain to Mrs Adams the diagnosis of systemic sclerosis, including the uncertain prognosis and lack of curative treatment.

Key issues to explore

How does she currently view her problems? Does she appreciate that she may have a serious chronic condition, and that the disease may progress beyond the symptoms of her Raynaud's? Approach this by asking what she was told at the last clinic appointment: was it mentioned that her cold fingers could be a feature of a more widespread disease? This is a 'warning shot' before explaining the diagnosis.

Key points to establish

- Tests have suggested that she may develop more than cold fingers in the future: they are associated with a disease called systemic sclerosis, or scleroderma, which means 'hard skin'. In this condition the skin, usually of the hands and feet, swells and thickens and becomes stiff, tight and shiny.

- This 'hardening' or fibrosis can also affect internal organs, which can cause a variety of symptoms depending on which organ is involved.

- As and when other symptoms develop, they can be addressed

and treated. However, there is no effective treatment for the underlying condition.

- Regular reviews are required to direct symptomatic treatments, anticipate problems with screening tests and provide support.

- If the patient does develop other problems, referral to a regional centre with a relative special interest may be appropriate.

Appropriate responses to likely questions

Patient: I feel completely well other than the cold fingers. Why do you think I have anything more serious than cold fingers?

Doctor: that's a good question: it's because of the blood tests. They show that you have an antibody that is linked with a condition called scleroderma, and it is common for people with this condition to have cold hands – Raynaud's – for many years before they develop skin thickening or any other problems.

Patient: so what will scleroderma do to me?

Doctor: I'm afraid that I cannot say for certain, not because I'm hiding anything, but because I don't know. Sometimes it just causes very slow thickening of the skin, especially of the hands and feet. But sometimes it causes thickening of the tissues of internal organs, and that can lead to a variety of problems.

Patient: what sort of internal problems can scleroderma cause?

Doctor: I don't want to cause you unnecessary concern because all these things certainly don't happen to every patient, but it can cause problems with the gut, particularly difficulty with swallowing, a variety of problems with the lungs, and problems with the kidneys, including very high blood pressure.

Patient: I have never heard of this disease. How can I find out more?

Doctor: I can give you a leaflet on scleroderma today, and also the contact details for the Raynaud's and Scleroderma Association.

Patient: what can you do if the scleroderma starts causing serious problems?

Doctor: I'm afraid that we don't have any good treatment that will cure the scleroderma: we don't have anything that will make it go away, but what we can do is to help the problems that it causes. For instance, if it causes problems with indigestion or swallowing, then there are tablets that we can recommend – strong anti-indigestion tablets – that can help. If it causes problems with your blood pressure, then it's important to try to control this very carefully to prevent serious complications.

Patient: if you can't treat this disease, then why are you telling me about it?

Doctor: as I said, we don't have any treatment that will cure scleroderma, but we can do things that will help. By monitoring you in clinic we can try to pick up any problems early on, rather than waiting until things have got really bad. For instance, we would keep a careful check on your blood pressure and your lungs, and we would recommend treatment if problems were developing. Good treatment of blood pressure would be very important in cutting down the chances of you developing kidney failure, or other problems.

1.3.3 Back pain

Scenario

Role: you are a junior doctor working on a general medical ward.

You have admitted a 58-year-old woman for urgent investigation. She has a 2-week history of low back pain which is now keeping her awake at night. Over the past 2 days she has noticed progressive numbness and weakness of both legs, and also sphincteric weakness. She had breast cancer with axillary node involvement 4 years ago, but was told at her last outpatient appointment in the oncology clinic 6 months ago that she was 'fine'. On examination she has bilateral lower limb sensory impairment and lower motor neuron weakness. A plain radiograph of the spine shows at least one suspicious lesion.

Your task: to explain to her that she has cord compression of uncertain cause but with a strong suspicion of malignancy. The plan will be for her to have MRI of the spine and that surgery will probably be recommended, but that this will not be curative.

Key issues to explore

Your discussion with the patient should cover the following areas:

- her understanding of the problem;
- your explanation of her symptoms;
- the probable underlying cause;
- the treatments available;
- the likely prognosis.

Key points to establish

- That there is a problem with the patient's spine: it is pressing on her spinal cord and causing a blockage of the nerve signals to the lower half of her body.

- That this is a serious problem, probably related to her breast cancer, which needs urgent investigation and may require surgical intervention.

- That, even in the worst case, there will always be support and a plan of management.

In routine clinical practice (and in PACES, although the offer will inevitably be declined) encourage the presence of a close friend or relative if the patient wishes it. As well as providing support, this will spare the patient the necessity of repeating the explanation and may improve her overall understanding of the problem.

Appropriate responses to likely questions

Patient: it's not the breast cancer come back, is it?

Doctor: I don't know, but I'm afraid that there is a good chance that it could be the cancer. We won't know for certain until we have done some tests. We'll start off with a scan, an MRI scan, of the spine and then probably perform an operation to relieve any pressure on the spine and take samples for analysis. If it is the cancer, we will arrange for you to see the cancer specialist to talk about further treatment.

Patient: but at the clinic a few months ago, the oncologist told me that everything was fine.

Doctor: I know, because at that time you hadn't got any back pain or any problems with your legs. If this is the cancer coming back, then it seems as though that's happened just in the last few months.

Patient: if the oncologist had done a scan of my back when I saw them in the clinic a few months ago, would they have found anything?

Doctor: that's a good question, but I'm afraid that I don't know the answer. Scans of the spine aren't organised as a routine, only if there seems to be a problem. However, this is something that you could discuss with the oncologists if and when you see them.

Patient: I'm afraid to have surgery in case it makes things worse. Are there any alternatives?

Doctor: you're right in saying that all surgery has risks, but this is not something we're going to race into. The surgeons will look at your scans very carefully and will discuss things with you before you make the final decision. They will only recommend going ahead if they agree that there is a good chance of success. If you didn't have surgery, your legs might get worse and it would be difficult to know what was causing the problem or how to treat it. Is there anything in particular about the surgery that is worrying you?

Patient: if it's the cancer, will they be able to remove it during the operation?

Doctor: if it is possible to remove it, then the surgeons would do so. However, trying to remove the whole tumour may well damage your spinal cord so it's likely that the surgeons will just take enough to relieve any pressure. If further treatment is necessary, then radiotherapy treatment or medication will probably be recommended, but this is something on which the oncologists would advise.

Patient: does this mean that I can't be cured, that I have terminal cancer?

Doctor: if it is cancer, then you are right in thinking that we probably won't be able to get rid of it completely. But having said that, there are treatments that can work pretty well and it is possible for some people to live a relatively healthy and normal life for some time, even though the cancer is not completely removed.

Further comments

It is important that you are realistic in your explanations. This patient will undoubtedly need to have trust and confidence in her medical team in the future. Although it is important to be as positive as you reasonably can be in your attitude, a falsely over-optimistic assessment at this stage is likely to result in increased distress and loss of trust in the medical team in the future.

1.3.4 Widespread pain

Scenario

Role: you are a junior doctor in a rheumatology outpatient clinic.

You are seeing a 38-year-old woman who is attending the clinic for her first follow-up appointment. She was first seen in the clinic 6 weeks ago (by the consultant), when she gave a 3-year history of widespread pain, profound fatigue and poor-quality sleep. These symptoms were associated with significant disability, and she reported spending much of her day in bed and being heavily dependent on her family. The notes record that she was 'sad, withdrawn and angry'. Examination revealed very widespread tenderness with

numerous tender 'trigger points', but movement of her joints was unrestricted and no neurological abnormality could be detected.

The consultant felt that a diagnosis of fibromyalgia was likely, with some evidence of associated depression. Various investigations including FBC, erythrocyte sedimentation rate, C-reactive protein, bone/liver/kidney/muscle biochemistry, thyroid function tests, a screen for autoimmune/vasculitic disease and a CXR were performed and all were normal.

Your task: to explain the diagnosis of fibromyalgia to the patient and suggest a graded exercise programme, and also the possible benefits of treatment for depression.

Key issues to explore

This consultation would be likely to be difficult, even for an experienced clinician. It is important to:

- find out what the patient thinks is causing her problems and what her expectations are – discussions are likely to be easier if you are aware of the patient's perspective;

- pursue the role that depression and other psychological factors might be playing in the illness.

Key points to establish

It is essential to establish an atmosphere of trust, taking the patient's physical symptoms seriously and acknowledging their reality.

- Explain fibromyalgia as a pattern of muscular pain that can be severe and distressing, but which is not associated with any tissue damage.

- Explain that factors such as sleep disturbance, loss of physical fitness (conditioning) and low mood can perpetuate the pain and make it worse. Some patients find it difficult to accept that depression can cause pain, but most will see how pain and sleep disturbance can cause depression. It is rarely productive to get drawn into a 'chicken or egg' argument about pain and depression, and it is usually easier and more helpful to explain how vicious circles between these factors can worsen the pain (see Fig. 23), viewing low mood as a practical problem to be solved in helping to overcome the pain.

- Explain that treatment is not easy and that a complete, rapid cure is unlikely, but also that addressing the perpetuating factors can improve function and quality of life for most patients.

Appropriate responses to likely questions

Patient: you are saying all the tests are normal and that there is nothing wrong with my muscles. Are you saying it is all in my mind?

Doctor: no, your pain is real and is clearly causing you distress and affecting your life. Many kinds of rheumatic pain do not lead to changes in the blood or abnormalities on X-rays. Nevertheless, it is good that fibromyalgia is not associated with any long-term damage to the tissues.

Patient: I don't see how I can do more exercise when exercise just makes the pain worse.

Doctor: this is a very common concern for people with fibromyalgia, because exercise can certainly make the pain and tiredness worse. Nevertheless, we know that graded exercise programmes are one of the most helpful treatments for patients with fibromyalgia. The key thing is to approach exercise in the right way, and this usually needs help from a physiotherapist. You need to start with an amount of exercise that you can cope with easily, repeat this regularly, and just gradually increase the amount you are doing. You will only improve if you are able to exercise three times a week or more. At first the exercise will cause some discomfort, but if you are able to come back and do the same again within a day or two, then this is fine. However, if you get so much pain after exercise that you cannot do anything for a week, then you have started at too high a level.

Patient: I know that amitriptyline is an antidepressant. Are you suggesting that I take it because you think my main problem is depression?

Doctor: you are right that amitriptyline is an antidepressant, but low doses of amitriptyline and similar drugs are often used in the treatment of long-standing pain, particularly when the pain disturbs sleep. The doses used to manage pain are much lower than those used in cases of depression. I'm suggesting that you take it simply because I think it might help.

Patient: do you think my main problem is depression?

Doctor: I honestly find it very difficult to know. For obvious reasons, people with painful conditions often become depressed and depression makes any sort of pain worse. Treating depression can sometimes be easier than treating pain and it can certainly do a lot to improve your quality of life.

Patient: if I take amitriptyline I'll become addicted to it and I'll get side effects, won't I?

Doctor: no, it isn't addictive. It's generally safe and well tolerated, although it can cause morning drowsiness in some people, especially at the beginning of treatment.

Patient: what about my other problems with irritable bowels? How will they be affected by your treatments? Lots of tablets upset my stomach.

Doctor: people with fibromyalgia often have a lot of pain in other parts of their bodies, and irritable bowel syndrome is very common. In most cases treatments for fibromyalgia, such as amitriptyline, tend to improve irritable bowel syndrome.

Patient: it isn't just the pain, the fatigue is just as bad. Why am I so tired?

Doctor: tiredness is one of the most distressing symptoms in fibromyalgia, and is also a big problem in many other painful conditions. One of the most important causes of the tiredness is sleep disturbances due to pain, and these often improve with drugs such as amitriptyline.

1.3.5 Explain a recommendation to start a disease-modifying antirheumatic drug

Scenario

Role: you are a junior doctor in a rheumatology outpatient clinic.

Mrs Susan Terrell, a 40-year-old secretary, has recently been diagnosed with erosive rheumatoid arthritis after she presented with a 3-month history of disabling joint pains affecting her wrists and fingers. She has a strongly positive rheumatoid factor and has had a persistently elevated serum C-reactive protein of 40–75 mg/L since presentation, both of which are adverse prognostic factors. Although it has been explained to her that treatment with a disease-modifying antirheumatic drug (methotrexate) is her best hope of preserving joint function in the long term, she is unconvinced of the need to start treatment with this drug at this juncture on account of its possible adverse effects.

Your task: to explain to Mrs Terrell why it is in her best interests to take methotrexate.

Key issues to explore

The decision whether to take any drug should depend on the balance of benefits and risks. Anxiety about drug-induced adverse effects is entirely understandable, and methotrexate can certainly be toxic, but the key issues to explore here are the patient's perceptions of the benefits and risks to her.

Key points to establish

- Do not be dismissive of the patient's concerns: recognise her anxiety regarding the impact of the diagnosis and what the future might hold.

- Explain the reasoning behind the recommendation to commence methotrexate rather than use symptomatic treatments alone, ie she has active disease with adverse prognostic indices comprising radiological evidence of joint erosions coupled with a persistently elevated C-reactive protein and a positive rheumatoid factor.

- Emphasise that the risk–benefit ratio of treatment in this situation is heavily tilted towards treatment.

- Explain the potential long-term consequences of not undertaking treatment with a disease-modifying antirheumatic drug.

- Offer to introduce her to a clinical nurse specialist in rheumatology for more detailed discussion.

Appropriate responses to likely questions

Patient: how confident are you that methotrexate will not cause me any problems?

Doctor: as you know, it's impossible to guarantee that any drug will not cause problems. Deciding whether or not to recommend any drug is always a matter of balancing benefits and risks, but most people who take methotrexate do not get any problems with it and it's a very effective drug for treating rheumatoid arthritis in many cases.

Patient: but how many people get problems with it?

Doctor: adverse effects such as nausea, loss of appetite and diarrhoea occur in up to 1 in 10 patients, but most of these individuals usually get better on their own without the need to stop treatment. Low blood counts may occur in up to 1 in 20 patients, but these should be detected by routine monitoring, which is necessary for anyone taking the drug, before they cause a problem.

Patient: which adverse effects would you be most concerned about?

Doctor: like any medication which dampens the activity of the immune system, methotrexate may suppress production of white blood cells in the bone marrow and increase your susceptibility to infections. It also has the potential in a few patients,

less than 5% of cases, to cause liver problems or lung inflammation.

Patient: if I get these problems, do they always get better if the drug is stopped?

Doctor: yes, in most patients both bone marrow suppression and liver or lung problems are reversible. Regular follow-up and blood test monitoring means that we would pick up evidence of them at an early stage. It would be equally important that you told us if you felt unwell or developed a cough or shortness of breath while you were on the drug, so that we could check things over promptly.

Patient: are there any other drugs that attack the disease that I could take instead?

Doctor: yes, there are other drugs which modify disease activity, but all of them have side effects, many similar to those of methotrexate. Methotrexate is the one that's been around the longest and none of the other drugs are clearly better, so that's why we recommend methotrexate in the first instance.

Patient: if you were afflicted with rheumatoid arthritis, would you take methotrexate?

Doctor: yes, I would take methotrexate or one of the other disease-modifying antirheumatic drugs if I had evidence of active erosive disease, because of the strength of evidence showing that early treatment prevents further joint damage.

Patient: why can't I wait and see how things go?

Doctor: you can wait if you want to, but that's not what we recommend. Damage is occurring in your joints – we can see it on the X-rays – and if that damage gets worse, then there isn't any treatment that will turn the clock back.

1.4 Acute scenarios

1.4.1 Fulminant septicaemia in an asplenic woman

Scenario

A 50-year-old asplenic woman presents to the Emergency Department with a 2-day history of fever and confusion. Her observations on admission confirm fever (39°C), tachycardia (150 bpm) and hypotension (BP 80/40 mmHg). She carries a splenectomy card stating that she underwent splenectomy 7 years ago for refractory immune thrombocytopenic purpura. As a junior medical doctor on duty, you suspect, given her asplenia, that she is septicaemic and initiate immediate treatment with broad-spectrum antibiotics.

Introduction

Asplenic patients are prone to overwhelming infection, particularly with encapsulated bacteria, because of their impaired ability to produce antibodies against capsular polysaccharide antigens of *Streptococcus penumoniae*, *Haemophilus influenzae* and *Neisseria meningitidis*. This is a direct consequence of the loss of splenic marginal zone B lymphocytes. In addition, the loss of approximately one-quarter of the body's total macrophage population renders patients susceptible to certain other blood-borne bacteria and some intraerythrocytic protozoa (Table 20).

Causes of hyposplenism are shown in Table 21.

TABLE 20 ORGANISMS CAUSING OVERWHELMING INFECTION IN ASPLENIC PATIENTS

Bacteria	Parasites
Streptococcus pneumoniae	Malaria
Streptococcus suis (from pigs and farm animals)	
Haemophilus influenzae	*Babesia* spp. (from tick bites)
Neisseria meningitidis	
Staphylococcus aureus	
Klebsiella pneumoniae	
Salmonella enteriditis	
Capnocytophaga canimorsus (DF-2) (from dog bites)	

TABLE 21 CAUSES OF HYPOSPLENISM

Splenectomy	Functional hyposplenism
Trauma	Sickle-cell anaemia
Haematological autoimmunity	Essential thrombocythaemia
Haematological malignancy	Lymphoproliferative disease
	Coeliac disease
	Inflammatory bowel disease

History of the presenting problem

Is there a history of dog bite or travel abroad?

This is important to ascertain because asplenic patients are at particular risk of infection with *Capnocytophaga canimorsus* (a Gram-negative bacillus found in canine saliva) and protozoal infections such as *Plasmodium* spp.

Other relevant history

What measures were or could have been taken to reduce the infective risks associated with asplenia before or after splenectomy?

Was the patient immunised with 23-valent pneumoccocal polysaccharide vaccine (Pneumovax), *Haemophilus* conjugate vaccine and meningococcal type C conjugate vaccine before splenectomy? Current guidelines from the British Committee for Standards in Haematology recommend that vaccination be performed at least 2 weeks before elective splenectomy or as soon as possible after emergency splenectomy.

Examination

> In any patient with overwhelming sepsis, consider hyposplenism.

This woman's profound hypotension indicates that she is extremely ill. Aside from repeating her vital signs, note the following in order to establish a baseline from which you can judge whether she is improving or deteriorating over the next 30 minutes or so.

- Peripheral perfusion: are her peripheries hot or cold and, if cold, how far proximally does this extend?

- Respiration: is she cyanosed? Does she look exhausted? If either of these are present, then call for assistance from the intensive care unit (ICU) sooner rather than later. Can she speak in sentences or only a few words at a time? Do not be falsely reassured by a normal respiratory rate (12–16/minute) if the patient looks tired and can hardly speak: it means that they are tiring and may arrest soon. Check pulse oximetry, but note that it may not be possible to get a proper reading in a patient who is peripherally vasoconstricted.

- She is confused: check score on the Glasgow Coma Scale. Is there meningism?

- Are there any clues that the patient may have a particular cause of septicaemia? Some patients with meningococcal septicaemia in particular may present with signs of disseminated intravascular coagulation (DIC) (see *Haematology*, Sections 1.4.4, 2.3.2 and 2.6), including skin purpura and digital gangrene. Examine the lungs: is there consolidation to indicate that the underlying condition is almost certainly pneumonia?

Investigation

To establish the diagnosis

In view of the high probability of septicaemia, send blood cultures before starting immediate antimicrobial therapy. The patient will require urethral catheterisation to monitor urine output. Send urine for culture, and also swabs/specimens from any other sites that might be infected. In selected cases other specific tests will be required, eg thick and thin films for malaria.

Organise a CXR to look for lobar consolidation, likely to be due to pneumococcal pneumonia in this context, and also for features suggesting acute respiratory distress syndrome.

To establish a baseline/presence of complications

- Check electrolytes and renal, liver and bone function.

- FBC.

- Clotting screen (possibility of DIC).

- Inflammatory markers (C-reactive protein and erythrocyte sedimentation rate) to assess severity of tissue damage.

- Check arterial blood gases to assess oxygenation and ventilation and for acidosis.

Management

This woman clearly requires resuscitation. Full details of how to approach a very ill patient can be found in *Acute Medicine*, Section 1.2.2, but the key issues include the following.

- Oxygenation: give high-flow oxygen via a reservoir bag, aiming to keep oxygen saturation at >92%.

- Fluid resuscitation: give colloid or 0.9% saline rapidly (as fast as the cannulae will allow) to raise the JVP to about 8–10 cm but reassess clinically after every litre of fluid has been given to check for pulmonary oedema. Stop rapid infusion if breathing deteriorates in any way. The insertion of a central venous line to monitor central venous pressure (CVP) may be helpful, but note that the first priority is to give fluid to an obviously hypotensive patient, not to try to insert a CVP line. The presence of hypotension that is refractory to fluid challenge or hypotension in association with pulmonary oedema indicates that the patient is *in extremis*: call for urgent help from the ICU.

- Antimicrobials: in this case where septicaemia is suspected.

- Support of failing systems: if this woman does not respond to the treatments indicated above, then she may require one or more of the following: mechanical ventilation, inotropic support or haematological support (fresh frozen plasma or platelet transfusion).

What principles should guide your choice of antimicrobials?

Until the results of blood cultures are available you should choose a broad-spectrum antimicrobial with bactericidal activity against the pathogens most likely to cause septicaemia in an asplenic host (Table 20). Most hospitals will have their own 'antibiotic policy', but unless there are unusual features to the case, such as recent foreign travel or a dog bite, then a third-generation cephalosporin in conjunction with an aminoglycoside would be appropriate until the results of cultures are available.

Further comments

The risk of serious infection following splenectomy is related to the age at surgery and the presence of underlying disease. The infection rate is particularly high in children under the age of 5 years (>10%). Although the period of greatest risk in all asplenic patients is the first 2 years following surgery, delayed infection may occur more than 20 years later, thus underlining the need for constant vigilance.

What measures would you adopt to minimise a recurrence of septicaemia in the future?

If and when the patient recovers, ensure that she is optimally

TABLE 22 VACCINATION RECOMMENDATIONS FOR HYPOSPLENIC ADULTS

Vaccine	Revaccination schedule	Comments
Polyvalent (23-valent) pneumoccoccal polysaccharide (Pneumovax)	5 years	Consider monitoring antibody levels. If the Prevenar (pneumococcal conjugate) vaccine is given, then consider an early booster dose to cover additional serotypes
Polyvalent (7-valent) pneumococcal conjugate (Prevenar)	Not known	Consider using prior to pneumococcal polysaccharide vaccine, as it is likely to give long-term protection
Haemophilus conjugate	Not routinely recommended	Use if previously unvaccinated
Meningococcal type C conjugate	Not routinely recommended	Use if previously unvaccinated
Meningococcal A and C polysaccharide	Prior to travel to high-risk area	Short-term protection only
Influenza vaccine	Annual	

protected against further episodes of sepsis due to encapsulated bacteria by vaccinating her with the relevant vaccines (Table 22). Although no formal evidence is available, it is likely that asplenic patients will derive additional protection from immunisation with the newly introduced pneumococcal conjugate vaccine by virtue of its greater immunogenicity. The need for booster immunisations should be dictated by antibody levels and reviewed at 5-yearly intervals. It is also prudent to offer patients annual influenza immunisation to minimise the risk of secondary bacterial infection following influenza.

Lifelong antibiotic prophylaxis using oral penicillin is recommended by the Chief Medical Officer in the UK, although the evidence for its efficacy is unclear.

All patients should carry a splenectomy card and a Medic-Alert bracelet stating their asplenic status, and should be educated regarding the risks associated with animal bites and travel to malarious areas.

How can splenic function be assessed?

The assessment of functional hyposplenism in patients with intact spleens is a difficult area since the traditional marker, Howell–Jolly bodies (Fig. 35), may be insufficiently sensitive in many early cases. Alternative methods of assessing splenic function include quantification of the circulating pitted red cell count by image contrast microscopy (Fig. 36), which reflects physiological function of phagocytosing effete red cells in the spleen, and radionuclide imaging to assess splenic uptake of isotopes. There are no reliable methods for directly assessing the important immunological functions of the spleen.

1.4.2 Collapse during a restaurant meal

Scenario

A 19-year-old medical student is admitted to the Emergency Department with facial swelling, difficulty in breathing and a generalised urticarial rash. Her symptoms began minutes after starting a meal with friends in a local restaurant. You are called to see her urgently.

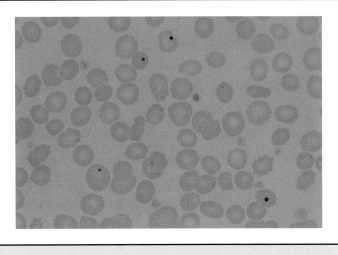

▲ **Fig. 35** Blood film depicting Howell–Jolly bodies (intraerythrocytic nuclear fragments) in a patient after splenectomy for immune thrombocytopenic purpura. (Courtesy of Dr D. Swirsky, Leeds General Infirmary.)

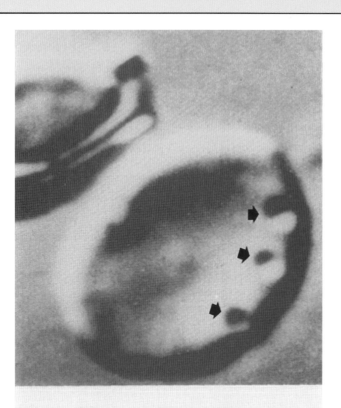

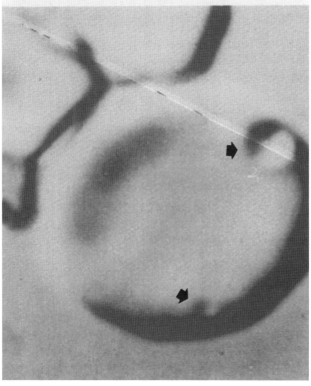

▲ **Fig. 36** Interference phase-contrast microscopy showing red cells with surface indentations or 'pocks' in an asplenic patient. 'Pocks' (arrows) occur in more than 12% of the red cells of patients with asplenia. (Reproduced with permission from Feder HM and Pearson HA. Assessment of splenic function in familial asplenia. *N. Engl. J. Med.* 1999; 341: 211, copyright © 1999 Massachusetts Medical Society.)

Introduction

Anaphylaxis occurs when there is systemic mast cell degranulation as a result of IgE-mediated binding to an allergen. Symptoms usually start within a few minutes of contact with the allergen and progress rapidly.

- More common after ingestion of an oral allergen: angio-oedema, laryngeal obstruction, wheeze, colicky abdominal pain with vomiting or diarrhoea.

- More common after intravenous exposure to allergen: hypotension.

- Cutaneous features occur in almost every episode of anaphylaxis: urticaria and flushing.

History of the presenting problem

In all cases of possible anaphylaxis the history is crucial, both to make the diagnosis and to prevent future episodes.

> Anaphylactic reactions usually occur within minutes of encountering the allergen: life-threatening reactions virtually never occur more than 30 minutes after contact.

The priority in this case is clearly to start treatment immediately and you should not delay in order to seek a detailed history, but you need to know what she ate to prevent recurrence. Get her friends to contact the chef at the restaurant in order to obtain a list of all the ingredients from her meal as soon as possible, but note that any food she ate more than 1 hour prior to the anaphylaxis is most unlikely to be the cause. Beware of hidden allergens: nuts, nut oils and spices are very common allergens that may be overlooked. Contact with latex and insect stings is unlikely to be relevant here, but should be considered in other cases.

Other relevant history

Previous episodes

Has the patient had any previous episodes, perhaps less severe? Does she have any known allergies? Atopic people (with eczema, asthma or hay fever) have a greater risk of anaphylaxis.

Drug history

The following drugs make treatment of anaphylaxis difficult or dangerous and should be avoided in future.

- Epinephrine will cause severe hypertension if given to patients on beta-blockers due to unopposed stimulation of α-adrenergic receptors.

- Tricyclic antidepressants, monoamine oxidase inhibitors and cocaine potentiate epinephrine and increase the risk of arrhythmias and hypertension.

Other medical conditions

A history of heart disease or hypertension, most unlikely in this case, would increase the risks of epinephrine treatment, but faced with life-threatening anaphylaxis the balance of benefits and risks very clearly favours treatment.

Examination

> Although the scenario described here follows the traditional format, with management following on from history, examination and investigation, in practice the clinical urgency of the situation means that immediate acute management of anaphylaxis takes precedence.
>
> This is a medical emergency: your patient has typical features of anaphylaxis and without prompt treatment she may die from respiratory tract obstruction, bronchoconstriction or hypotension. If she looks as though she is about to arrest, then call the cardiac resuscitation team immediately. Do not wait for her heart to stop!

When the patient is *in extremis* you should take no more than a few seconds for a brief assessment. Aside from noting vital signs, the key issue is to look for evidence of upper and/or lower airway obstruction.

- Can the patient speak?

- Can she swallow?

- Is she cyanosed?

- Is she using her accessory muscles to support breathing?

- Look in her mouth, but do not force open because this may occlude a critically compromised airway. Note the degree of facial, tongue and pharyngeal swelling.

- Stridor or wheeze: remember that absence of these may indicate very poor air entry and incipient respiratory arrest.

- Count her respiratory rate, but note that a normal value is not always reassuring (see Section 1.4.1).

- Chest movement: does her chest seem to be expanding normally? Is there indrawing of the intercostal muscles?

- Check pulse oximetry.

Other features to note include erythema, urticaria, rhinitis, vomiting or diarrhoea. Does she have a Medic-Alert bracelet?

Immediate management

While you are conducting the assessment, give high-flow oxygen via a reservoir bag and prepare emergency drugs. If airway obstruction is the dominant problem, the patient will be most comfortable sitting; if it is hypotension, then lying flat will be best. After this, proceed as follows.

- Give epinephrine 0.5 mg (0.5 mL of 1:1000) intramuscularly: most

patients with anaphylaxis or anaphylactoid reactions respond promptly to this treatment, but repeat after 5 minutes if there is no response or if symptoms recur.

- Establish intravenous access; if the patient is hypotensive, give 1–2 L of physiological (0.9%) saline.

- Give an antihistamine, such as chlorpheniramine 10–20 mg, and hydrocortisone 100–500 mg (each by intramuscular or slow intravenous injection) to help minimise later reactions.

- Recheck the BP and listen to her chest: nebulised salbutamol (5 mg) will help any residual bronchoconstriction; intravenous salbutamol may be necessary if the patient has recently taken a beta-blocker.

Investigation

The diagnosis here is almost certainly anaphylaxis, but sometimes all is not what it appears to be and a case that seems initially to be a straightforward episode of anaphylaxis becomes much less so with time. There are other causes of facial and laryngeal swelling (Table 23), and panic attacks can be dramatic. Do not forget C1 inhibitor deficiency, especially if the response to epinephrine is poor.

> Consider panic attacks: these may cause dramatic breathlessness, with loud upper airway noises and occasionally erythema, but without the other features of anaphylaxis.

Measurement of serum mast cell tryptase is useful in demonstrating that the presenting episode was associated with demonstrable mast cell degranulation, ie was

TABLE 23 DIFFERENTIAL DIAGNOSIS OF FACIAL AND LARYNGEAL SWELLING

Frequency	Diagnosis
Common	Allergy, including anaphylaxis
	Anaphylactoid reactions (usually to drugs)
	Idiopathic and angiotensin-converting enzyme inhibitor-induced angio-oedema
	Salicylate hypersensitivity
	Infection: erysipelas, dental infections, parotitis and quinsy
	Trauma, including burns
Must consider	C1 inhibitor deficiency

anaphylactic or anaphylactoid. Serial samples should be taken, ideally at 1 and 4 hours after onset with a further sample at 24 hours, by which time raised tryptase levels should have returned to baseline. Even a single measurement can be invaluable if the diagnosis is later questioned.

Specific IgE can be estimated for suspect allergens as dictated by the clinical history, but note that radioallergosorbent or immunoCAP tests may occasionally be negative immediately after an episode of anaphylaxis. If in doubt, repeat at a later date. Skin-prick tests may be performed at a later date in clinic.

Further management

After resuscitation the patient is likely to be well, but she should be kept under observation for at least 12 hours since biphasic anaphylactic reactions occasionally occur. During this time:

- ensure that asthma management, if required, is optimal;

- prescribe self-injectable epinephrine and train her in its use (Fig. 37);

- advise her to avoid likely allergens, including hidden allergens such as nuts, pending results of further assessment (see Section 1.3.1);

- refer her to an allergy clinic, making sure the history and details of possible allergens are documented.

Further comments

Asthma and food allergy

In patients with food allergy, poorly controlled asthma is an important risk factor for fatal anaphylaxis, underlining the need for optimal asthma control in these patients.

1.4.3 Systemic lupus erythematosus and confusion

Scenario

A 35-year-old woman of Afro-Caribbean origin presents with an acute confusional state. She first came to medical attention 2 years ago when she presented with joint pains and oedema. A diagnosis of systemic lupus erythematosus (SLE) was made; renal biopsy revealed grade IV

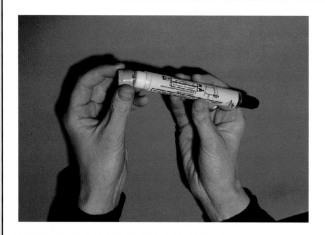
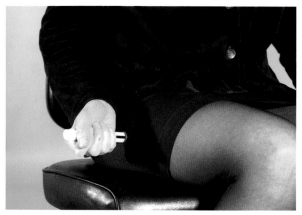

▲ **Fig. 37** Use of EpiPen. (**a**) Take cap off the back of the EpiPen. (**b**) Holding the pen as shown, press firmly to the lateral part of the thigh, through clothes if necessary. A click will be felt as the epinephrine is injected. Hold for 10 seconds. After epinephrine self-administration, patients should seek urgent medical attention, because the benefit may be temporary. A second 'back-up' epinephrine dose should be provided for use if symptoms do not improve or if they recur en route to the hospital.

glomerulonephritis, and she was initially treated with intravenous pulses of methylprednisolone (followed by oral prednisolone) and cyclophosphamide. Since then her lupus has been active and difficult to control at times. For the last 6 months she has been on prednisolone 15 mg daily and mycophenolate 1 g bd. She has now developed an acute confusional state, the cause of which is not clear and her condition is deteriorating.

On examination her vital signs are not grossly abnormal: temperature 37.4°C, pulse 80 bpm, respiration 14/minute, BP 132/82 mmHg. Her peripheral circulation is normal and pulse oximetry shows an oxygen saturation of 98% on air. Her score on the Glasgow Coma Scale is 13/15 and her Abbreviated Mental Test score is 6/10. Neurological examination is difficult, but there are no clear focal signs and no meningism.

Introduction

Neurological symptoms in a patient with SLE merit urgent investigation. Your aim is to distinguish between the following:

- neuropsychiatric SLE;
- central nervous system (CNS) or other infection in an immunocompromised individual;
- side effect of drug treatment, eg prednisolone;
- unrelated neurological/psychiatric illness.

This can be a very difficult differential diagnosis, but crucially important because the treatment of these conditions is radically different.

History of the presenting problem

Is the lupus active?

Neurological involvement in lupus usually occurs on a background of active systemic disease, but may occasionally occur anew. You should therefore ask relevant questions to assess whether the patient's lupus is active (eg malar rash, mouth ulcers, alopecia, Raynaud's, fatigue, inflammatory arthritis or pleurisy). If she is incapable of coherent conversation, ask a relative or partner.

Is this neuropsychiatric lupus?

Neuropsychiatric SLE may present with diffuse or focal symptoms. Ask about the following:

- headache;
- seizures;
- problems with vision;
- limb weakness and numbness;
- psychotic symptoms.

How much immunosuppressive treatment has the patient received?

A patient such as this, who has been given pulsed methylprednisolone, cyclophosphamide and other 'aggressive' treatments, is clearly prone to immunosuppression-related infection. In contrast, someone who has received only a modest dose of steroids, perhaps with azathioprine, is at much lower risk.

Has the patient been taking her medications?

It is important to check drug compliance: failure to take medications in a patient with a background of active SLE will predispose the individual to develop a flare.

What features would support a diagnosis of infection?

Pyrexia with obvious evidence of meningism or septicaemia should raise the possibility of meningitis. However, be aware that many of the usual clinical manifestations of sepsis such as fever may be absent in the patient who is immunosuppressed.

> Opportunistic infection may masquerade as neuropsychiatric SLE in patients on prolonged immunosuppressive therapy, and a recent increase in steroid dosage may suggest steroid-induced psychosis.

Other relevant history

Has anything like this happened before and, if so, what was the diagnosis? Does this patient have any history of psychiatric disorders?

Examination

Look carefully for evidence of lupus activity, eg rash, inflammatory arthritis or pericardial/pleural rubs. Given the presentation with confusion, particular emphasis on the neurological examination is required, so look carefully for the following.

- Meningism: if present this would suggest an infective cause.

- Fundi for papilloedema and/or exudates: papilloedema, signifying an increase in intracranial pressure, is unusual in neuropsychiatric SLE and would point to one of the alternative diagnoses. Retinal exudates may occur with both lupus and opportunistic infections such as toxoplasmosis.

- Cranial and peripheral nerves for mononeuritis multiplex, which would suggest active lupus vasculitis.

- Limbs/trunk/thorax for evidence of transverse myelitis: isolated transverse myelitis is a recognised complication of lupus and would characteristically manifest as a paraparesis with a sensory level.

Investigation

This will be dictated by the nature of the presentation. The differential diagnosis of an acute confusional state is very wide. If the patient looks as though she has a sepsis syndrome, eg cool or warm peripheries, hypotension and a high fever (not present in this case), then she should be treated accordingly, acknowledging that the differential diagnosis will be wider than usual in someone who is immunosuppressed. Neuropsychiatric SLE does not cause circulatory compromise.

Immunological

> **Neuropsychiatric SLE is primarily a clinical diagnosis.** There is no single reliable laboratory or radiological marker of the condition. A good clinician assessing appropriate serum, cerebrospinal fluid (CSF) and imaging studies has the best chance of coming to the correct conclusion.

Urgent serology is required to assess lupus activity. Check antinuclear antibodies, antibodies to double-stranded DNA, complement C3 and C4 levels, erythrocyte sedimentation rate and C-reactive protein (CRP). Anti-neuronal and anti-ribosomal P antibodies have been promoted as markers of neuropsychiatric SLE, but are rarely used in practice because of a combination of methodological difficulties and poor sensitivity. Although many cases of neuropsychiatric SLE are associated with worsening serology, exceptional cases may occur with stable serology. A raised CRP is unusual in lupus itself and should raise suspicions of infection.

Antiphospholipid antibodies (anti-cardiolipin and lupus anticoagulant) are useful in delineating patients with the antiphospholipid syndrome, who may present with confusion secondary to thrombotic disease.

Other tests

The following will be required.

- Dipstick urine for protein and blood: if positive for protein, quantitate urinary albumin/creatinine ratio; if positive for blood, use microscopy to analyse urine for red cell casts. If these tests are significantly more abnormal than they were at the patient's last routine review, then they suggest that she might have active lupus nephritis, which would make neuropsychiatric SLE more likely.

- Check FBC, electrolytes, renal/liver/bone function tests, blood cultures, and urine cultures.

- Brain imaging: a gadolinium-enhanced MRI scan would be the preferred test, but if one is not readily available then proceed to a contrast-enhanced CT scan.

- Lumbar puncture: perform as soon as imaging has excluded raised intracranial pressure/mass effect.

> **Investigation of suspected neuropsychiatric lupus**
> - Urgent brain imaging is required to exclude space-occupying lesions. A gadolinium-enhanced MRI scan is the imaging modality of choice, but note that a negative scan does not rule out CNS lupus.
> - Lumbar puncture: examination of CSF is essential for excluding opportunistic infection; a non-specific cellular pleocytosis, rise in protein and CSF oligoclonal bands occur in 30% of cases of neuropsychiatric lupus.

Management

Urgent specialist advice is required for management of this patient, but the important general message is that neuropsychiatric SLE requires aggressive immunosuppressive therapy, usually using parenteral steroids and cyclophosphamide, with concomitant antimicrobial therapy if infection cannot be excluded. Opportunistic CNS infection should be treated appropriately.

Further comments

The heterogeneity of neuropsychiatric SLE suggests that multiple aetiological factors, ranging from vascular injury to intracranial vessels to antineuronal and antiphospholipid antibodies, are responsible for driving the diverse clinical manifestations of the condition. Cerebral lupus is a diagnosis of exclusion because of the lack of a diagnostic marker and the real difficulties in differentiating between neuropsychiatric lupus and infection of the CNS.

1.4.4 Acute hot joints

Scenario

Case A

A 73-year-old woman presents with a 24-hour history of a painful, swollen and hot right knee. She feels generally unwell and has a temperature of 38.1°C. She has had minor pain and stiffness in both knees for many years.

Case B

A 42-year-old man presents with a hot swollen left elbow. He gives a history of two attacks of severe pain and redness of the big toes over the last 2 years. He is overweight and drinks four or five pints of beer several nights a week.

Case C

A 21-year-old man develops a painful swollen right knee 1 week after returning from a holiday in Spain. He subsequently develops pain and swelling in the left midfoot. He denies any recent episodes of diarrhoea or genitourinary symptoms.

Introduction

What are the differential diagnoses for each case?

- Case A: septic arthritis, pseudogout (pyrophosphate arthritis), gout and haemarthrosis.

- Case B: septic arthritis and gout.

- Case C: septic arthritis and reactive arthritis.

Which diagnosis should be considered in all these cases?

Septic arthritis is the primary concern in the assessment of the acute hot joint. Septic arthritis is not the commonest cause of an acute monoarthritis (Table 24) but it is the most serious and has serious potential for severe joint damage and life-threatening septicaemia. If sepsis has been considered and excluded, the main differential diagnosis is between a crystal arthritis and a postinfective reactive arthritis. The history and examination may give pointers towards the correct diagnosis, but sepsis can never be completely excluded on this basis alone. The most important tool in the assessment of the acute hot joint is aspiration of synovial fluid for microscopy, including crystals, and culture.

TABLE 24 DIFFERENTIAL DIAGNOSIS OF ACUTE HOT JOINTS

Frequency of disorder	Examples
Common	Crystal arthritis
	• Gout (Case B)
	• Pseudogout (Case A)
	• Reactive arthritis (Case C)
	Non-gonococcal septic arthritis caused by pyogenic bacteria
	• *Staphylococcus aureus* (70%)
	• Other Gram-positive cocci (20%)
	• Gram-negative bacilli (10%)
Rare	Haemarthrosis
	Other spondyloarthritides
	Other infections
	• Gonococcal arthritis (becoming more common but still rare in the UK, more common in the USA and Australasia)
	• Lyme disease
	• Tuberculosis
	Palindromic rheumatoid arthritis (RA)
	Monoarticular presentation of RA
	Osteonecrosis (especially involving the hip)

The hot joint

- The best diagnostic tool is synovial fluid aspiration.
- Always consider the possible diagnosis of septic arthritis.

History of the presenting problem

The history of joint swelling is usually straightforward but helps little with the differential diagnosis. A history of trauma may point to haemarthrosis. Rapid onset of pain and systemic malaise can occur in all the common causes, but severe systemic symptoms and a focus of infection should increase the suspicion of sepsis. A slow subacute onset makes pyogenic bacterial sepsis less likely, but the possibility of tuberculosis should be considered. The differential diagnosis is influenced by age: crystal arthritis is the most common cause in elderly people, whereas reactive arthritis tends to occur in sexually active young adults. Gout and reactive arthritis are more common in men.

Other relevant history

Consider the diagnoses listed in Table 24. Which of these fits the picture best?

Risk factors for sepsis

Is there a history of penetrating injury (either near the joint or elsewhere) that might have acted as a portal of entry? Do not forget intravenous drug abuse. Is there a history of immunosuppression (especially corticosteroid treatment)?

Previous similar episodes

Episodic, severe, flitting monoarthritis raises particular suspicions of gout, especially if the first metatarsophalangeal joint has been involved. Palindromic RA may produce a similar picture.

Chronic rheumatological disease

A history suggestive of pre-existing osteoarthritis in the hot joint may point to pseudogout. Patients with RA have an increased risk of sepsis (independent of treatment, but steroid therapy increases the risk further).

Risk factors for gout

Gout is far more common in men, particularly those who are obese, those who drink heavily and those with a family history of the condition. Diuretics (especially thiazides and furosemide) are a common predisposing factor, especially in the elderly. Gout hardly ever occurs in women, except in the context of diuretic usage or renal impairment.

Infection

Is there any evidence of infection that might have triggered a reactive arthritis? Rheumatologists reserve the term 'reactive arthritis' for a specific syndrome of acute non-infectious mono- or oligo-arthritis with a predilection for the large joints of the legs that occurs after bacterial gastrointestinal infection (*Salmonella*, *Shigella*, *Campylobacter* or *Yersinia* spp.) or sexually acquired chlamydial infection. Arthritis can occur alone or together with ocular and mucocutaneous disease, when the label 'Reiter's syndrome' can be used. Ask the patient about any recent travel, diarrhoeal illness and genitourinary symptoms such as penile or vaginal discharge.

Taking a sexual history

It may be necessary to take a sexual history, but this should be sensitively handled because patients are usually unaware of any possible link between their painful knee and their sex life. This discussion should therefore be left to the end of the consultation, after the rest of the history and examination have been performed, and the topic should be introduced carefully, with explanation, perhaps as follows:

'I need to ask one or two more questions to try to work out why your knee is giving you trouble . . .'

'There are many reasons why it might be . . .'

'Some infections can cause the problem . . .'

'In particular, some genital infections can do this . . .'

'Are you at risk of any of these . . . ?'

'Have you had any problems in that department?'

'Have you had any discharge or ulceration on your penis/vagina?'

'Have you had sex with any new partners recently?'

(See *Clinical Skills*, Clinical Skills for PACES – History-taking for PACES.)

Examination

General features

A sick febrile patient should always be considered to have sepsis until proven otherwise (check their temperature, pulse and BP) but remember that sepsis can be present in a patient who initially appears clinically well, especially if they are elderly or immunosuppressed.

Specific features

- Confirm that the swelling is articular rather than periarticular or subcutaneous. Is an effusion present? Erythema around the joint can occur in gout but should raise a very strong suspicion of sepsis.

- Are the other joints normal, or is there evidence of a more widespread acute inflammatory arthropathy? Are there features of a chronic arthritis preceding the acute illness?

- Look for features suggestive of reactive arthritis/Reiter's syndrome: conjunctivitis/uveitis; scaly rashes on the palms and soles; balanitis; and urethral discharge.

- Look for tophi, which can occur on any pressure point.

Investigation

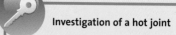

Investigation of a hot joint

Aspiration of synovial fluid is vital for accurate diagnosis. Techniques are not difficult, but if you are not confident then ask someone else. On call, these skills are most likely to be found amongst the orthopaedic team. Do not defer aspiration because you lack this skill (see Section 3.5).

Joint aspiration

A few drops of fluid are sufficient for microscopy and culture (Fig. 38). The macroscopic appearance of synovial fluid may give some clues:

- grossly purulent fluid suggests sepsis;

- blood-stained fluid may suggest haemarthrosis, but also occurs in pseudogout.

Fluid should be sent for urgent:

- polarised light microscopy for crystals;

- Gram stain for organisms;

- culture.

Gout only rarely coexists with sepsis (unless there is an ulcerating tophus) but pseudogout can, so it may be best to wait 24 hours for culture results before concluding that pseudogout is the primary diagnosis.

Other tests

Blood cultures are mandatory when sepsis is suspected. Other tests provide less useful information.

- FBC: white cell count, particularly the neutrophil count, is typically raised in acute sepsis, but it may be normal.

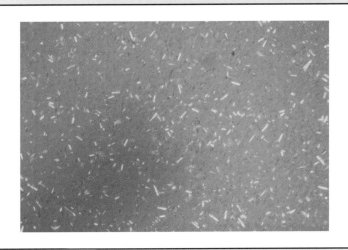

▲ **Fig. 38** Monosodium urate crystals in synovial fluid from acute gout observed by polarised light microscopy.

- Serum urate often drops in an acute attack of gout so may be unhelpful.

- Inflammatory markers, particularly C-reactive protein, are rarely diagnostically helpful, but are useful in measuring the subsequent response to therapy.

- Autoantibody testing is hardly ever helpful in this context.

- A clotting screen should be performed in those with haemarthrosis.

- Joint radiographs are largely unhelpful as they show evidence of chronic joint disease only, although chondrocalcinosis may be seen in a patient with pseudogout.

Management

Immediate management should be admission to hospital if there is strong suspicion of sepsis or mobility is severely restricted (and appropriate support at home cannot be arranged). If sepsis is unlikely, the patient may be managed as an outpatient with early follow-up.

Start empirical antibiotic therapy if sepsis is clinically likely, ie the patient looks ill or there is purulent synovial fluid/organisms on Gram stain. In adults, use high-dose flucloxacillin plus a third-generation cephalosporin initially. Antibiotics can be withdrawn if cultures are negative at 24 hours. The minimum period of antibiotic treatment for joint sepsis is 6 weeks (usually including 2 weeks where drugs are given intravenously).

> ⚠ Beware prior antibiotic treatment masking the diagnosis of sepsis.

Further comments

- Orthopaedic assessment is useful: arthrotomy/joint wash-out may be indicated. Orthopaedic surgeons should always deal with suspected sepsis in a prosthetic joint.

- NSAIDs may give useful symptom control, but avoid them if possible in the presence of renal impairment (often present in this context). Also beware of past or current history suggestive of peptic ulceration, reflux or NSAID intolerance.

- Treatment of non-septic arthritides with intra-articular steroids may be indicated. In most patients do this only after negative culture, although some may be injected at the time of initial assessment (eg recurrent gout). If in doubt, wait.

- Consider unusual infections (eg tuberculosis and fungal) in patients with immunosuppression or a history of foreign travel.

- Avoid weight-bearing on a severely inflamed joint, although splintage is not usually necessary. Arrange for early mobilisation as inflammation subsides; physiotherapy input will be required.

- Do not forget longer-term issues: screening for chlamydial infection in sexually active patients with non-crystal non-septic arthritis; gout prophylaxis; and gout as a surrogate marker for diabetes, hypertension and hyperlipidaemia.

1.4.5 A crush fracture

Scenario

A 65-year-old woman develops severe low thoracic back pain and right flank pain while gardening. She has a history of thyrotoxicosis and smokes 10 cigarettes per day. She is reviewed in the Emergency Department by the urologists for suspected renal colic, but investigation of her urinary tract is normal and she is referred to the physicians. You are asked to see her.

Introduction

A genitourinary cause for her symptoms has been excluded so the remaining differential diagnoses include:

- vertebral collapse due to osteoporosis;

- vertebral collapse due to other causes, eg malignancy;

- mechanical thoracic back pain and radiculopathy;

- gastrointestinal disease, eg pancreatitis;

- aortic aneurysm.

The most likely cause of a vertebral crush fracture in a woman of 65 years is osteoporosis, but trauma (not likely to be relevant in this case) and local vertebral pathology (especially secondary tumours or myeloma) should be considered. The most common sites for osteoporotic vertebral fractures are mid-dorsal and the thoracolumbar junction, giving potential for confusion with other causes of chest and flank pain.

Important considerations if the diagnosis is osteoporotic collapse are the cause (postmenopausal, corticosteroid-induced, myeloma, etc) and the severity, which is predictive of risk of further fractures.

> The risk of osteoporotic fracture is influenced heavily by the risk of falling. This risk should be assessed and treatable causes addressed (see *Medicine for the Elderly*, Sections 1.1.1 and 2.3).

History of the presenting problem

Osteoporotic fracture
The diagnosis of possible osteoporotic fracture will often have been made before referral to you, but the condition should be considered in spinal pain with the following characteristics:

- sudden onset;

- provoked by movement;

- ameliorated by rest;

- present especially in postmenopausal women and others at increased risk of osteoporosis;

- associated with nerve root irritation or entrapment, which may produce referred pain or paraesthesiae with dermatomal distribution.

Other causes of the fracture
Are there any clues to a malignant process? Think about the possibilities as you take the history. Check if she has had any of the following symptoms recently.

- Malaise or weight loss.

- Difficulty breathing or a productive cough: this might indicate respiratory pathology (lung cancer) or anaemia (gastrointestinal bleeding, bone marrow secondaries or myeloma) in this context.

- Indigestion or change in her bowels (gastrointestinal malignancy).

- Bone pain elsewhere (secondaries or myeloma).

Other relevant history

Osteoporosis
A history of femoral neck fracture, Colles' fracture or clinical/radiological evidence of a previous vertebral fracture (Fig. 39) are the best surrogate markers of the severity of bone loss and future fracture risk.

Causes of osteoporosis
Ask about the following.

- Menstrual history: at the age of 65 years she will certainly be postmenopausal, but what was her age at menopause and has she had a hysterectomy/oophorectomy or prolonged amenorrhoea at any time, eg anorexia nervosa?

- Steroid treatment: risk depends on the dose and duration of treatment.

- Frequency of exercise.

- Dietary history: in particular, does she have an adequate calcium intake?

- Family history.

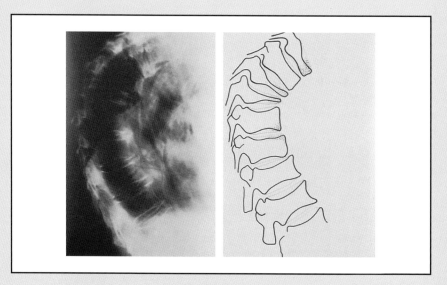

▲ **Fig. 39** Multiple osteoporotic fractures in the thoracic spine. (Courtesy of Dr M. Pattrick.)

Risk of falls

Ask about the following:

- previous falls;

- pre-existing neurological or locomotor disease;

- postural dizziness;

- alcohol use;

- use of psychotropic drugs.

Other causes of vertebral fracture

Has she got a history of malignancy or 'problems with the blood'?

Examination

General features

Does the patient look as though she might have malignancy? Your surgical colleagues may have examined the woman thoroughly, but also they may not, so take particular care to look for the following: weight loss/cachexia, pallor, lymphadenopathy, breast lump, and abnormal chest, abdominal or rectal signs.

Could the patient have a secondary cause for osteoporosis? Is there evidence of thyrotoxicosis, hypogonadism (in a man) or Cushing's disease?

Specific features

The level of the vertebral fracture may be marked by a palpable step. Look for diffuse dorsal kyphosis as a marker of long-standing severe bone loss.

Look for the following to assess the risk of falling.

- Visible unsteadiness/frailty.

- Postural drop in BP.

- Neurological signs: in particular, is there a sensory level, sphincter disturbance and/or weakness in the legs as pointers towards possible cord compression?

Investigations

These will obviously be dictated by the findings on history and examination.

Consideration of secondary causes

The need to pursue secondary causes of osteoporosis varies depending on the patient's age, other risk factors, ill-health and clinical suspicion. The following tests should be considered:

- FBC;

- renal and liver function;

- bone biochemistry (raised alkaline phosphatase may suggest osteomalacia or secondaries; hypercalcaemia may suggest malignancy, especially myeloma);

- immunoglobulins and serum and urine electrophoresis (to exclude myeloma in elderly people);

- thyroid function;

- testosterone (in men);

- CXR;

- investigations for Cushing's syndrome (see Endocrinology, Sections 2.1.1 and 3.2).

Diagnosis of osteoporosis

The gold standard for the diagnosis and planning of treatment is bone densitometry at two sites, usually the hip and lumbar spine. The presence of a fracture consistent with osteoporosis in the presence of risk factors is often enough to make the diagnosis. Histology is rarely useful and even more rarely obtained.

Management

Pain may be severe and require opiates. Consider supplementary approaches such as TENS (transcutaneous electrical nerve stimulation) and epidural analgesia. Calcitonin will improve acute pain. Avoid immobility, as this will increase the risk of bronchopneumonia and venous thromboembolism (consider prophylactic heparin).

Treat secondary causes of osteoporosis, if identified, although most symptomatic osteoporosis will be postmenopausal and managed by the following.

- Lifestyle modification: avoid falls, but encourage safe exercise.

- Optimisation of calcium intake.

- Bisphosphonates are now the standard treatment for osteoporosis. Hormone-replacement therapy is no longer routinely used because of the increased risk of malignancy. It is important to explain to the patient how bisphosphonates should be taken, eg if taking weekly risedronate, the patient must take it on an empty stomach and remain upright for a further 30 minutes before further eating or drinking.

2.1 Immunodeficiency

2.1.1 Primary antibody deficiency

Aetiology/pathophysiology/pathology

Common variable immunodeficiency (CVID) is an acquired antibody deficiency. It comprises a heterogeneous group of diseases in which B cells are present (Fig. 40) but which fail to produce IgG, IgA and sometimes IgM. Some variants are associated with sarcoid-like granulomas. Autoimmunity (organ specific and haematological) is common. There may be coexistent T-cell defects.

Evidence against an intrinsic B-cell defect in CVID

- B cells in CVID are capable of secreting immunoglobulins *in vitro* with appropriate stimulation.
- Infection with viruses (HIV, hepatitis C) can sometimes reverse hypogammaglobulinaemia in CVID.

Epidemiology

The incidence is estimated at 1 in 10,000 to 1 in 50,000. It may be sporadic or inherited in an autosomal dominant manner with variable phenotype; affected family members may have autoimmunity alone, IgA or IgG subclass deficiencies, or CVID. The great majority (95%) present in adulthood.

Clinical presentation

Common
Complications of antibody deficiency Complications include bacterial infections, especially of the respiratory and gastrointestinal tracts and of the skin (Fig. 41).

Autoimmunity Organ-specific (especially thyroid disease and pernicious anaemia).

- Haematological: anaemia, neutropenia and thrombocytopenia.
- Arthritis: reactive or septic; consider the possibility of *Mycoplasma* spp. if cultures are negative.

B cells in CVID exhibit a curious paradox

Despite their inability to mount antibody responses to exogenous antigens, patients with CVID do mount antibody responses to self-antigens, resulting in autoimmune disease.

Granulomas These include lung infiltrates and hepatosplenomegaly (Fig. 42).

Uncommon
- Coeliac-like enteropathy.
- Diseases associated with T-cell deficiencies such as herpes zoster.

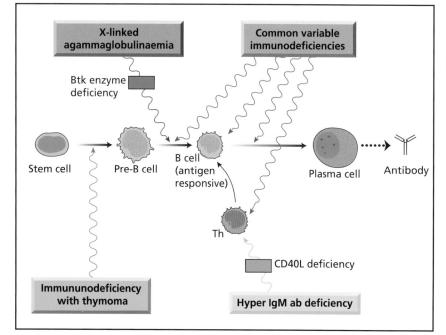

▲**Fig. 40** Overview of the steps in B-cell maturation and the levels at which more common defects in antibody production may occur. (Reproduced with permission from Chapel H, Haeney M, Misbah S and Snowden N. *Essentials of Clinical Immunology*, 4th edn. Oxford: Blackwell Science, 1999.)

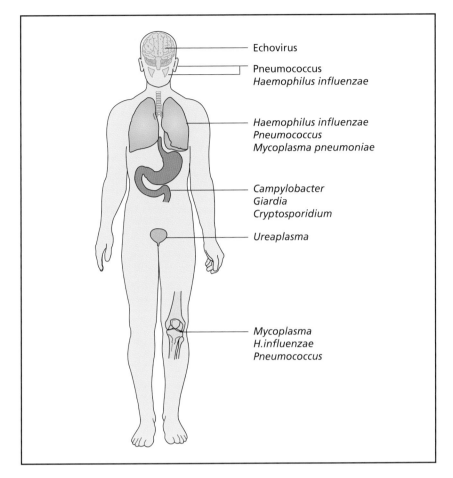

Echovirus

Pneumococcus
Haemophilus influenzae

Haemophilus influenzae
Pneumococcus
Mycoplasma pneumoniae

Campylobacter
Giardia
Cryptosporidium

Ureaplasma

Mycoplasma
H.influenzae
Pneumococcus

▲**Fig. 41** Infectious complications of CVID. (Courtesy of Dr A.D.B. Webster.)

Rare

- Nodular lymphoid hyperplasia.

- Thymoma.

Common physical signs

- Signs of bronchiectasis (see *Respiratory Medicine*, Section 2.4).

- Lymphadenopathy and hepatosplenomegaly.

- Arthritis.

- Thyroid enlargement.

Uncommon physical signs

- Wasting.

Investigation

- Serum IgG, IgA and IgM: IgG subclasses are of limited value. Assess the severity of antibody deficiency by measuring antibodies to past immunisations (tetanus and diphtheria) and common pathogens (*Streptococcus pneumoniae* and *Haemophilus influenzae* type b). If baseline antibody levels are low, proceed to test immunisation and measure antibody levels in 4 weeks.

- CD3, CD4, CD8, CD19 lymphocyte markers (to quantify total, helper and cytotoxic T-cell and B-cell numbers, respectively). Most patients with CVID have normal numbers of circulating B cells; a minority have no B cells and clinically resemble those with X-linked agammaglobulinaemia.

- Blood count and differential.

Differential diagnosis

- Secondary antibody deficiencies: the result of drugs (gold, penicillamine, cytotoxics and antiepileptics); associated with lymphoproliferative disease (particularly chronic lymphocytic leukaemia, myeloma or lymphoma); and post bone-marrow transplantation.

- Bruton's (X-linked) agammaglobulinaemia: peak age of presentation 4 months to 2 years of age. Presents with absent B cells, absent lymphoid tissue, and no granulomas or autoimmune disease.

- Combined immunodeficiencies: T-cell-associated infections are more prominent (see Section 2.1.2) and usually present in early childhood.

Hyper-IgM syndromes

These are characterised as follows.

- CD40 ligand deficiency is the best characterised.

- X-linked.

- Low IgG, high or normal IgM.

- T-cell numbers are normal but functionally defective with a high risk of long-term opportunistic infection, particularly *Pneumocystis* pneumonia or cryptosporidial sclerosing cholangitis.

- Bone-marrow transplantation should be considered.

- Other causes of hyper-IgM syndromes include uracil-*N*-glycosylase deficiency, CD40 deficiency (features and management as for CD40 ligand deficiency) and activation-induced cytidine deaminase deficiency (less severe, T-cell function normal and managed as for CVID).

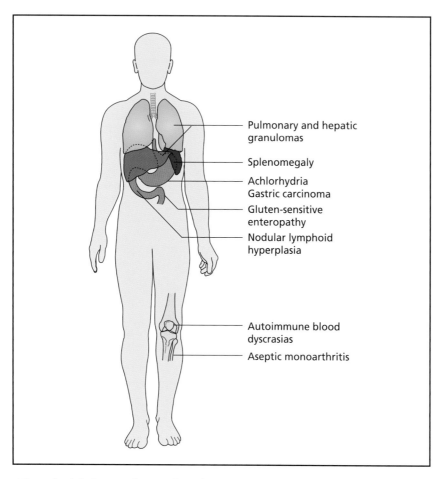

Pulmonary and hepatic granulomas

Splenomegaly

Achlorhydria
Gastric carcinoma

Gluten-sensitive enteropathy

Nodular lymphoid hyperplasia

Autoimmune blood dyscrasias

Aseptic monoarthritis

▲**Fig. 42** Non-infectious complications of CVID. (Courtesy of Dr A.D.B. Webster.)

X-linked lymphoproliferative disease (Duncan's syndrome)

This disease, a defect in SAP (signalling lymphocyte-activation molecule-associated protein), usually presents with overwhelming Epstein–Barr virus infection or lymphoma, but occasionally with a CVID-like picture. Bone-marrow transplantation may be considered.

Treatment

Emergency

Prompt treatment of all infections with a high-dose prolonged course of antibiotics (typically 2 weeks for bacterial chest infection).

Long term

Regular subcutaneous or intravenous immunoglobulin therapy at 1-week or 3-week intervals respectively (see Section 3.7). Aim to achieve trough serum IgG levels well within the normal range.

> **Trough serum IgG levels maintained at >5 g/L prevents deterioration in lung function.**

Complications

Common

- Bronchiectasis secondary to recurrent infection.

- Anaemia, thrombocytopenia and neutropenia (haematological autoimmunity, splenomegaly and vitamin deficiencies resulting from malabsorption).

Uncommon

- Increased risk of lymphoma (23–100 fold).

- Gastric carcinoma (50-fold increase).

> **Difficulties in the diagnosis of lymphoma in CVID**
>
> Lymph-node biopsies in patients with CVID may reveal a bizarre histology mimicking lymphoma. Biopsies should therefore be reported by a histopathologist experienced in examining tissue from patients with immune deficiency.

Rare

- Severe opportunistic infections caused by T-cell deficiency such as *Pneumocystis* pneumonia.

Prognosis

Morbidity

- Of those with CVID, 75% suffer frequent or chronic infections.

- 14% have structural damage, such as bronchiectasis.

Mortality

The mean age at death for all patients who have antibody deficiencies is 40.5 years, but the range is wide. The main causes of death are sepsis, chronic lung disease, lymphoma and other malignancies.

Prevention

The mean delay in diagnosis of 7.5 years accounts for a great deal of the morbidity and mortality. Serum immunoglobulins should be checked in anyone with unusually severe, prolonged or recurrent bacterial infections, or granulomatous disease.

FURTHER READING

Goldacker S and Warnatz K. Tackling the heterogeneity of common variable immunodeficiency. *Curr. Opin. Allergy Clin. Immunol.* 2005; 5: 504–9.

2.1.2 Combined T-cell and B-cell defects

Aetiology/pathophysiology/pathology

Inherited genetic defects result in the failure of normal development or maturation of T lymphocytes and B lymphocytes, or the build-up of metabolites toxic to developing lymphocytes (Table 25). Without T-cell help, the production of antibodies by B cells is severely limited.

Epidemiology

These defects are a heterogeneous group of conditions. They usually have autosomal recessive or sex-linked inheritance. In France the incidence of SCID is estimated to be 1 in 100,000 live births.

Clinical presentation

Common

- Presents in infancy.

- Recurrent infections, sometimes with unusual 'opportunistic' organisms (see rare presentations below for details), and a slow response to treatment.

- Pneumonia, skin infections, eczema and persistent diarrhoea.

- Failure to thrive.

- Features of associated syndromes.

> Persistent lymphopenia in an ill baby is an important clue pointing towards SCID.

Uncommon

- Graft-versus-host disease (GVHD) from immunocompetent maternal cells or transfused blood.

- Invasive disease from BCG given at birth.

Rare

- Adult presentation: usually has a milder phenotype.

- Papilloma viruses: warts, or cervical or anal intraepithelial neoplasia.

- Herpes viruses: herpes simplex 1 and 2, severe varicella-zoster and Epstein–Barr virus-associated disease.

- Lymphoproliferation and lymphomas.

- JC virus: associated with progressive encephalopathy.

- Bacterial infections, especially

Time of presentation	Disorder	Key features
Severe combined immunodeficiency (SCID) during infancy	Adenosine deaminase (ADA) deficiency[1]	Marked T- and B-cell lymphopenia, reduced serum immunoglobulin Autosomal recessive
	Common cytokine receptor γ-chain deficiency (γ-chain shared by IL-2, IL-4, IL-7, IL-9 and IL-15)	Marked T-cell lymphopenia, reduced serum immunoglobulin, normal or increased B-cell numbers X-linked
	Janus kinase 3 deficiency	As for cytokine receptor γ-chain deficiency Autosomal recessive
	Recombinase-activating gene1/2 deficiency	Marked T- and B-cell lymphopenia, reduced serum immunoglobulin
	Omenn syndrome	Increased serum IgE, eosinophilia, reduced serum immunoglobulin, B-cell numbers normal or reduced
	IL-2 receptor α-chain deficiency	T-cell lymphopenia, serum immunoglobulin and B-cell numbers normal
	Purine nucleoside phosphorylase deficiency	T-cell lymphopenia, reduced serum urate, serum immunoglobulin normal or reduced
Presenting in later life, including adulthood	X-linked hyper-IgM (CD40 ligand deficiency)	Reduced serum IgG and IgA, increased or normal IgM

TABLE 25 COMBINED IMMUNODEFICIENCY DISORDERS

1. Milder forms of SCID may present in adulthood, eg ADA deficiency.
IL, interleukin.

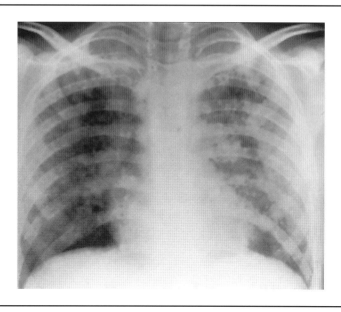

▲**Fig. 43** CXR showing bilateral lung shadowing caused by *Pneumocystis carinii* pneumonia.

respiratory tract and intracellular bacteria such as *Salmonella* spp.

- Mycobacterial disease, including tuberculosis.

- Fungal infections: mucocutaneous *Candida* infection, *Pneumocystis* pneumonia (Fig. 43) and invasive cryptococci.

- Protozoal disease: cryptosporidial diarrhoea and cholangitis, and *Toxoplasma* cerebral abscess.

Physical signs
Common signs are:

- poor growth and structural organ damage from repeated infections;

- active infections often present.

Investigations
Babies with clinical features suggestive of SCID and lymphopenia (lymphocytes $<1.5 \times 10^9$ in a newborn) should be referred urgently to a regional centre (see Section 3.3).

Differential diagnosis
Secondary immunodeficiency, such as HIV or lymphoid malignancy.

Treatment

Short term

- Avoid live vaccines.

- Irradiate blood products.

- Active diagnosis and early aggressive treatment of infections.

⚠️ To avoid GVHD, blood products should be irradiated before transfusion in patients with suspected cellular immune defects.

Long term
Prophylaxis of infection
Intravenous immunoglobulin and an antibiotic (co-trimoxazole), which provides cover against *Pneumocystis* and bacterial infections.

Correction of defect In some cases enzyme replacement (eg in ADA deficiency) may be possible, but success is limited. Alternatively:

- consider bone-marrow transplantation if a human leucocyte antigen match is

available, although success rates are low in adults;

- gene therapy has had some success in a handful of children with single-gene disorders where no matched bone-marrow donor exists.

Complications
Structural damage from recurrent infections:

- malignancy, especially lymphoma;

- vasculitis resulting from immune dysregulation.

Prognosis

Morbidity
Morbidity is severe due to recurrent infections.

Mortality
Most affected individuals die in infancy or early childhood. For those surviving until adulthood, prognosis is poor if prior bone-marrow transplantation has not been carried out. Death occurs from uncontrolled infection or malignancy.

Prevention
Prenatal diagnosis is often possible. Early bone-marrow transplantation in selected affected infants may be curative.

Disease associations
Combined immunodeficiencies often occur in association with other congenital diseases, particularly cardiac, haematological, neurological (including learning difficulties) or skeletal (including dysmorphic facies).

FURTHER READING

Buckley RH and Fischer A. Bone marrow transplantation for primary immunodeficiency diseases. In: Ochs HD, Smith CIE and Puck JM, eds.

Primary Immunodeficiency Diseases: A Molecular and Cellular Approach, 2nd edn. Oxford: Oxford University Press, 2006: 669–87.

Candotti F and Blaese RM. Gene therapy. In: Ochs HD, Smith CIE and Puck JM, eds. *Primary Immunodeficiency Diseases: A Molecular and Cellular Approach*, 2nd edn. Oxford: Oxford University Press, 2006: 688–705.

Cavazzana-Calvo M, Hacein-Bey S, de Saint Basile G, *et al*. Gene therapy of human severe combined immunodeficiency (SCID)-X1 disease. *Science* 2000; 288: 627–9.

2.1.3 Chronic granulomatous disease

Aetiology/pathophysiology/pathology

Chronic granulomatous disease (CGD) is due to an inherited defect of one of four *phox* genes, which encode subunits of nicotinamide adenine dinucleotide phosphate (NADPH) oxidase, the enzyme that catalyses the phagocyte respiratory burst (Fig. 44), resulting in the defective killing of engulfed organisms.

Epidemiology

- Rare: incidence is 1 in 250,000.

- 67% of cases present in infancy, but diagnosis is occasionally delayed until early adulthood.

- 65% are X-linked and 35% have autosomal recessive inheritance.

Clinical presentation

Common

Infections Pneumonia, lymphadenitis, skin infections, hepatic abscesses, osteomyelitis, perianal suppuration and enteric infections. Organisms are usually catalase positive (Table 26).

Granulomas As chemotaxis and phagocytosis are unimpaired, ineffective killing by phagocytes results in the formation of granulomas; these manifest as lymphadenopathy, hepatosplenomegaly, Crohn's disease-like enteropathy with diarrhoea, dermatitis or obstructive hydronephrosis.

Miscellaneous Anaemia of chronic disease, gingivitis and asymptomatic chorioretinopathy.

Investigations

Screen with nitroblue tetrazolium test (NBT, see Fig. 5) or dihydrorhodamine fluorescence test (see Section 1.1.4). If the screening test is abnormal, check for the presence of NADPH oxidase subunits and associated gene defects.

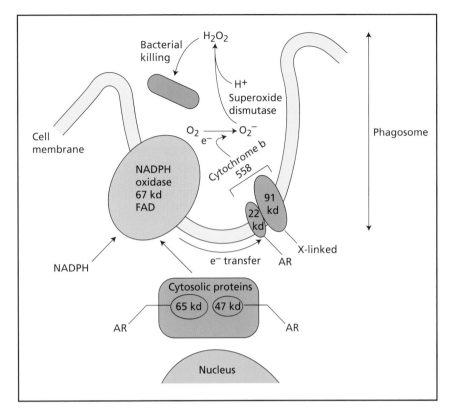

▲ **Fig. 44** Diagrammatic representation of components of the NADPH oxidase system within a phagosome, depicting bacterial killing and the site of abnormalities in CGD. AR, autosomal recessive; FAD, flavin adenine dinucleotide. (Modified with permission from Gallin JI and Malech HL. Update on chronic granulomatous diseases of childhood: immunotherapy and potential for gene therapy. *JAMA* 1990; 263: 1533–7.)

TABLE 26 COMMON PATHOGENS IN CGD

Bacteria	Fungi
Staphylococcus spp.	*Aspergillus* spp.
Escherichia coli	*Candida* spp.
Salmonella spp.	
Klebsiella spp.	
Serratia spp.	
Burkholderia spp.	

The NBT screening test may be misleadingly normal in some patients with CGD. Proceed to flow cytometric evaluation of the respiratory burst and genetic studies in case of diagnostic doubt.

Differential diagnosis

- Idiopathic abscesses without obvious immunodeficiency.

- Crohn's disease.

- Neutrophil glucose-6-dehydrogenase, myeloperoxidase or glutathione peroxidase deficiency.

Other neutrophil defects

Common

- Neutropenia: usually secondary to medication or disease. Treat/withdraw the causative agent. Consider granulocyte colony-stimulating factor (G-CSF).

Rare

- Cyclical neutropenia: 3-weekly cycle of neutropenia, associated with infection. Neutrophil count may be normal or high by the time the patient presents. Check neutrophil count three times weekly for 1 month. Treat with antibiotic prophylaxis (co-trimoxazole) or, exceptionally, G-CSF to cover the predicted times of neutropenia.
- Leucocyte adhesion molecule deficiencies (CD18/CD11 and CD15): marked neutrophilia (even during infection-free intervals) caused by defective leucocyte–endothelial interaction, impaired pus formation and poor wound healing. Severe phenotypes present in childhood and require bone-marrow transplantation.

Treatment

Emergency

This requires early empirical treatment of the suspected infection with broad-spectrum antimicrobials.

Short term

- Aggressive search for source and organism; cultures of blood and a sample from the possible site(s) of infection. Drain large abscesses.

Take biopsies; excision biopsy of inflammatory masses and lymph nodes is preferable because of the risk of fistula formation.

- Initiate early empirical parenteral antibiotic treatment. Consider adjunctive interferon (IFN)-γ. Prolonged treatment is usually required.

- Granulomas may be troublesome. Steroids (prednisolone 0.5 mg/kg, reducing after a few weeks) can help, but take care that any infections are controlled with antibiotics.

Long term

- Antimicrobial prophylaxis with co-trimoxazole and itraconazole.

- Consider IFN-γ 0.05 mg/kg three times weekly, which reduces infections despite the persistence of defective respiratory burst.

- Bone-marrow transplantation is curative, but the risks outweigh the benefits for most patients.

- Gene therapy offers a promising future treatment.

Complications

- Chronic suppurative perianal disease.

- Anaemia of chronic disease.

- Structural damage caused by abscesses or granulomas.

Prognosis

Morbidity

Morbidity from infections and granulomas is significant.

Mortality

Of patients with CGD, 30–50% survive to adulthood. Their prognosis is likely to improve significantly with better prophylaxis and treatment.

Prevention

Primary

Prenatal diagnosis is possible.

Secondary

- Avoidance of fungal spores (composts, rotting hay, humidifiers and marijuana).

- No smoking.

- Immediate cleaning of all abrasions and rinsing with 2% hydrogen peroxide.

- Meticulous perianal hygiene and avoidance of constipation.

- Careful dental cleaning, flossing and use of mouthwash.

Disease associations

McLeod's syndrome

This is a mild haemolytic anaemia caused by poor expression of erythrocyte Kell antigens. Patients with McLeod's syndrome require Kell-negative products if transfusion is required.

FURTHER READING

Ott MG, Schmidt M, Schwarzwaelder K, *et al*. Correction of X-linked chronic granulomatous disease by gene therapy augmented by insertional activation of MDS-1, EVT1, PRDM 16 or SETBP-1. *Nat. Med*. 2006; 12: 401–9.

Rosenzweig SD and Holland SM. Phagocyte immunodeficiencies and their infections. *J. Allergy Clin. Immunol*. 2004; 113: 620–6.

2.1.4 Cytokine and cytokine-receptor deficienicies

Aetiology/pathophysiology/pathology

Mutations in the genes for interleukin (IL)-12, IL-12 receptor,

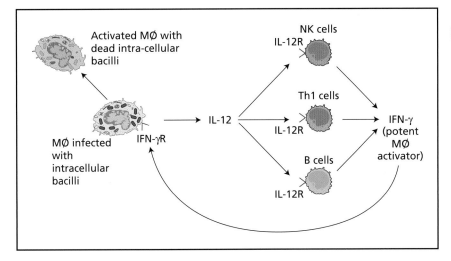

▲ **Fig. 45** Role of the IL-12/IFN-γ pathway in protective immunity. IL12R, interleukin-12 receptor; IFNγ, interferon-γ; MØ, macrophage; IFNγR, interferon-γ receptor; NK, natural killer; Th1, T helper 1.

> ⚠ Atypical mycobacteria are resistant to some conventional antituberculous drugs, such as isoniazid, rifabutin, ethambutol, azithromycin and ciprofloxacin. Some second-line antituberculous drugs may be useful despite apparent resistance *in vitro*. Expert advice is required.

IL-12 signalling pathway and the interferon (IFN)-γ receptor (Fig. 45) are associated with defective macrophage and T-helper (Th)1 cell function, leading to failure to eradicate mycobacteria. Functional defects of the IL-12/IFN-γ pathways can present in adulthood. These may be idiopathic or caused by IFN-γ antibodies.

Other cytokine and cytokine receptor deficiencies

Mutations in the common γ chain of IL-2, IL-4, IL-7, IL-9 and IL-15 receptors and IL-2 or IL-7 deficiency result in severe combined immunodeficiency.

Epidemiology
These are rare inherited autosomal dominant or recessive disorders, although instances of disease presenting in middle age may be acquired.

Clinical presentation

Common
Disseminated disease as a result of environmental mycobacteria of low virulence, or after BCG immunisation.

Uncommon
Recurrent *Salmonella* infection.

Physical signs
The signs are similar to those for mycobacterial disease in immunocompetent individuals.

Investigation
IFN-γ production by activated lymphocytes is reduced in IL-12, IL-12 receptor and IFN-γ receptor deficiencies. Routine immunological investigations are normal or non-specific, but clinical features will suggest the need for further investigation.

Differential diagnosis
Consider other primary or secondary T-cell defects, particularly late-stage HIV infection.

Treatment
- Antibiotic treatment of mycobacterial disease: prolonged treatment with multiple agents is likely to be required.

- IFN-γ.

Complications
Complications are those of uncontrolled mycobacterial disease.

Prognosis

Morbidity
There is considerable morbidity from mycobacterial disease and its treatment.

Mortality
- Very high.

- Long-term control of disease is possible in variants that respond to IFN-γ.

Prevention
Avoid BCG in close family members until the defect has been excluded.

Disease associations
- Some individuals have increased susceptibility to *Salmonella* spp.

- Occasional association with CD4 lymphopenia.

FURTHER READING

Casanova JL and Abel L. Genetic dissection of immunity to mycobacteria: the human model. *Annu. Rev. Immunol.* 2002; 20: 581–620.

Döffinger R, Helbert MR, Barcenas-Morales G, *et al*. Autoantibodies to interferon-gamma in a patient with selective susceptibility to mycobacterial infection and organ-specific autoimmunity. *Clin. Infect. Dis.* 2004; 38: E10–E14.

2.1.5 Terminal pathway complement deficiency

Aetiology/pathophysiology/ pathology

- Inherited deletion of the terminal complement (C5–C9) gene.

- Lack of complement-mediated lysis results in inefficient clearance of neisserial infections.

Epidemiology

Autosomal recessive inheritance.

Clinical presentation

Common

- Recurrent invasive meningococcal disease.

- Asymptomatic relative.

Primary complement deficiency with meningococcal infection

The following are pointers towards primary complement deficiency in patients with meningococcal infection:

- unusual meningococcal serotype;
- recurrent disease;
- family history of meningococcal disease.

Uncommon

- Disseminated gonococcal disease.

Physical signs

There are usually no physical signs specifically associated with complement deficiency.

Investigations

Assess integrity of the complement pathway by checking haemolytic complement activity (classical pathway CH50 and alternative pathway AP50). The absence or marked reduction of both CH50 and AP50 suggests deficiency of terminal complement proteins C5–C9 (see Fig. 46 and Table 1).

- Complement proteins are labile.
- Samples for haemolytic complement activity should therefore be sent to the laboratory immediately.

Differential diagnosis

- Consider external connection to subarachnoid space: head injury, erosive sinus disease and after pituitary surgery.

- Properdin or factor D deficiency (AP50 will be absent, CH50 will be normal).

- Other immunodeficiency.

Treatment

Emergency

This involves the prompt treatment of neisserial infection (see *Infectious Diseases*, Sections 1.3.2, 1.3.11 and 2.5.2).

Short term

Chemoprophylaxis of household contacts (see *Infectious Diseases*, Sections 1.3.11 and 2.1).

Long term

- Prophylactic antibiotics.

- Meningococcal immunisation.

- Annual influenza immunisation.

Complications

The complications are those of neisserial disease (see *Infectious Diseases*, Sections 1.3.2, 1.3.11 and 2.5.2).

Prognosis

Meningococcal disease may not be as severe in the presence of complement deficiency. However, there is a significant risk of permanent disability or death.

Meningococcal disease tends to be less severe in complement-deficient patients, presumably reflecting the requirement for an intact complement pathway to cause bacterial endotoxin release.

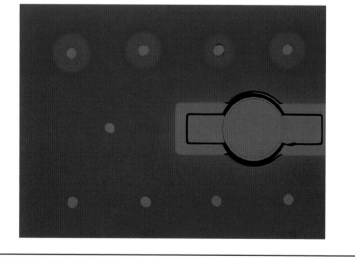

▲ **Fig. 46** Haemolytic complement screening test for complement deficiency. This test measures the ability of complement in the patient's serum to lyse antibody-coated erythrocytes via the classical pathway. The coated erythrocytes are embedded in a gel. Control and test sera are placed in wells and left overnight. Normal sera containing complement components C1–C9 lyse the erythrocytes, seen as a ring around the well (top row). Sera that are completely deficient in one or more complement components do not cause lysis (middle and bottom rows).

Prevention

Primary

Primary prevention is by genetic counselling and screening of relatives at risk.

> **Other complement deficiencies**
>
> - C1q, C2 or C4 deficiency: C1q deficiency is strongly associated with systemic lupus erythematosus, followed in turn by homozygous C4 and C2 deficiency. Individuals with such deficiencies may be antinuclear antibody negative, but are more likely to be Ro positive.
> - Mannan-binding ligand deficiency results in a predisposition to bacterial infections. However, this is usually evident only if another immunodeficiency is present.
> - C3 deficiency causes glomerulonephritis and a predisposition to bacterial infections.

> **FURTHER READING**
>
> Mathew S and Overurf GD. Complement and properdin deficiencies in meningococcal disease. *Pediatr. Infect. Dis. J.* 2006; 25: 255–6.

2.1.6 Hyposplenism

Aetiology/pathophysiology/pathology

The spleen is the major lymphoid organ for blood-borne antigens. Splenic macrophages remove bacteria, immune complexes and abnormal erythrocytes from the circulation.

> **Immunological consequences of asplenia**
>
> - Removal of a large reservoir of polysaccharide-responsive B cells.

> - Impaired clearance of encapsulated bacteria and intracellular protozoans (*Plasmodium* and *Babesia* spp.).
> - Necessity for higher antibody levels for macrophages to clear encapsulated bacteria.

Clinical presentation

Common

- Asymptomatic: known because of underlying condition.
- Fulminant septicaemia.

Uncommon

- Howell–Jolly bodies noted on blood film.

Rare

- Congenital asplenia, with cardiac abnormalities and biliary atresia.

Physical signs

There are usually no physical signs except for a splenectomy scar.

Investigations

- If blood film shows Howell–Jolly bodies (see Fig. 35), this suggests functional hyposplenism. However, the absence of Howell–Jolly bodies does not reliably exclude hyposplenism. Proceed to functional studies of splenic function (pitted red-cell count and radioisotope uptake) in cases of diagnostic uncertainty.
- Ultrasonography to confirm anatomical absence.
- Pneumococcal, *Haemophilus influenzae* type b and meningococcal antibodies: higher antibody levels are required for protection in asplenic individuals.

Treatment

Emergency

Urgent investigation and immediate empirical treatment of any febrile illness.

Long term

- Pneumococcal, *Haemophilus* and meningococcal immunisation (see Section 1.4.1 for recommendations on immunisation).
- Annual influenza vaccination.
- Lifelong penicillin prophylaxis.

Complications

Common

Fulminant septicaemia, especially with encapsulated organisms (pneumococci, *Haemophilus influenzae* type b and meningococci).

Uncommon

- Severe malaria.

Rare

- Babesiosis.
- Infection with *Capnocytophaga canimorsus* (from dog bite).

Prognosis

There is a significant lifelong risk of death from overwhelming infection.

Disease associations

- Haemoglobinopathies.
- Coeliac disease.
- Inflammatory bowel disease.
- Bone marrow transplantation.

> **FURTHER READING**
>
> Newland A, Provan D and Myint S. Preventing severe infection after splenectomy. *BMJ* 2005; 331: 417–18.

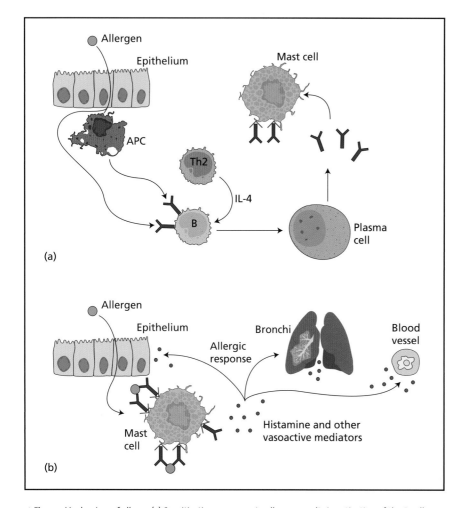

(a)

(b)

▲ **Fig. 47** Mechanism of allergy. (**a**) Sensitisation: exposure to allergen results in activation of the B cell, which becomes an IgE-secreting plasma cell. Secreted IgE binds to IgE receptors on mast cells. (**b**) Re-exposure to the same allergen results in cross-linking of preformed allergen-specific IgE on the mast cell surface. This causes the mast cell to degranulate. The release of histamine and other vasoactive substances from the granules causes the clinical manifestations of allergy or, if severe, anaphylaxis. APC, antigen-presenting cell; IL, interleukin; Th2, T-helper cell type 2.

2.2 Allergy

2.2.1 Anaphylaxis

Aetiology/pathophysiology/pathology

The mechanisms of allergy (Fig. 47) involve sensitisation (exposure to allergen and specific IgE production) followed by mast cell degranulation (re-exposure to allergen binds preformed IgE on mast cell surface, inducing the release of histamines and other vasoactive mediators).

Epidemiology

There are very few data on the overall incidence of anaphylaxis, which is currently estimated at 1 in 10,000 of the population annually. Common allergens include foods, drugs, insect venoms or latex.

Clinical presentation

Definition of anaphylaxis

One or more of these symptoms:

- laryngeal oedema;
- bronchoconstriction;
- hypotension.

Anaphylaxis is caused by IgE-mediated mast cell degranulation. Abdominal cramps with severe vomiting and diarrhoea may occur. Anaphylactoid reactions are caused by non-IgE-mediated mast cell degranulation but are otherwise identical.

Common

- Facial, tongue or throat swelling.
- Wheeze.
- Syncope.
- Feeling of impending doom.

Uncommon

- Abdominal cramps.
- Diarrhoea and vomiting.

Physical signs

Common

- Urticaria, angio-oedema, skin erythema or extreme pallor.
- Stridor or wheeze.
- Hypotension.

Investigations

- Mast cell tryptase (within 6 hours) as a marker of mast cell degranulation in cases of diagnostic uncertainty.
- Skin-prick testing of suspect allergens, with positive and negative controls (Figs 48 and 49).
- IgE: total and specific to suspect allergens (radioallergosorbent test).

Tryptase

Tryptase levels are a marker of mast cell degranulation.

- Elevated serum β-tryptase levels are useful in differentiating anaphylactic/anaphylactoid reactions from other disorders with similar clinical manifestations.

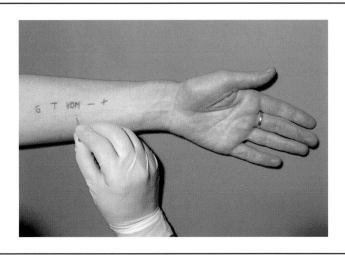

▲ **Fig. 48** Skin-prick testing: a drop of a standardised extract of the suspect allergen is placed on the skin. The superficial layer of the skin is lifted with a needle tip (or pricked with a lancet) through the drop. Positive (histamine) and negative (diluent) controls are included.

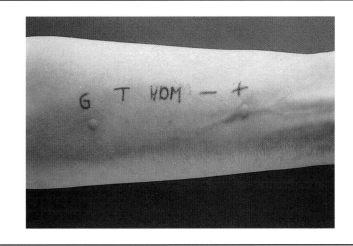

▲ **Fig. 49** Skin-prick test reactions are read at 15 minutes. The mean diameter of the weal (not the flare) is recorded. Reactions more than 3 mm greater than the negative control are significant.

> • Since β-tryptase is stable, stored serum or serum obtained *post mortem* should be assayed if anaphylaxis is suspected.

Differential diagnosis

- Panic attack.
- Asthma.
- Syncope.
- C1 inhibitor deficiency.
- Mastocytosis.
- Ruptured hydatid cyst (rare).

Treatment

See Fig. 50.

Emergency

- Oxygen.
- Intramuscular epinephrine.
- Intravenous crystalloid.

> Epinephrine is the drug of choice because it immediately counteracts the vasodilatation and bronchoconstriction of anaphylaxis.

> ⚠ Anaphylaxis in individuals on pre-existing beta-blockers may prove to be refractory to epinephrine. Consider the use of cardiac inotropes in such cases.

Short term

- Antihistamines.
- Corticosteroids.

Long term

- Identification and avoidance of allergen.
- Desensitisation: bee or wasp venoms and, in rare cases, drugs.
- Patients should have a Medic-Alert bracelet and carry epinephrine in an easily injectable form (eg Epi-Pen or Ana-Kit) (see Fig. 37).

Prognosis

Significant numbers of deaths occur. Previously healthy young adults are often the victims.

Disease associations

- Atopy (predisposition to asthma, eczema or hay fever).

Occupational aspects

- Beekeepers (due to bee stings).
- Medical personnel (due to latex).

FURTHER READING

Lieberman P. Anaphylaxis. *Med. Clin. North Am.* 2006; 90: 77–95.

Lieberman P *et al.* On behalf of the Joint Task Force on Practice Parameters. The diagnosis and management of anaphylaxis: an updated practice parameter. *J. Allergy Clin. Immunol.* 2005; 115: S483–S523.

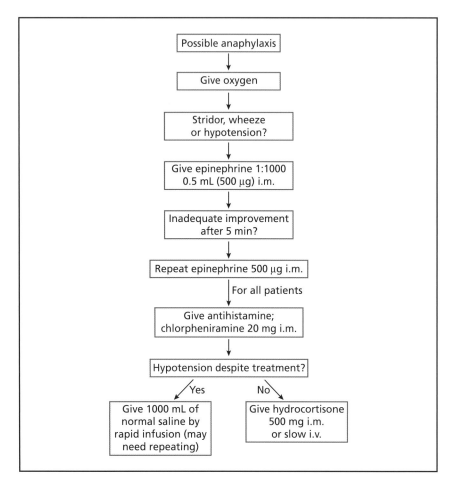

▲**Fig. 50** Algorithm for the treatment of anaphylaxis. (Adapted with permission from Consensus Guidelines of the Project Team of the Resuscitation Council, UK.)

pigmentosa (see Section 1.8) and dermographism. SM presents with episodic flushing, diarrhoea and palpitations caused by the release of mast cell mediators. Organ infiltration may result in hepatosplenomegaly, lymphadenopathy and bone pain.

Physical signs

- Mainly confined to urticaria and the pigmented plaques of urticaria pigmentosa.

- Dermographism and Darier's sign may be present.

Investigation

The key investigations are to demonstrate mast cell proliferation on skin and bone marrow trephine biopsies (Figs 51 and 52), coupled with biochemical evidence of elevated mast cell mediators (plasma tryptase and urinary methylhistamine).

Establish the presence of mast cells in SM: immunophenotyping using monoclonal antibodies to CD117 and mast cell tryptase is useful in distinguishing atypical mast cells from basophils.

Differential diagnosis

See Table 4.

Treatment

The principles of management of SM are based on the following.

- Inhibition of mast cell mediator release using combined histamine H_1 and H_2 receptor blockade to alleviate cutaneous symptoms and reduce gastric acid production respectively. This approach will suffice for patients with mild symptoms.

2.2.2 Mastocytosis

Aetiology/pathophysiology/pathology

Mastocytosis encompasses a spectrum of disorders characterised by mast cell proliferation. This may be confined to the skin, as in cutaneous mastocytosis, or affect other organs (eg bone marrow, gut and bones) as in systemic mastocytosis (SM).

The recent demonstration of mutations (Asp816→Val) in the gene encoding the mast cell c-kit tyrosine kinase receptor (CD117) in the majority of patients with SM lends support to the view that SM is a clonal haematopoietic neoplasm. The Asp816→Val mutation results in ligand-independent activation of the c-kit receptor, resulting in uncontrolled mast cell proliferation. In contrast, cutaneous mastocytosis is not associated with the c-kit mutation.

Epidemiology

The precise prevalence is unknown. The estimated frequency of cutaneous mastocytosis is said to be 1 in 1,000 to 1 in 8,000 of dermatology outpatient visits.

Clinical presentation

Presentation depends on which organs are affected. Cutaneous mastocytosis is characterised by urticaria, the fixed reddish-brown maculopapules of urticaria

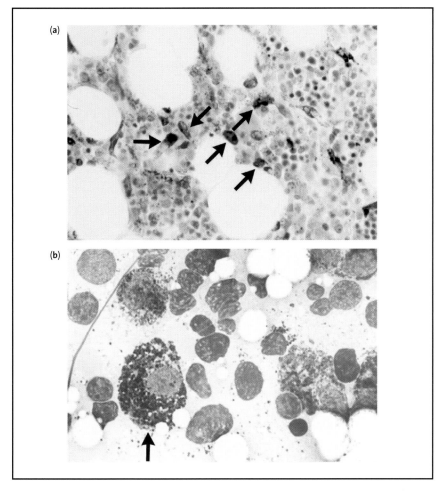

▲ **Fig. 51** Bone marrow biopsy specimen with staining for acid-fast bacilli. (**a**) Mast cells (arrows) on a bone-marrow aspirate (×400). (**b**) Typical normal-appearing mast cell (arrow) (×1000). (Reproduced with permission from Sawalha *et al. N. Engl. J. Med.* 2003; 349: 2255–6, copyright © 2003 Massachusetts Medical Society.)

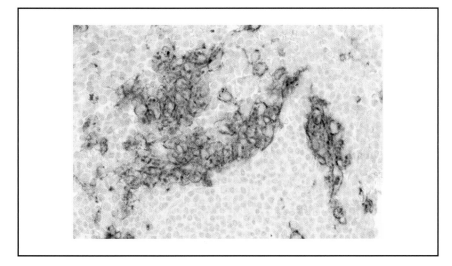

▲ **Fig. 52** Bone marrow biopsy specimen with immunohistochemical staining for CD117 (to detect c-kit) showing numerous mast cells. (Reproduced with permission from Sawalha *et al. N. Engl. J. Med.* 2003; 349: 2255–6, copyright © 2003 Massachusetts Medical Society.)

- Use of cytoreductive therapy such as interferon alfa in patients with aggressive disease associated with organ infiltration.

Imatinib, a tyrosine kinase inhibitor that inhibits c-kit, shows promise in the minority of patients with SM who do not have the Asp816→Val mutation.

Prognosis

In general, SM progresses very slowly. For the small minority of sufferers who develop an associated myeloproliferative or lymphoproliferative disorder, the prognosis depends on the haematological disorder.

FURTHER READING

Valent P, Akin C, Sperr WR, *et al.* Diagnosis and treatment of systemic mastocytosis: state of the art. *Br. J. Haematol.* 2003; 122: 695–717.

2.2.3 Nut allergy

Aetiology/pathophysiology/pathology

Nut allergy is due to IgE-mediated mast cell degranulation precipitated by contact with peanuts (strictly speaking these are pulses not nuts) or tree nuts (brazil, almond, walnut or hazelnut) (see Fig. 47). T-cell clones from patients with nut allergy overproduce interleukin-4 while underproducing interferon-γ, consistent with a T-helper 2-like cytokine profile.

Epidemiology

Nut allergy is more common in atopic individuals. It follows sensitisation to nuts, usually in early childhood.

Clinical presentation

Common

- Lip tingling, swelling, angio-oedema and urticaria.

- Anaphylaxis, with laryngeal oedema or bronchoconstriction.

Rare

- Anaphylaxis with hypotension.

Investigations

- Detailed dietary history.

- Skin-prick testing or specific serum IgE measurements.

- Oral challenge if diagnosis remains uncertain.

⚠ Skin-prick and challenge testing should take place where there are facilities for resuscitation, ideally in an allergy clinic.

Differential diagnosis

- Allergy to other foods.

- C1 inhibitor deficiency.

Treatment

Emergency

If anaphylaxis occurs, the emergency treatment is as follows:

- intramuscular epinephrine (see Section 2.2.1);

- antihistamines;

- corticosteroids.

Long term

Avoidance of allergen is the cornerstone of treatment since allergen immunotherapy is not an option at present. Sublingual immunotherapy with hazelnut extract has shown promise in patients with hazelnut allergy,

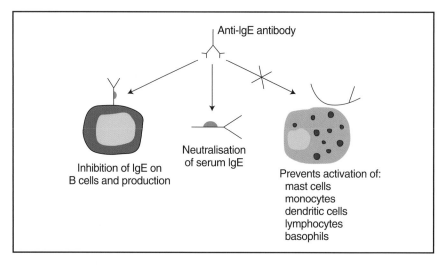

▲ **Fig. 53** Mechanism of action of anti-IgE antibodies as a treatment for allergic disease. The anti-IgE antibody binds to the section of the IgE molecule that associates with the high-affinity Fcε receptor. (Reproduced with permission from the BMJ Publishing Group; from Holgate ST. Science, medicine, and the future: allergic disorders. *BMJ* 2000; 320: 231–4.)

but requires validation in larger randomised trials. Humanised monoclonal anti-IgE (omalizumab, Fig. 53) is beneficial in patients with severe peanut allergy but the need for regular injections and its prohibitive cost make it unlikely that this treatment will be widely used at present.

Prognosis

This is unknown, but there are several deaths from nut allergy each year in the UK.

Prevention

Primary

Avoidance of contact with nuts in infancy and childhood, especially if there is a family history of atopy. Peanut products may be hidden in processed foods or creams and ointments (such as arachis oil).

Secondary

- Constant avoidance: detailed dietary advice is required. Most patients do not 'outgrow' peanut allergy, underlining the need for indefinite vigilance.

- Self-injectable epinephrine (see Fig. 37).

Disease associations

- Asthma.

- Hay fever.

- Eczema.

🔑 Patients with a food allergy and poorly controlled asthma are at particular risk of anaphylaxis.

Further allergies

Other allergies may include the following:

- tree nuts (common even if main allergy is to peanuts);

- other foods (eg eggs, milk and fresh fruit);

- common airborne allergens (pollen, house-dust mite, animal dander and moulds);

- pulses (peas, lentils and beans).

FURTHER READING

Teuber SS and Beyer K. Peanut, tree nut and seed allergies. *Curr. Opin. Allergy Clin. Immunol.* 2004; 4: 201–3.

TABLE 27 IMMUNOLOGICAL CLASSIFICATION OF DRUG HYPERSENSITIVITY

Type	Mechanism	Clinical picture	Examples
I	Immediate hypersensitivity	Anaphylaxis Urticaria and angio-oedema Bronchospasm	Penicillins
II	Cytotoxic antibodies	Haematological cytopenias	Penicillins Heparin
III	Immune complex	Drug-induced lupus Vasculitis Serum sickness	Minocycline Carbimazole
IV	T-cell mediated	Contact dermatitis Interstitial nephritis	Topical antibiotics NSAIDs Halothane Hepatitis

Susceptibility to drug reactions is poorly understood, but genetic factors have been identified for some drug-induced syndromes, eg genetically determined slow acetylation of the triggering drug is associated with drug-induced lupus and with co-trimoxazole sensitivity in HIV. Some immunological diseases are also associated with an increased risk of adverse drug reactions, particularly HIV infection and systemic lupus erythematosus (SLE).

Clinical presentation

Drug hypersensitivity can affect any system of the body and mimic many other forms of disease (Table 28). Cutaneous drug reactions are discussed in *Dermatology*, Section 2.7.

Investigations

The diagnosis of drug allergy is based largely on the history and the recognition of typical patterns of drug reaction, eg acute interstitial nephritis and toxic erythema of the skin are highly suggestive of drug reactions.

When there is a mild reaction to a therapeutically important drug, drug challenge is sometimes justified, but this must always be used cautiously. Skin tests (a local form of challenge testing) can be useful in immediate hypersensitivity (anaphylaxis) and contact dermatitis induced by topical medication.

2.2.4 Drug allergy

Aetiology/pathophysiology/pathology

Immunological reactions to drugs can be classified according to the four subtypes of hypersensitivity (Table 27 and see *Scientific Background to Medicine 1*, Immunology and Immunosuppression). However, the immunological mechanisms underlying many drug reactions, particularly those affecting the skin, remain unclear. In practice, the line between immunological and non-immunological reactions to drugs is often blurred. Non-immunological adverse reactions to drugs are discussed in *Clinical Pharmacology*, Adverse Drug Reactions.

Epidemiology

Incidence figures vary enormously from drug to drug. Crude estimates suggest that between 1 and 10% of prescriptions are complicated by some form of allergic adverse reaction.

TABLE 28 DRUG REACTIONS THAT MIMIC OTHER SYNDROMES

Syndrome	Examples of triggering drugs
Systemic lupus	Minocycline Hydralazine
Myasthenia gravis	D-Penicillamine
Pemphigus	D-Penicillamine
Pulmonary fibrosis	Amiodarone Nitrofurantoin Some cytotoxics
Pulmonary eosinophilia	NSAIDs Antibiotics
Vasculitis	Antibiotics Thiazides Carbimazole
Immune haemolytic anaemia	Methyldopa Penicillin
Neutropenia	Carbimazole
Thrombocytopenia	Gold salts Diuretics Heparin

Detection of drug-specific IgE has been described in some types of drug-induced anaphylaxis, particularly to the penicillins, but is unreliable. No other clinically useful blood tests for drug allergy have been described.

Allergic to penicillin

A negative skin test to both the major and minor determinants of penicillin suggests that a patient is unlikely to develop anaphylaxis on exposure.

Differential diagnosis
Beware of drug reactions that mimic idiopathic systemic diseases, eg SLE (see Table 28).

Treatment

- Supportive care depending on organ system involved.

- Treatment of immediate hypersensitivity: antihistamine and epinephrine.

- Other forms of hypersensitivity: consider corticosteroids.

- The overwhelming majority of reactions will resolve on drug withdrawal.

FURTHER READING

Greenberger PA. Drug allergy. *J. Allergy Clin. Immunol.* 2006; 117: S464–S470.

- - - - - - - - - - - - - - - -

Gruchalla RS and Pirmohamed M. Antibiotic allergy. *N. Engl. J. Med.* 2006; 354: 601–9.

2.3 Rheumatology

2.3.1 Carpal tunnel syndrome

This is the most common entrapment neuropathy; it presents commonly in rheumatology clinics.

Aetiology/pathophysiology/ pathology
The median nerve is easily compromised in the tight space of the carpal tunnel. Anything that makes the space tighter will induce carpal tunnel syndrome. The following mnemonic covers important causes.

C Crystal arthritis (Colles' and other fractures)
R Rheumatoid arthritis
A Amyloidosis (acromegaly)
M Myxoedema
P Pregnancy
E Elusive (no cause identified)
D Diabetes (drugs)

Clinical presentation
The median nerve receives sensory input from the radial three-and-a-half fingers (Fig. 54). However, symptoms are often more diffuse than this. The patient often describes paraesthesia in the whole hand or even extending up the arm, which is usually uncomfortable and often painful (the pain may also be the result of the underlying cause). The symptoms are usually worse at night and early in the morning, and a history of nocturnal paraesthesia alone should suggest the carpal tunnel syndrome. Patients often describe shaking their hand(s) to improve the symptoms. Motor symptoms are usually less prominent, although the hand may feel generally weak.

Physical signs
It should be emphasised that examination may be entirely normal if the symptoms are intermittent

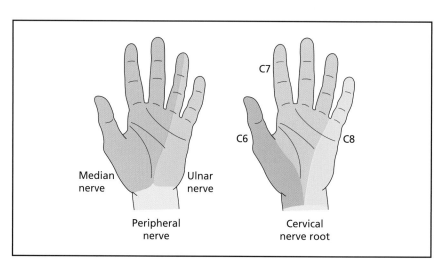

▲**Fig. 54** Sensory innervation of the palmar surface of the hand.

(usually nocturnal). A sensory discrepancy on the radial and ulnar side of the ring finger is highly suggestive of a median nerve lesion. Fixed sensory changes, weakness of thumb abduction and wasting of the thenar eminence are usually only found in severe cases and (in the presence of wasting) long-standing median nerve compression.

Two provocation tests are often used:

- percussion over the median nerve (Tinel's test);
- maintenance of fixed flexion of the wrist (Phalen's test).

These tests are positive if they produce transient sensory disturbance with a similar quality to the original symptoms. If positive, they are of good predictive value.

Investigations

A definitive diagnosis can be made using nerve conduction studies, although these may sometimes be normal in very mild intermittent compression. Electrophysiology is not obligatory in every case. Use only where the diagnosis is uncertain or where the result will affect your management. Many surgeons require electrophysiological confirmation before carpal tunnel decompression.

> Consider also an investigation of underlying cause, although these patients may have underlying thyroid disease and thus will have a very low threshold for thyroid function testing.

Differential diagnosis

Cervical root compression and peripheral neuropathy are the main differential diagnoses. Although a C6/7 nerve root lesion may give similar sensory symptoms, it would

not cause motor symptoms in the hand (supplied by T1). Ulnar nerve lesions are easy to distinguish by the pattern of sensory disturbance.

Treatment

This is dictated by the severity of the symptoms. Many mild cases with occasional symptoms need no treatment. Conversely, intervention will be needed in most cases with severe unremitting symptoms. Most cases lie somewhere in between.

- Night-time splintage of the wrists is often used in mild compression, although there is little evidence that this is effective.

- Injection of corticosteroids into the carpal tunnel is a simple outpatient treatment that may produce prolonged relief of symptoms, particularly in cases of recent onset or with an underlying inflammatory cause.

- Surgical decompression is the definitive treatment and is highly effective unless permanent nerve damage has occurred, which is usually in severe long-standing cases (possibly predictable from electrophysiology).

2.3.2 Osteoarthritis

Aetiology/pathophysiology/pathology

> Osteoarthritis is a process of joint failure rather than a disease. It can occur as a primary disorder or secondary to other insults to the joint.

The usual description of 'wear and tear' is misleading. Osteoarthritis (OA) is best considered the result of an inadequate attempt by cartilage and periarticular bone to repair itself after injury. The following are the cardinal pathological features (Fig. 55).

- Progressive disruption and loss of articular cartilage.

- Remodelling of periarticular bone, usually leading to new bone formation (osteophytes in hypertrophic OA) but sometimes to bone destruction (atrophic or erosive OA).

- Secondary changes in synovial membrane and other soft tissues.

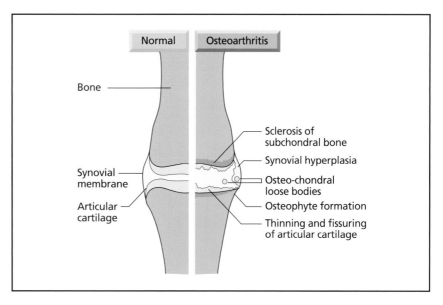

▲**Fig. 55** Joint changes in OA.

- Genetic factors are important: there is usually a strong family history in generalised nodal osteoarthritis. The underlying genetic defects are not yet identified. OA associated with calcium pyrophosphate crystal deposition is a common feature of hereditary haemochromatosis.

Other aetiological factors include:

- obesity;

- trauma or other disruptions to joint anatomy (such as a previous fracture or congenital hip dysplasia);

- acquired hip disease (eg Perthe's or slipped femoral epiphysis);

- occupation;

- inflammatory joint disease.

Epidemiology

OA is very common. It can be detected radiologically in 25% of 45 year olds and virtually everyone over the age of 65 (Fig. 56). Severe disease and hand involvement are more common in women.

Clinical presentation

OA usually presents with pain and functional impairment, but it may be asymptomatic, particularly in the cervical and lumbar spine. Clinical features depend on the joint involved. The most common pattern of polyarticular osteoarthritis is generalised nodal OA, which is characterised by the following:

- distal and proximal interphalangeal joint involvement;

- involvement of the base of the thumb (first carpometacarpal joint);

- hip, knee, cervical and lumbar spine involvement;

- perimenopausal onset.

If the OA has an atypical joint distribution (see Section 1.2.2), consider the secondary causes of OA.

1. Congenital:
   (a) Leg hypermobility.
   (b) Leg length discrepancies.
   (c) Hip dislocation.
   (d) Dysplasias.

2. Metabolic disorders:
   (a) Haemochromatosis.
   (b) Ochronosis.
   (c) Storage disorders, eg Gaucher's disease.
   (d) Haemoglobinopathies.

3. Endocrine disorders: acromegaly.

4. Neuropathic joints (Charcot's).

5. Other:
   (a) Chronic inflammatory/septic arthritis.
   (b) Osteonecrosis.

Physical signs

Tenderness, bony swelling (reflecting osteophyte formation), painful restriction of movement and crepitus are the usual findings. The formation of Heberden's and Bouchard's nodes in the distal and proximal interphalangeal joints, respectively, is pathognomonic. The base of the thumb often has a square appearance (see Fig. 25). Note also the muscle wasting around affected joints and the evidence of nerve or nerve root entrapment (most commonly carpal tunnel syndrome and cervical or lumbar root entrapment; more rarely, but more seriously, spinal cord compression).

Investigations/differential diagnosis

See Section 1.2.2.

Treatment/prognosis

A definitive, curative medical treatment for OA remains a remote prospect. The overall outcome depends as much on muscle strength and overall fitness as on joint damage.

OA of the hand

Outcome in OA of the hand is usually good, with long-term function usually preserved despite pain. Pain is often worse at onset, as osteophytes grow, and tends to settle with time. Severe changes at the base of the thumb may be associated with a worse functional outcome. Surgery may be helpful in relieving pain, but is less useful in improving hand function.

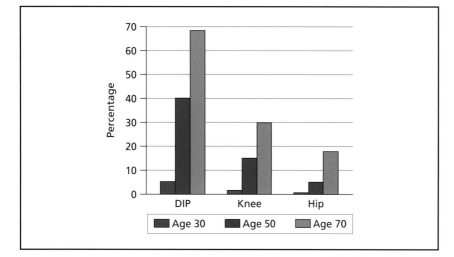

▲ **Fig. 56** Percentage prevalence of radiological changes of OA at three different sites and at three different ages in white people living in Western Europe. DIP, distal interphalangeal joint.

OA of the hip and knee

Hip and knee OA is progressive only in a minority, but it may cause severe pain and disability in this subgroup. Severely impaired mobility and rest pain are the main indications for joint replacement. The outcomes from hip and knee replacement are excellent. Arthroplasty of other joints is less widely used, but the outcomes from shoulder and elbow replacement are improving.

2.3.3 Rheumatoid arthritis

Rheumatoid arthritis (RA) is a chronic systemic inflammatory disease characterised by a distinct pattern of joint involvement. The primary site of pathology is the synovium and it is commonly accompanied by extra-articular manifestations of the disease.

Aetiology

The aetiology is unknown, although current evidence supports a combination of genetic and environmental factors acting in concert. Genetic and environmental factors have both been implicated in the susceptibility of an individual to, and in determination of severity of, RA. Strong evidence for a genetic contribution comes from twin studies with human leucocyte antigens (HLA), which are thought to explain about half of the genetic predisposition. There is a strong association with particular HLA antigens: HLA-DR4 and HLA-DR1 ('rheumatoid epitope' or 'shared epitope', respectively). Over 70% of patients with erosive seropositive disease are likely to be HLA-DR4 positive (compared with 25% of the normal population). Environmental factors include hormonal and reproductive factors, socioeconomic factors, diet, cigarette smoking and infection.

Epidemiology

The annual incidence in the UK is estimated to be 36 per 100,000 women and 14 per 100,000 men. RA occurs worldwide in all ethnic groups. The peak incidence of onset is in the sixth decade.

Pathology

Changes in early disease are confined to the synovial microvasculature, with endothelial swelling, polymorph infiltration and thrombotic occlusion. In late disease, the synovium is heavily infiltrated by lymphocytes, macrophages and plasma cells and it resembles an immunologically active lymph node. Rheumatoid nodules (Fig. 57) have a characteristic histological appearance with central fibrinoid necrosis surrounded by fibroblasts. Although several lines of evidence suggest that T cells and macrophages play a key role in RA, recent evidence attesting to the efficacy of rituximab (monoclonal anti-CD20) has re-ignited interest in the role of B cells in the pathogenesis of RA.

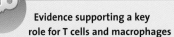

Evidence supporting a key role for T cells and macrophages in RA

- Synovial lymphoid infiltrates consist mainly of clonally expanded CD4+ T cells, which express markers of immunological memory (CD45RO) and activation (CD69).
- CD4+ T cells are in close proximity to antigen-presenting cells in the synovium.
- T-cell-derived and macrophage-derived cytokines such as interleukin (IL)-6, tumour necrosis factor (TNF)-α and IL-1 are abundantly expressed in rheumatoid joints.
- Treatment with anti-TNF is of proven benefit in RA.

Clinical presentation

Common

The pattern of joint involvement is typically symmetrical, affecting hands (see Fig. 24), wrists, elbows and shoulders, but usually sparing the distal interphalangeal joints. Several distinct patterns of onset are recognised (see Section 1.1.14 and 1.2.3).

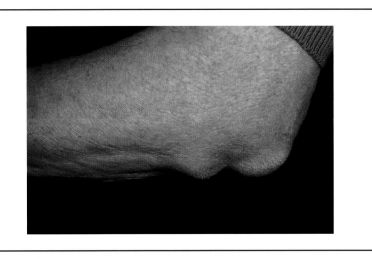

▲**Fig. 57** Subcutaneous rheumatoid nodules in a patient with seropositive RA.

> ### Criteria for RA
>
> The following are the revised criteria of the American College of Rheumatology for the classification of RA (1987).
>
> - Morning stiffness (duration >1 hour, lasting >6 weeks).
> - Arthritis of at least three areas (soft-tissue swelling or fluid >6 weeks).
> - Arthritis of hand joints (wrist, metacarpophalangeal joints or proximal interphalangeal joints >6 weeks).
> - Symmetrical arthritis (at least one area >6 weeks).
> - Rheumatoid nodules (as observed by physician).
> - Serum rheumatoid factor.
> - Radiological changes (as seen on anteroposterior films of wrists and hands).
>
> The presence of four criteria is required for diagnosis of RA.

Physical signs

Common

Acute synovitis of an involved joint leads to pain, swelling, stiffness and loss of function. Chronic active disease leads to joint damage and the characteristic deformities of RA (see Fig. 31 and Section 1.2.3). Rheumatoid nodules are seen only in patients with positive rheumatoid factor (Fig. 57).

Uncommon

- Extra-articular manifestations (see Table 19).

Investigations

The diagnosis of RA is based on a collection of clinical features rather than on a specific pathognomonic abnormality. Investigations are helpful in assessing disease severity and prognosis.

Blood count

Red cell count Many patients with active disease are anaemic. Aetiology of anaemia is multifactorial.

> ### Causes of anaemia in RA
>
> - Normochromic normocytic anaemia caused by chronic disease itself.
> - Hypochromic microcytic anaemia secondary to iron deficiency (gastrointestinal bleeding caused by NSAIDs).
> - Macrocytic anaemia resulting from folate deficiency (sulfasalazine and methotrexate) or vitamin B_{12} deficiency (associated pernicious anaemia).
> - Haemolysis (drug induced: sulfasalazine and dapsone).
> - Bone marrow suppression (drug induced: sulfasalazine, gold and cytotoxic agents).
> - Hypersplenism as in Felty's syndrome.

White cell count This may be normal. It is elevated in patients with severe disease or infection or in those on steroid therapy. Leucopenia may be drug induced or secondary to peripheral consumption, as in Felty's syndrome.

Platelet count This is usually normal. Thrombocytosis is a feature of active disease whereas thrombocytopenia may be caused by drug-induced marrow suppression or Felty's syndrome.

Acute-phase indices

Both the erythrocyte sedimentation rate (ESR) and C-reactive protein are elevated in active disease and correlate with disease severity.

Rheumatoid factor

Rheumatoid factor is positive in 70% of patients. High titres are usually associated with severe RA, particularly with extra-articular features. The role of rheumatoid factor as a marker of RA is increasingly being supplanted by antibodies to cyclic citrullinated peptide, which have recently been shown to be highly specific for RA and are predictive of aggressive disease.

Radiology

Small joints of the hands and feet are affected early in the disease. Typical changes include:

- soft-tissue swelling;
- periarticular osteoporosis;
- loss of joint space;
- marginal erosions (regarded as a characteristic feature of RA).

Synovial fluid analysis

See Sections 1.1.14 and 3.5.

Synovial biopsy

Synovial histology is rarely necessary and is not pathognomonic. It is sometimes useful in excluding tuberculosis in a patient with monoarticular disease.

Differential diagnosis

See Section 1.1.14.

Treatment

The following are the aims of any treatment:

- relief of symptoms;
- suppression of active disease and arrest of disease progression;
- restoration of function to affected joints.

To achieve these aims, a multidisciplinary team approach is vital, encompassing rheumatologists, occupational therapists, physiotherapists, nurses, social workers and orthopaedic surgeons. Patient education is equally crucial. Ensure that the patient understands the chronicity of disease with its exacerbations and remissions.

Active-phase treatment consists of local measures and treatment with drugs.

Local measures

- Splints to rest joints.

- Physiotherapy.

- Intra-articular steroids (see Section 3.6).

These measures are very useful where one or more joints continues to be painful despite simple analgesics and NSAIDs. The duration of symptomatic relief is variable (2–4 weeks).

Drug treatment

The traditional pyramidal approach to drug therapy, in which NSAIDs are used as first-line agents with the late introduction of disease-modifying antirheumatic drugs (DMARDs), is no longer valid because the assumptions underpinning this approach have been shown to be incorrect.

The following traditional assumptions regarding drug treatment of RA are now known to be erroneous:

- RA is a benign disease;
- aspirin and NSAIDs are non-toxic therapies;
- DMARDs are too toxic for routine use.

Current consensus favours the early use of DMARDs in view of:

- their efficacy as a group in arresting disease progression;

- the recognition that the risks associated with untreated disease may be greater than the toxicity of drug treatment.

NSAIDs These drugs provide symptomatic relief by suppressing inflammation, but they do not influence the underlying disease process. Most patients with RA require daily treatment. Additional simple analgesics, such as paracetamol with or without opiates, are useful if pain relief is inadequate.

DMARDs This is a heterogeneous group of drugs comprising sulfasalazine, methotrexate, leflunomide, chloroquine/hydroxychloroquine, gold, steroids, azathioprine and cyclophosphamide. Methotrexate is now the first-line DMARD provided there are no contraindications. Used increasingly early in disease, DMARDs are slow-acting drugs that inhibit cytokine-mediated inflammatory damage, thereby preventing joint destruction and preserving joint function. Regular monitoring is required to prevent toxicity (Table 29).

Steroids These are administered via either the intra-articular or the intramuscular route. Both afford temporary relief lasting 2–12 weeks, and are useful in two situations:

- acute exacerbations of disease;

- as a stop-gap measure before DMARDs start acting.

Oral steroids are rarely justified, although intravenous steroid pulses are useful as a short-term measure for severe disease exacerbations, eg rheumatoid vasculitis.

Cytotoxic therapy This is rarely used, and is usually reserved for resistant disease.

New agents in the treatment of RA

Cyclooxygenase-2 inhibitors

Celecoxib and rofecoxib selectively inhibit cyclooxygenase (COX)-2, the COX isoform expressed in inflammatory lesions, in contrast to COX-1 which is constitutively expressed in most tissues. COX-2 inhibitors are useful in RA because they inhibit synovial prostaglandin production while sparing intestinal prostaglandin synthesis, which is mediated by COX-1. The main advantage of COX-2 inhibitors over conventional NSAIDs is the lower risk of gastrointestinal ulceration. The lowest dose of COX required to control a patient's symptoms should be used. Recent guidance from the Committee on Safety of Medicines states that COX-2 inhibitors should not be used in patients with hypertension or a history of ischaemic heart disease on account of the increased cardiovascular risks associated with long-term COX-2 inhibition.

TABLE 29 SIDE EFFECTS OF DMARDs

Drug	Side effects
Gold	Mouth ulcers, rash, bone marrow suppression, nitritoid reaction (flushing) and proteinuria
Sulfasalazine	Nausea, vomiting, rash, mouth ulcers, hepatotoxicity, bone marrow suppression and transient azoospermia
Methotrexate	Nausea, vomiting, mouth ulcers, hepatotoxicity, bone marrow suppression, pneumonitis and renal damage
Leflunomide	Diarrhoea, hypertension, hepatotoxicity and bone marrow suppression

TNF inhibitors Three TNF inhibitors are currently licenced for treating severe RA. Infliximab and adalimumab (monoclonal anti-TNF antibodies) and etanercept (a soluble TNF receptor) act by potently binding TNF and consequently reducing the pro-inflammatory effects of this cytokine. Patients can be treated with the anti-TNF drugs only if they have failed to obtain relief from at least two DMARDs, one of which must be methotrexate, and they must have a composite score (Disease Activity Score) derived from various disease activity markers (eg ESR or swollen joint count) of >5.1. Patients on anti-TNF drugs have to be monitored closely as they may be more prone to developing unusual serious adverse events, such as infections, (particularly extrapulmonary tuberculosis), demyelination, congestive cardiac failure and possibly malignancies (lymphoma).

Anti-B cell therapy The recent success of rituximab (anti-CD20) in patients with severe RA unresponsive to conventional DMARDs and anti-TNF therapies has led to a reappraisal of the immunopathogenic role of B lymphocytes in RA.

Surgery

Joint replacement is indicated once irreversible joint damage has occurred. The overall outcome after knee and hip replacement is favourable, with promising results being seen with elbow and shoulder replacement.

Prognosis

Severe disabling disease occurs in 10% of cases of RA. Major causes of death are cardiovascular disease, infection, vasculitis and secondary amyloidosis.

Poor prognostic factors in RA

- **Female patients or young male patients.**
- Severe disease and/or severe disability at presentation.
- Extra-articular disease.
- High concentration of rheumatoid factor.
- Evidence of early (first 3 years) erosions on radiological examination.
- HLA-DR4.

FURTHER READING

Emery P. Treatment of rheumatoid arthritis. *BMJ* 2006; 332: 152–5.

Hyrich KL, Watson KD, Silman AJ, *et al*. Predictors of response to anti-TNF (alpha) therapy among patients with rheumatoid arthritis: results from the British Society of Rheumatology Biologics Register. *Rheumatology* 2006; 45: 1558–65.

Looney RJ. Discovering that B cells are important in rheumatoid arthritis. *J. Rheumatol.* 2005; 32: 2067–9.

Simpson C, Franks C, Morrison C, *et al*. The patient's journey: rheumatoid arthritis. *BMJ* 2005; 331: 887–9.

2.3.4 Seronegative spondyloarthropathies

Definition of seronegative spondyloarthritis

Generic term for a group of rheumatological disorders characterised by:

- sacroiliitis;
- peripheral arthritis (usually affecting large joints, predominantly the lower limbs);
- mucocutaneous inflammation;
- significant familial aggregation.

Rheumatoid factor is absent (hence seronegative).

These disorders include the following:

- ankylosing spondylitis (AS), features of which may occur in all the other syndromes;

- psoriatic arthritis;

- reactive arthritis;

- enteropathic arthritis (associated with inflammatory bowel disease).

Considerable overlap may occur between these syndromes and, in some patients, the generic label 'seronegative spondyloarthropathy' may be more appropriate than any of the above.

Aetiology/pathophysiology/pathology

Genetic factors are important, with human leucocyte antigen (HLA)-B27 being the most clearly defined association (Table 30). Infectious agents (mucosal or skin) are thought to be the most important environmental trigger. This is best defined for reactive arthritis, with infectious agents including the following:

- *Chlamydia trachomatis*;

- *Salmonella* spp.;

- *Shigella* spp.;

- *Campylobacter jejuni*;

- *Yersinia enterocolitica*.

The inflammatory process probably results from an immune response against non-viable bacterial antigens sequestered in musculoskeletal tissues, perhaps leading to a secondary autoimmune response. The cardinal pathological feature is enthesitis, an enthesis being the junctional tissue between the muscle/ligament/tendon and bone. Enthesitis is responsible for spinal inflammation in AS and localised problems such as plantar fasciitis

TABLE 30 PREVALENCE OF HLA-B27	
Disease	**Percentage prevalence**
UK controls	5–10
Ankylosing spondylitis	95
Reactive arthritis	80
Psoriatic arthritis (total)	20
Psoriatic spondylitis	50

and Achilles tendonitis. Enthesitis is also probably the first pathological change in joint inflammation in these disorders.

Epidemiology

All these disorders show either a male preponderance or equal gender distribution, in contrast with most chronic immunological rheumatic diseases.

Ankylosing spondylitis

AS has a prevalence of 0.1–0.2% in white populations. It is strongly associated with HLA-B27, although only around 2% of individuals who are HLA-B27 positive develop AS. It is rare in Afro-Caribbean populations, reflecting their low prevalence of HLA-B27. The male to female ratio is around 4:1, with peak onset in late adolescence or early adulthood.

Reactive arthritis

Reactive arthritis is typically a disorder of young adults. Most patients report a positive family history. The frequency of reactive arthritis after an enteric infection caused by *Salmonella*, *Shigella* or *Campylobacter* has been reported to be in the order of 1–4%, with HLA-B27 predisposing to more chronic and more severe disease.

Psoriatic arthritis

Rates of psoriatic arthritis have been estimated as 0.04–0.1%. The male to female ratio is 1:1, with mean age of onset between 30 and 50 years.

There is an increased prevalence in HIV-positive populations.

Clinical presentation

> **Common features that may occur in all spondyloarthropathies:**
>
> - insidious onset of spinal pain and restriction;
> - localised enthesitis, eg plantar fasciitis and Achilles tendonitis;
> - large-joint synovitis;
> - acute uveitis (painful red eye).

Ankylosing spondylitis

Spinal symptoms predominate so look for:

- involvement of whole spine (Fig. 58);

- patient may have large-joint oligoarthritis in lower limbs, especially the hips.

Reactive arthritis

This often begins acutely: severe systemic disturbance may be present and mimic sepsis (which should be actively excluded). Common features include the following.

- A history of diarrhoea or urethritis up to 1 month before the articular disease. However, these features are often absent, particularly in post-chlamydial reactive arthritis. A triggering infection can be reliably identified in only about 50% of patients.

- The spectrum of the disease ranges from purely articular to multisystem disease.

- The most common presentation is acute lower-limb large-joint monoarthritis or oligoarthritis in a young male.

- Patients often present with enthesitis (inflammation of the insertion of tendon into bone), such as Achilles tendinitis or plantar fasciitis.

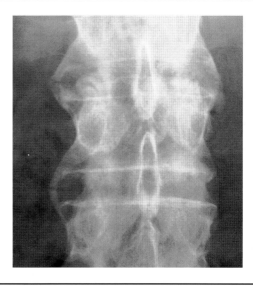

▲ **Fig. 58** Spinal fusion in AS. (Courtesy of Dr M. Pattrick.)

- Scaly psoriasis-like eruption on hands/feet (keratoderma blennorrhagica).

- Eroded appearance to glans penis (circinate balanitis).

- Conjunctivitis is more common than uveitis.

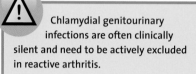

Chlamydial genitourinary infections are often clinically silent and need to be actively excluded in reactive arthritis.

Psoriatic arthritis
There are several patterns, which may overlap (percentages are of total psoriatic arthritis population):

- distal interphalangeal joint (7–17%) (see Fig. 28);

- asymmetrical oligoarthritis (30–55%);

- symmetrical polyarthritis, similar to rheumatoid arthritis (20–40%);

- arthritis mutilans (not unlike rheumatoid, but grossly destructive and often with telescoping digits) (2–15%);

- sacroiliitis and spondylitis (5–30%).

Dactylitis (sausage-like finger or toe swelling, usually affecting only one or two digits) is a distinctive feature, occurring in around 25% of patients. The severities of the skin and joint disease are not correlated. Aggressive arthritis can be accompanied by very mild psoriasis and vice versa. Some patients may have joint disease that is highly suggestive of psoriatic arthritis, but no obvious skin disease. Skin disease may appear many years later.

Enteropathic arthritis
There are two patterns (which again may overlap):

- large-joint lower-limb oligoarthritis or monoarthritis (activity tends to mirror the severity of bowel inflammation);

- AS.

Uncommon features

- Aortitis, which may lead to aortic incompetence.

- Pulmonary fibrosis (AS).

- Spinal discitis, which may lead to instability and spinal cord and nerve root compression.

- Amyloid (as in all chronic inflammatory disease).

Physical signs
It is necessary to assess spinal disease in AS, as follows.

Lumbar spine
Restricted movement is almost always found, usually more so than in mechanical back pain and usually in all directions. The modified Schoeber's test is used for serial measurement: the increase in distance following forward flexion of two points 15 cm apart, one 5 cm below and one 10 cm above a line drawn between the dimples of Venus (see Fig. 32).

Thoracic spine
Dorsal kyphosis often develops as disease progresses. Chest expansion is the best index: <5 cm is abnormal.

Cervical spine
This is globally restricted, with the neck being forced into a flexed position by dorsal kyphosis. Place the patient with his or her back to a wall: can the patient touch the wall with his or her occiput? If not, measure the occiput to wall distance.

Investigations

Synovial fluid
Microscopy and culture are essential to exclude sepsis and crystal arthritis.

Blood tests
Measures of the acute-phase response are useful:

- to distinguish inflammatory from non-inflammatory back pain;

- to assess disease activity/response to treatment.

Ascertainment of HLA-B27 status is of limited diagnostic value because it is present in around 5–10% of the population, but it may be of limited use in completing the diagnostic jigsaw.

Identifying a triggering cause
Look for a triggering cause in reactive arthritis.

- *Chlamydia* spp. are the most common triggering cause, and may be clinically silent. Chlamydial serology is of little use. Diagnosis can be made only by detection of the organism in the genital tract (antigen detection or polymerase chain reaction). Referral to a genitourinary physician may be required.

- Diagnosis of *Campylobacter/Shigella/Salmonella* infection may be possible by culture if the patient has recently had diarrhoea, but this is unlikely to be successful if the gastrointestinal symptoms have settled.

- In practice, the clinical picture is often suggestive of reactive arthritis, but no triggering organism is identified.

Think about HIV

Remember that florid reactive arthritis and psoriatic arthropathy may be presenting features of HIV infection.

Radiology

Sacroiliitis This may be asymptomatic. It is worth looking for in unexplained monoarthritis and oligoarthritis because the presence of bilateral sacroiliitis makes the diagnosis of a spondyloarthropathy very likely. Beware of unilateral sacroiliitis: this may be due to sepsis, so consider aspiration or biopsy.

Spinal radiographs These are indicated in back pain of an inflammatory pattern. Sacroiliitis and vertebral changes may be diagnostic long before the classic bamboo spine develops.

MRI There is increasing evidence that MRI is able to detect acute spinal lesions even in the early stages of sacroiliitis/AS. This tool is being used in research to monitor disease progression and responsiveness to therapy.

Peripheral joint disease Look for erosions and use to assess the progress of damage.

Occult inflammatory bowel disease Consider small-bowel radiology/large-bowel endoscopy in:

- 'reactive arthritis' with persistent bowel symptoms;

- erythema nodosum;

- persistent monoarthritis/oligoarthritis with an acute-phase response or anaemia that seems out of proportion to the articular disease.

Differential diagnosis

- Spinal disease: beware infective or neoplastic spinal pathology, especially in an older patient. Mechanical back pain may sometimes give a very inflammatory picture.

- Monoarthritis: consider sepsis and crystal arthritis (see Section 1.18).

- Oligoarthritis: consider crystal arthritis, rheumatic fever in a younger patient or Lyme disease if the patient has travelled to, or is resident in, an endemic area. Dactylitis is also a feature of sarcoid arthropathy.

- Polyarthritis: parvovirus arthritis and other postviral arthritides, also rheumatoid disease.

- Joint and mucocutaneous disease: systemic lupus erythematosus and Behçet's syndrome.

- Joint and gut disease: vasculitis, Whipple's disease and coeliac disease.

Treatment

Short term

- Exclude sepsis, symptomatic NSAIDs for pain and stiffness, and intra-articular corticosteroid injections.

- Treat any associated sexually transmitted infection in reactive arthritis (this has little or no influence on the joint disease).

- Control inflammatory bowel disease.

Long term

- Lifelong daily exercise plan via physiotherapists for spinal disease.

- Sulfasalazine and methotrexate are useful in peripheral joint

disease, but have little or no impact on spinal disease.

- Methotrexate is particularly useful in cases of psoriatic arthritis.

- Anti-tumour necrosis factor therapy is now licensed for severe AS and psoriatic arthritis.

Prognosis

Ankylosing spondylitis

Many patients do well, with only a minority having severe disabling disease. Joint replacement is necessary in 15% of cases (most often for hips).

Poor prognostic features in AS

- **Onset in adolescence.**
- **High acute-phase response.**
- **Extraspinal joint disease.**

Reactive arthritis

- Remission in more than 70% at 1 year and 85% at 2 years, but relapse can occur in 30–50% of patients, perhaps provoked by recurrent exposure to a triggering infection.

- Persistent long-term disease in 10–30% of patients.

- Persistence and recurrence more likely if HLA-B27 is present.

Psoriatic arthritis

The outcome of psoriatic arthritis depends on the pattern. Asymmetrical oligoarthritis has a good long-term outcome. A mutilans picture is associated with considerable disability.

FURTHER READING

Nash P, Mease PJ, Braun J, *et al.* Seronegative spondyloarthropathies: to lump or split. *Ann. Rheum. Dis.* 2005; 64(Suppl. 2): ii9–ii13.

2.3.5 Idiopathic inflammatory myopathies

Aetiology/pathophysiology/pathology

Usual classification

- Primary idiopathic polymyositis (PM).
- Primary idiopathic dermatomyositis (DM).
- PM or DM with malignancy.
- Juvenile DM (not discussed here).
- PM or DM with another connective tissue disease.
- Inclusion body myositis.
- Rare forms of idiopathic myositis, eg eosinophilic myositis, focal myositis and orbital myositis.

These myopathies are usually considered to be autoimmune disorders. They are paraneoplastic in 10% of cases. The immunological mechanism of muscle damage is largely via T cells in PM and via antibody and complement in DM. Striated muscle involvement predominates, although cardiac and smooth muscle can be involved. Skeletal muscle pathology usually shows lymphocytic infiltration and fibre damage.

Epidemiology

These are rare disorders, with an incidence of around 5 per 10 million annually. The female to male ratio is about 2:1, although the sexes are equally affected by paraneoplastic myositis.

Clinical presentation

Muscle

This is usually affected by proximal weakness rather than pain. The assessment of the patient with proximal weakness is discussed in Section 1.1.11. Non-skeletal

involvement may produce cardiac failure, respiratory failure and oropharyngeal dysfunction.

Skin

The following are important features:

- nail-fold capillary dilatation, usually visible to the naked eye;

- development of scaly rashes on light-exposed skin, eg metacarpophalangeal joints (Gottron's papules);

- heliotrope rash (lilac-coloured rash on the eyelids);

- angio-oedematous changes, particularly on the face.

Lung

Intercostal and diaphragmatic weakness occurs in severe cases, which can lead to respiratory failure. Vital capacity should be monitored in inpatients. Interstitial lung disease, clinically indistinguishable from cryptogenic fibrosing alveolitis/idiopathic pulmonary fibrosis, occurs in around one-fifth of cases. The lung disease may be the presenting feature, initially with mild muscle changes. It is often associated with the presence of the anti-Jo-1 antibody, which is discussed further in Section 3.2.1.

Investigations

Assay of creatine kinase (CK) is the best marker of muscle inflammation, although it is not specific to myositis (see Section 1.1.11). CK is also a useful marker of response to treatment. PM and DM may occasionally present with a normal CK. Screening for malignancy and use of muscle biopsy, electromyography and muscle imaging are discussed in Section 1.1.11. A raised alanine aminotransferase (ALT) may occasionally be due to myositis; CK should therefore be included in the screen for causes of a raised ALT.

Detection of autoantibodies is often helpful, although around one-third of patients with PM/DM do not have any recognised pattern of autoantibodies. The presence of high-titre antinuclear antibodies greatly increases the diagnostic likelihood of PM/DM or other connective tissue disease. A variety of distinctive patterns of autoantibody production are seen in defined subtypes of myositis and overlap syndromes. These patterns are usually detected using screening tests for antibodies to extractable nuclear antigens. These include anti-Jo-1, anti-U1 ribonucleoprotein and anti-PM-Scl, which are all associated with syndromes that include myositis, lung disease and scleroderma-like changes.

Differential diagnosis

See Section 1.1.11.

Do not automatically assume that:

- a normal CK level excludes myositis;
- a raised CK level is the result of myositis without additional investigation;
- lymphocytic infiltrates in a muscle are always caused by myositis.

Treatment

Corticosteroids form the mainstay of treatment, initially at high doses. Most patients require a steroid-sparing drug as the dose of steroids is reduced. Methotrexate can be used if there is no evidence of inflammatory lung disease. Another alternative is azathioprine. Ciclosporin as monotherapy or in combination with methotrexate, other immunosuppressant drugs including intravenous cyclophosphamide, and high-dose intravenous immunoglobulin can all be used where the response to treatment is poor. Assessing response to treatment is usually by serial measurement of CK and muscle strength. Lung function tests including transfer factor and high-resolution CT of the lungs are useful in patients with inflammatory lung disease. Physiotherapy is an important adjunct to pharmacological treatment.

Reassessment

Where response to treatment is poor, consider re-biopsy to reassess the following.

- Initial diagnosis: is this really PM/DM? Inherited myopathies can sometimes be confused. Inclusion body myositis is a variant of PM that is much less responsive to immunosuppression. Patients with inclusion body myositis also often have distal muscle weakness as well as proximal weakness.
- Treatment or disease: could persistent weakness be corticosteroid induced?

Skin and lung involvement will usually respond in parallel with the muscle disease, but topical steroids and antimalarials may be useful in skin disease and more aggressive immunosuppression may be required for lung disease. Rapid, non-specific deterioration may reflect the progression of underlying malignancy rather than the muscle disease itself.

Prognosis

Morbidity

Although most patients will show some response to immunosuppression, the morbidity of those with PM and DM is high. Overall, more than 50% of patients will have some long-term muscle weakness. The response to treatment in DM and myositis associated with

other connective tissue diseases is better than in PM. Onset over the age of 65 is a poor prognostic sign.

FURTHER READING

Dalakas MC and Hohlfeld R. Polymyositis and dermatomyositis. *Lancet* 2003; 362: 971–82.

Targoff IN. Polymyositis and dermatomyositis in adults. In: Isenberg DA, Maddison PJ, Woo P, Glass DN, Breedveld FC, eds. *Oxford Textbook of Rheumatology*. Oxford: Oxford University Press, 2004: 895–914.

2.3.6 Crystal arthritis: gout

Aetiology/pathophysiology/ pathology

Poorly soluble crystals

A variety of poorly soluble crystals can be found in joints, some of which can induce inflammation, including the following.

- Monosodium urate: the cause of gout.
- Calcium pyrophosphate: the cause of pseudogout.
- Apatite: possibly associated with aggressive forms of osteoarthritis (rare and not discussed further here).

Formation of monosodium urate crystals is a consequence of hyperuricaemia, which in turn results from overproduction or inefficient renal excretion of uric acid (or a combination of the two). The biochemistry of uric acid formation and its relationship to cell turnover is discussed in *Scientific Background to Medicine 1*, Biochemistry and Metabolism – Nucleotides. Poor excretion is probably the major factor in most cases of gout. Obesity, diuretic usage and alcohol consumption are the main environmental causes, but

genetic factors play a strong modulating role. Drugs are an important contributory cause, particularly diuretics and ciclosporin.

Crystals tend to form in joints, subcutaneously, and in the kidney and renal tubules. Subcutaneous crystals tend to form discrete masses or tophi. The crystals induce inflammation by activating leucocytes and/or the complement cascade.

Epidemiology

Gout is common, affecting more than 1% of the population, and is the most common cause of the acute hot joint. Gout is predominantly a male disease, and only occurs in significant numbers of women among those over the age of 60, when it is almost invariably associated with diuretic usage.

Clinical presentation

A number of overlapping syndromes are associated with urate crystal deposition:

- acute gout;
- tophaceous gout;
- nephrolithiasis;
- uric acid nephropathy.

Acute gout

This usually presents with an episodic, self-limiting, flitting monoarthritis or oligoarthritis. This is most commonly of the first metatarsophalangeal joint and knee, but can produce an asymmetrical polyarthritis. Extra-articular acute attacks can occur in bursae (especially the olecranon). The inflammation is usually severe and exquisitely painful, although polyarthritic gout tends to be less florid. The attacks may be associated with systemic ill-health and fever. Precipitants include the following:

- alcohol excess;

- intercurrent illness (including surgery), particularly if dehydration is pesent;

- starvation;

- introduction of any drug that interferes with the handling of uric acid (including allopurinol).

The joint generally returns to normal between attacks.

Tophaceous gout

Widespread tophus formation can occur on a background of recurrent long-standing acute gout, but it can also occur in elderly women on diuretics in the absence of acute attacks (see Fig. 27). Tophi are usually pea-sized, but can be very large. They tend to occur on pressure points, such as extensor surfaces, and on the pinnae.

Nephrolithiasis

Uric acid crystals account for around 8% of all renal/ureteric calculi. They are radiolucent.

Uric acid nephropathy

Hyperuricaemia is a common finding in renal impairment, usually as a consequence of impaired kidney function, hypertension or drug treatment, rather than the cause. The important exception is acute uric acid nephropathy which occurs in high cell turnover states, particularly leukaemias and lymphomas during the early stages of chemotherapy. Systemic illness and poor renal perfusion increase the risk of renal failure.

Physical signs

For physical signs see Section 1.2.6. Gout and sepsis are the only common causes of a red-hot joint, and it is important to differentiate the two by joint aspiration if there is any doubt. Gout may also mimic infection by producing spreading cellulitic changes, which may desquamate as recovery occurs. The affected joint is usually red, hot, swollen and very tender and painful to palpation.

Investigations

- Aspiration of synovial fluid is the only definitive diagnostic test (see Section 3.5). The crystals are negatively birefringent under polarised light microscopy and are needle-shaped (Fig. 38). Uric acid crystals can be found between acute attacks, and the diagnosis can be made by aspiration of a quiescent joint: only a tiny amount of fluid is required. Crystals can also be seen in material aspirated from bursae and tophi.

- Measurement of serum uric acid is of little value: hyperuricaemia is far more common than clinical gout and furthermore the level may be normal during an acute attack.

- Uric acid excretion can be used to define overproducers and underexcretors, but this is rarely of clinical value.

- Assess renal function and consider screening for common comorbid conditions: hypertension, diabetes mellitus and hypercholesterolaemia (metabolic syndrome X/insulin resistance syndrome).

- Radiographs may be useful in chronic disease: periarticular tophi produce a distinctive punched-out pattern, which can be distinguished from other erosive arthropathies.

Differential diagnosis

This includes the causes of the acute hot joint discussed in Section 1.4.4. Chronic tophaceous gout can be confused with:

- rheumatoid arthritis;

- psoriatic arthritis;

- nodal osteoarthritis.

Treatment

Short term

NSAIDs These are the mainstay of acute treatment. However, beware the use of NSAIDs in cases of renal impairment, because marked deterioration may occur in patients with congestive cardiac failure and ischaemic heart disease. Remember that:

- indometacin has acquired a reputation for being the most effective NSAID although there is little evidence for this;

- aspirin is usually avoided because it inhibits the excretion of urate.

Colchicine This may be poorly tolerated. In high doses it causes diarrhoea so has little to recommend it as a first-line treatment. However, it is sometimes used in low doses (500 µg bd) in patients who are unable to tolerate NSAIDs with good effect.

Corticosteroids These are invaluable, particularly in patients unable to tolerate NSAIDs. Intra-articular administration is preferred when one or a small number of joints are affected. Alternatively, consider a short 7–10 day oral burst (eg prednisolone 40 mg daily). Some advocate tailing off the dose over a week or two, but others do not feel that this is necessary.

Long term

Most of the predisposing causes of gout are reversible. Clearly there are good reasons for addressing these beyond the potential reduced risk of recurrent gout.

Prophylaxis

Prophylactic treatment should be considered in the following circumstances:

- recurrent acute attacks;
- chronic tophaceous gout;
- renal impairment;
- presence of leukaemias/lymphomas/bulky solid tumours prior to aggressive chemotherapy;
- inherited syndromes with uric acid overproduction, eg Lesch–Nyhan syndrome.

Allopurinol is the mainstay of prophylaxis, usually at a dose of 300 mg daily unless renal impairment is present. This is usually not started until around 2 weeks after an acute attack because it may initially precipitate further attacks. For this reason, a NSAID or low-dose colchicine is often co-prescribed for the first few weeks of allopurinol treatment. Allopurinol is usually well tolerated but can provoke severe mucocutaneous reactions, including Stevens–Johnson syndrome.

Recurrent gout on allopurinol usually reflects poor compliance or persistent high alcohol use, although some patients require dose increases of up to 900 mg daily (the aim being to normalise serum urate). Uricosuric drugs (probenecid and sulfinpyrazone) are occasionally useful when allopurinol is ineffective or not tolerated.

Beware the interaction between allopurinol and azathioprine in organ recipients and patients with systemic autoimmune disease. Azathioprine toxicity, including pancytopenia, may result because allopurinol inhibits xanthine oxidase, an enzyme responsible for metabolising azathioprine.

2.3.7 Calcium pyrophosphate deposition disease

Aetiology/pathophysiology/ pathology

This disease is poorly understood. Pyrophosphate crystals form in articular cartilage and are shed into the synovial fluid where they can provoke an inflammatory response. Pyrophosphate crystal formation occurs increasingly with age, but is also associated with a number of metabolic disorders:

- hereditary haemochromatosis;
- primary hyperparathyroidism;
- previous joint trauma (including surgery);
- previous intra-articular bleeding;
- hypophosphatasia (rare inherited alkaline phosphatase deficiency).

Epidemiology

Acute pseudogout is largely a disorder of elderly people, unless it is secondary to a metabolic disorder. Incidence is about half that of gout. Radiographic chondrocalcinosis is common.

Clinical presentation

Acute pseudogout

This disease presents like any other acute hot joint (see Section 1.4.4), often with striking fever and systemic illness. Intercurrent illness is the most common precipitant.

Chronic joint disease

The spectrum of disease ranges from a rheumatoid-like picture with synovitis to a variant of osteoarthritis. There is shoulder, elbow, wrist and metacarpophalangeal joint (especially second and third) involvement in the upper limb.

Investigations

The rheumatoid-like picture is not associated with rheumatoid factor, and is only occasionally associated with an acute-phase response. Diagnosis of the chronic joint diseases is largely radiological, looking for chondrocalcinosis (Fig. 59) and the distinctive pattern of degenerative joint disease.

Investigate potential secondary causes, especially haemochromatosis. Ferritin, serum iron and iron binding, calcium and alkaline phosphatase should be measured in most cases, especially in younger patients.

Treatment

Acute pseudogout is best managed with NSAIDs or intra-articular steroid injection once sepsis has been excluded. Low-dose colchicine has been used to prevent recurrent attacks. There are no specific treatments for chronic pyrophosphate arthropathies.

FURTHER READING

Dalbeth N and Haskard DO. Inflammation and tissue damage in crystal deposition diseases. *Curr. Opin. Rheumatol.* 2005; 17: 314–18.

2.3.8 Fibromyalgia

Aetiology/pathophysiology/ pathology

Attempts to understand the nature of this disorder within the conventional framework of physical musculoskeletal disease lead to little more than the Cheshire cat's smile. Detailed study has revealed no convincing evidence of musculoskeletal pathology, although the syndrome may arise

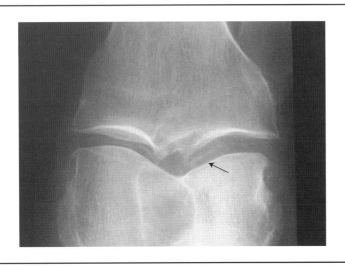

▲**Fig. 59** Chondrocalcinosis of the knee (arrowed).

- acute-phase markers (C-reactive protein and erythrocyte sedimentation rate);

- myeloma screen in patients >50 years old;

- antinuclear antibodies;

- CXR, especially in smokers.

'Red flag' features in widespread pain

You should suspect that fibromyalgia is *not* the diagnosis if any red flag features are present see Section 1.1.18

on a background of definite rheumatic disease (eg rheumatoid arthritis or spinal pain). There is considerable overlap with other so-called functional syndromes, particularly the chronic fatigue syndrome, and also a very high prevalence of psychiatric disorders, particularly depression.

Fibromyalgia is best considered a disorder of bodily perception, in which pain is perceived centrally in the absence of any peripheral cause. This is often intertwined with a tendency to somatise, meaning to express psychological distress in physical terms. Various factors seem to perpetuate the syndrome, including the following:

- sleep disturbance;

- a tendency to cope with pain and fatigue by withdrawal and rest;

- consequent profound loss of physical fitness;

- depression.

Epidemiology
The fibromyalgia syndrome is common but difficult to define precisely, which probably explains

why various studies report a prevalence of 0.5–10% in the general population.

Clinical presentation
Widespread pain, fatigue and disability, which is often profound.

Physical signs
None, apart from musculoskeletal tenderness.

Investigations
Fibromyalgia is a clinical diagnosis: there is no investigation that will 'prove' that the patient has the condition. The purpose of investigation is to exclude conditions that can present with similar manifestations. A reasonable set of tests in most cases would include the following:

- FBC;

- renal, bone and liver biochemistry;

- blood glucose;

- creatine kinase;

- thyroid function;

Treatment
Patients with fibromyalgia have a high level of disability, greater than that of those with rheumatoid arthritis. It is not acceptable simply to document the lack of severe physical disease in these patients and then discharge them: they deserve a constructive and positive approach to their diagnosis and management. Is a patient likely to be helped by the label of fibromyalgia? This is difficult to answer.

Argument against fibromyalgia
Placing a simple diagnostic label on a patient whose problems are at least partly the result of a tendency to express psychological distress in physical terms may serve only to perpetuate the patient's belief that the problems have an external physical cause. This may further divert attention from the real problems.

Argument for fibromyalgia
The diagnostic label can be used constructively to convince patients that their symptoms do fall into a recognised pattern, and to provide a framework for management. This

framework can then be used to discuss the relationship between the physical symptoms and the depression and other psychological factors. This is often a difficult area, with the potential for breakdown in communication unless it is handled tactfully.

It is often easier for a patient to accept that further investigation is unlikely to be helpful if it is felt that a diagnosis has been achieved.

What might help?

Regardless of whether or not the diagnosis of 'fibromyalgia' is applied, treatment can usefully be directed towards the factors that perpetuate the patient's disability. It is important that such treatment is presented as a process of rehabilitation in which the patient plays an active part.

- Sleep quality and pain can be improved with a low-dose tricyclic antidepressant, eg amitriptyline 10–50 mg nocte.

- Use analgesics if they are helpful, but withdraw if they are not.

- Physical fitness can be improved with a graded exercise programme.

- Depression, if present, may improve if treated with full-dose antidepressant therapy.

- Cognitive behaviour therapy may be very effective for both depression and in correcting abnormal or unhelpful beliefs about pain.

Be realistic about the prognosis (see below). Carefully assess any secondary gain and consider discussion with the family. And do not organise more and more investigations: try to limit further referrals.

Prognosis

Patients with a long history and a high degree of disability have a very poor prognosis. Involvement of pain management services and liaison psychiatry may be useful. The issues of the sick role, secondary gain and involvement of the family and carers may also need to be addressed.

2.4 Autoimmune rheumatic diseases

2.4.1 Systemic lupus erythematosus

Aetiology/immunopathogenesis

The cause of systemic lupus erythematosus (SLE) is unknown. It has a clear genetic element, as evidenced by the higher rate of concordance in monozygotic twins (25%) compared with dizygotic twins (3%). Risk factors include the human leucocyte antigen (HLA) haplotypes HLA-A1, -B8 and -DR3, complement C4 null alleles, and primary complement deficiency (of early components C1q, C1r, C1s, C4 and C2). Defective clearance of apoptotic cells has also been implicated in disease pathogenesis.

The onset of disease is triggered by ultraviolet (UV) light, drugs (eg minocycline, sulfasalazine, penicillamine, hydralazine and isoniazid) and possibly infection. There is a plethora of immunological abnormalities, characterised by marked polyclonal B-cell activation associated with hypergammaglobulinaemia and the production of autoantibodies.

Epidemiology

SLE is nine times more common in women than in men. Onset is commonly in the second and third decades. People of Afro-Caribbean and Asian origin are particularly susceptible. The prevalence of SLE in Afro-Caribbean women is 1 in 450, in Asian women 1 in 900 and in northern European women 1 in 2,000.

Factors responsible for exacerbations of SLE

- Exposure to sunlight (UV light).
- Psychological stress.
- Infections.
- Pregnancy and puerperium.
- Drugs, eg minocycline, sulfasalazine, penicillamine, hydralazine and isoniazid.

Clinical presentation

Many patients present with fever, arthralgia, fatigue and a skin rash. The symptoms may sometimes be very non-specific and lead to a delay in diagnosis. Additional features and major organ involvement (eg kidneys and the central nervous system) may occur at disease onset or evolve. SLE has a long-term course characterised by exacerbations and remissions.

Musculoskeletal manifestations

Flitting arthralgia associated with early morning stiffness is common (90%). The arthritis rarely progresses to a deforming arthropathy. Hand deformities resulting from tendon disease may cause a rheumatoid-like but non-erosive arthropathy (Jaccoud's arthropathy) in a minority of patients (Fig. 60). Only 4% of SLE patients develop erosions.

Skin and mucous membranes

UV light-induced skin photosensitivity is common. Malar rash (see Fig. 10) and recurrent mouth ulcers (see Fig. 11) occur in 50% of cases, non-scarring alopecia in 70% and Raynaud's phenomenon

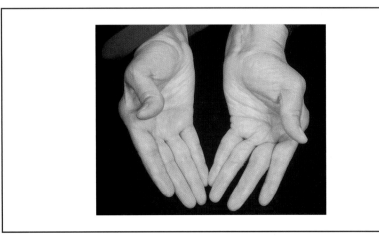

▲ **Fig. 60** Jaccoud's arthropathy in a patient with SLE.

is a feature in 25%. Lupus confined to the skin is characterised by distinctive rashes, ie discoid lupus (see Fig. 9) or subacute cutaneous lupus.

Kidney disease

Almost all patients with SLE have histological abnormalities on renal biopsy (see *Nephrology*, Section 1.9), but only 50% of patients develop overt renal disease. Screening for early disease should be carried out at each visit by analysing urine for blood and protein and by checking the patient's BP.

Nervous system

Neurological involvement affects up to two-thirds of patients at some point in their disease (see Section 1.4.3).

Pulmonary

Pleurisy with or without radiological evidence of effusion occurs in 40% of cases. Pulmonary emboli may occur in patients who are antiphospholipid positive. Inflammatory lung disease, shrinking lung syndrome and pulmonary hypertension are rare manifestations in SLE.

Cardiovascular

Pericarditis (30% of cases) is usually mild and very rarely progresses to tamponade. Non-infective thrombotic endocarditis (Libman–Sacks endocarditis) is rare and is associated with the antiphospholipid syndrome.

Haematological abnormalities

Normocytic normochromic anaemia, mild lymphopenia and mild thrombocytopenia occur in a substantial number of patients. Severe thrombocytopenia, severe leucopenia and haemolytic anaemia may sometimes occur. Reactive lymphadenopathy (40% of cases) and splenomegaly (10% of cases) occur, especially during disease activity. The antiphospholipid syndrome occurs in 20% of patients with SLE.

Overlap syndromes

This term describes patients who have coexisting features of two or more connective tissue diseases (Fig. 61). The following are common examples:

- scleroderma/SLE overlap;
- scleroderma/polymyositis overlap.

Mixed connective tissue disease

Patients are defined as having mixed connective tissue disease if they have features of:

- SLE;
- scleroderma;
- polymyositis.

This is defined on the basis of high antibody titres to U1

> **Neuropsychiatric manifestations of SLE (in decreasing order of frequency)**
>
> - Organic brain syndrome: cognitive impairment and psychosis (may be steroid induced).
> - Seizures.
> - Cranial neuropathy.
> - Peripheral neuropathy.
> - Stroke.
> - Movement disorder.
> - Transverse myelitis.
> - Headaches.

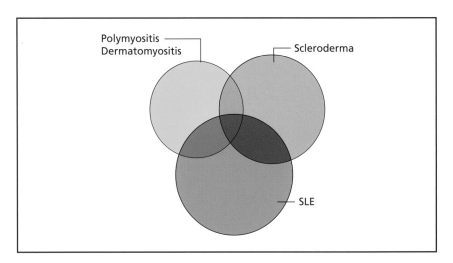

▲ **Fig. 61** Venn diagram depicting overlap of SLE, scleroderma and myositis.

ribonucleoprotein, arthritis/arthralgia (95% of cases), Raynaud's (85% of cases) and minimal renal disease. The existence of mixed connective tissue disease as a distinct diagnostic entity has since been questioned because none of the clinical or laboratory criteria used for the definition of the disease have proven specific.

Investigations
See Section 1.1.8.

Differential diagnosis
See Section 1.1.8.

Treatment

Mild disease
Mild disease confined to the skin and joints responds well to chloroquine, non-steroidal anti-inflammatory drugs (NSAIDs) and low-dose steroids either single or in combination.

Severe disease
Severe lupus with major organ involvement (kidneys and brain) requires more powerful immunosuppressive therapy using steroids and cyclophosphamide.

Phospholipid syndrome
Patients with the phospholipid syndrome require prophylactic antithrombotic therapy.

All cases
Long-term follow-up with regular monitoring of disease activity is essential. Do not forget general advice regarding sun exposure, potential problems of long-term steroids and oestrogen-based contraception.

Prognosis
The 5-year survival rate for patients with SLE is now over 90%. Patients with renal disease have a higher mortality rate than patients with non-renal disease. Mortality is caused by severe disease activity, sepsis and cardiovascular complications due to atherosclerosis leading to premature coronary heart disease. Screening for disease activity, excluding infection, and screening for risk factors for atherosclerosis are all important in the management of the lupus patient.

FURTHER READING
D'Cruz DP. Systemic lupus erythematosus. *BMJ* 2006; 332: 890–4.

2.4.2 Sjögren's syndrome

Sjögren's syndrome is a chronic autoimmune exocrinopathy predominantly affecting the salivary and lacrimal glands. The clinical picture is dominated by keratoconjunctivitis sicca (KCS) and xerostomia. It may occur by itself (primary Sjögren's syndrome) or in association with one of the connective tissue diseases or rheumatoid arthritis (secondary Sjögren's syndrome; Fig. 62). Primary Sjögren's syndrome is classically associated with anti-Ro and anti-La antibodies.

Epidemiology

- Marked female preponderance: male/female ratio is 1:10.

- Typically affects middle-aged women.

Aetiology/pathology
The cause of Sjögren's syndrome is unknown but is believed to be multifactorial and due to a combination of genetic and environmental factors. Genetic markers include human leucocyte antigen (HLA) subtypes HLA-DR3 and HLA-DQ2. Possible viral factors include hepatitis C, cytomegalovirus and Epstein–Barr virus. Inappropriate apoptosis has recently been implicated in disease initiation, while inhibition of apoptosis as a result of overexpression of the *bcl-2* oncogene has been implicated in the lymphoproliferation seen in established Sjögren's syndrome. The cardinal pathological lesion is inflammatory destruction of salivary glands, mediated by focal periductular CD4+ T-cell infiltrates.

Clinical presentation
KCS manifests as dry gritty eyes (Fig. 63) on a background of fatigue.

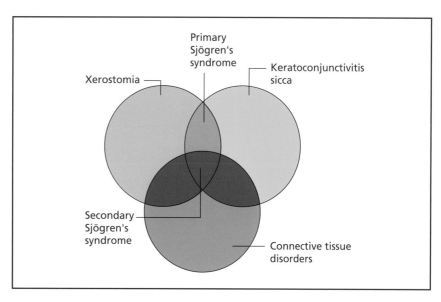

▲ **Fig. 62** Relationship between KCS, xerostomia, and primary and secondary Sjögren's syndrome. (Adapted with permission from Manthorpe R and Jacobsson LT. *Baillière's Clin. Rheumatol.* 1995; 9: 483–96.)

▲ **Fig. 63** Dry eyes in Sjögren's syndrome demonstrated by Schirmer's test: wetting of <5 mm of filter paper in 5 minutes is considered abnormal.

FURTHER READING

Fox RI. Sjögren's syndrome. *Lancet* 2005; 366: 321–31.

Hansen A, Lipsky PE and Dorner T. Immunopathogenesis of primary Sjögren's syndrome: implications for disease management and therapy. *Curr. Opin. Rheumatol.* 2005; 17: 558–65.

Poor salivary secretion leads to dysphagia for dry foods. Salivary gland enlargement (parotid and submandibular) occurs in 50% of cases. Other exocrine glands may be involved in Sjögren's syndrome, eg impaired glandular function in the nasal and sinus epithelium and the vagina, leading to recurrent sinusitis and dyspareunia respectively.

limitation of the damaging local effects of the sicca complex using the following:

- Artificial tears, sugar-free candies and chewing gum
- Meticulous dental hygiene
- Avoidance of diuretics and anticholinergic agents.

Extraglandular features of Sjögren's syndrome

- Non-erosive arthritis.
- Raynaud's phenomenon.
- Cutaneous vasculitis.
- Mixed cryoglobulinaemia.
- Alveolitis.
- Interstitial nephritis.
- Renal tubular acidosis.
- Mononeuritis multiplex.
- Risk of congenital heart block in babies of mothers with Sjögren's syndrome who are Ro antibody positive.

Immunosuppressive therapy is of little value in uncomplicated Sjögren's syndrome.

Complications

There is an increased risk of B-cell lymphoma, estimated to be 33-fold in an Italian study.

Lymphoma in Sjögren's syndrome

Consider lymphoma if there is:

- persistent cervical lymph node enlargement;
- persistent hard or nodular salivary or lacrimal gland enlargement;
- lung shadowing;
- monoclonal cryoglobulins;
- progressive fall in serum immunoglobulins.

Investigation

For laboratory findings, tests for KCS, the rose bengal test and tests for xerostomia, see Section 1.1.10.

Treatment

Therapy for Sjögren's syndrome is limited to symptomatic relief and

2.4.3 Systemic sclerosis (scleroderma)

Scleroderma is an autoimmune disorder characterised by the excessive deposition of collagen. It leads to fibrosis and vascular obliteration within the skin, and frequently within other organs including the lung, heart, kidneys and gastrointestinal tract.

Aetiology/immunopathogenesis

Despite wide-ranging immunological activation, it has been difficult to propose a single unifying immunopathogenic model for scleroderma. Several environmental agents (silica and organic solvents) have been implicated in disease initiation, but conclusive epidemiological evidence is lacking. A genetic component is exemplified by human leucocyte antigen (HLA) associations (various HLA-DR alleles) with certain disease subsets. One recent hypothesis argues that microchimerism as a result of persistence of fetal T cells in the mother might cause scleroderma by initiating a graft-versus-host response; another describes the presence of stimulatory autoantibodies against the platelet-derived growth factor receptor that can activate collagen gene expression in fibroblasts.

> **Key immunological features in scleroderma**
>
> - Skin and lung lesions infiltrated by activated CD4⁺ and CD8⁺ T cells.
> - Increased expression of adhesion molecules from the selectin/integrin and immunoglobulin gene superfamily.
> - Increased production of T-helper (Th)-1 and Th-2 cytokines: interleukin (IL)-1, IL-2, IL-4, IL-6, IL-8, tumour necrosis factor and transforming growth factor β.
> - Polyclonal B-cell activation leading to hypergammaglobulinaemia and autoantibody production.

TABLE 31 CLASSIFICATION OF SCLERODERMA

Disease extent	Features
Systemic	Diffuse cutaneous systemic sclerosis (DCSS) Limited cutaneous systemic sclerosis (LCSS) Systemic sclerosis without scleroderma Overlap syndrome
Localised	Morphoea (localised and generalised) Linear scleroderma

TABLE 32 FEATURES HELPFUL IN DIFFERENTIATING DCSS FROM LCSS

	DCSS	LCSS
Extent of skin thickening	Truncal and acral	Acral
Timing of relationship between skin thickening and Raynaud's phenomenon	Simultaneous or skin first	Prolonged Raynaud's phenomenon before skin
Joints and tendon	Contractures and tendon friction rubs	Infrequent involvement
Calcinosis	Uncommon	Prominent
Visceral involvement	Renal, myocardial, inflammatory lung disease	Pulmonary hypertension
Serum autoantibodies	Anti-Scl-70 (30%)	Anti-centromere (70%)

Epidemiology

There is an annual incidence of 18 per 10 million in the UK. The prevalence is estimated to be 1 in 10,000. The female/male ratio is 3:1 and the incidence increases with age: it is most common in those aged 30–50 years.

Clinical presentation

The classification of scleroderma is shown in Table 31.

Diffuse cutaneous scleroderma

The onset may be abrupt and may present as swollen hands (see Fig. 26), face and feet, which is also associated with new or recent onset of Raynaud's phenomenon. Fatigue is common and overt weakness may be present due to coexisting myositis. Examination reveals an inability to pinch skin folds, and the loss of skin lines and creases in involved areas. An evaluation of swallowing, breathing, renal and cardiac functions may reveal abnormalities (Table 32).

Limited cutaneous systemic sclerosis

Limited systemic sclerosis was previously known as CREST (*c*alcinosis, *R*aynaud's, *o*esophageal dysfunction, *s*clerodactyly, *t*elangiectasia). Typically the patients are female, aged 30–50 years, have a long history of Raynaud's phenomenon and have recent skin involvement limited to the hands, face and feet (Table 32). Other features include:

- calcium deposition in the skin (calcinosis) (Fig. 64);

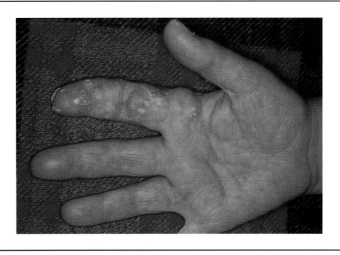

▲ **Fig. 64** Calcinosis cutis in the index finger of a patient with LCSS.

- dilated blood vessels (telangiectasia, Fig. 65) in the palms and face;

- oesophageal dysmotility with or without reflux (Fig. 66).

Systemic sclerosis without scleroderma

Some patients have visceral disease without cutaneous involvement. The presence of anti-centromere, anti-Scl-70 or anti-nucleolar antibodies is helpful in making the diagnosis.

Visceral involvement

The clinical spectrum of visceral involvement in scleroderma includes the following.

- Gastrointestinal tract: small mouth aperture and oesophageal hypomotility (90% of cases); malabsorption, wide-mouthed colonic diverticulae and rarely pneumatosis cystoides intestinalis; and faecal incontinence.

- Lungs: pulmonary fibrosis, aspiration pneumonia, recurrent chest infections, pleural thickening, effusion and calcification, spontaneous pneumothorax, pulmonary hypertension, pulmonary vasculitis and bronchoalveolar carcinoma.

- Cardiovascular system: pericarditis with effusion, myocardial fibrosis causing dysrhythmias and congestive cardiac failure.

- Kidney: hypertension, scleroderma renal crisis (accelerated hypertension) and progressive renal failure.

Investigations

Antinuclear antibodies
Antinuclear antibodies occur in 90% of patients. Three well-defined,

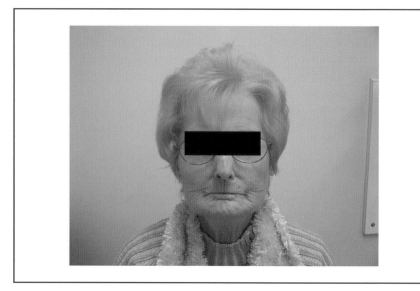

▲ **Fig. 65** Telangiectasia in a patient with LCSS.

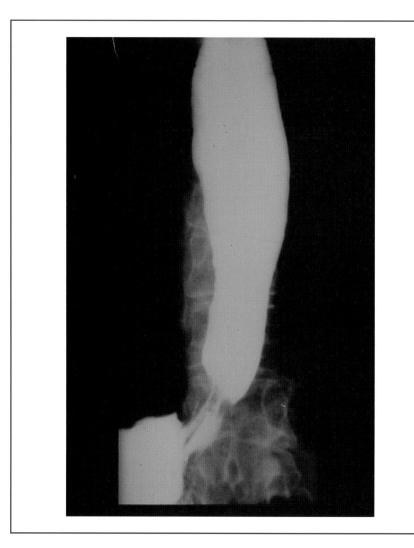

▲ **Fig. 66** Oesophageal dysmotility in a patient with scleroderma.

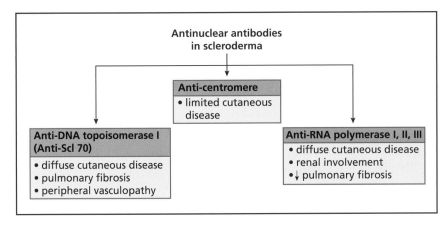

▲ Fig. 67 Antinuclear antibodies in scleroderma enable the definition of three mutually exclusive specificities.

FURTHER READING

Charles C, Clements P and Furst DE. Systemic sclerosis: hypothesis-driven treatment strategies. *Lancet* 2006; 367: 1683–91.

Hochberg MC, Silman AJ, Smolen JS, Weinblatt ME and Weisman MH, eds. *Rheumatology*. St Louis: Mosby, 2003.

Isenberg DA, Maddison PJ, Woo P, Glass DN and Breedveld FC, eds. *Oxford Textbook of Rheumatology*. Oxford: Oxford University Press, 2004.

mutually exclusive specificities have been defined for investigation (Fig. 67), each associated with certain clinical features.

Hand radiography
Look for loss of terminal phalangeal tufts and soft-tissue calcification (calcinosis).

Visceral involvement
Assess the extent of gastrointestinal involvement (use manometry, endoscopy and contrast studies) and lung involvement (use pulmonary function tests including transfer factor to look for restrictive defect, as well as high-resolution CT scans). Regular monitoring of blood pressure, renal function and urinalysis is essential in diffuse disease (owing to the risk of scleroderma renal crisis). Use Doppler echocardiography to detect pulmonary hypertension.

Treatment
Scleroderma is incurable. Treatment is aimed at:

- alleviating the symptoms of Raynaud's phenomenon;

- alleviating the symptoms of reflux oesophagitis and gastrointestinal hypomotility;

- preventing the progression of lung fibrosis by the use of immunosuppressive therapy;

- preventing the progression of pulmonary hypertension with prostaglandins (eg iloprost), endothelin antagonists (eg bosentan) and phosphodiesterase type 5 antagonists (eg sildenafil);

- preventing renal crisis by using a prophylactic low dose of an angiotensin-converting enzyme inhibitor.

The symptoms of Raynaud's phenomenon can be alleviated by stopping smoking, wearing thermal gloves, avoiding cold temperatures and prompt treatment of digital infections and ulcers. Oral vasodilators (calcium channel blockers) are useful for frequent attacks. Prostacyclin infusions are useful in treating severe digital ischaemia.

Prognosis
The 5-year survival rate ranges from 30 to 70%. Adverse prognostic features include male sex, extent of skin involvement, and heart, lung and renal disease.

2.5 Vasculitides

There is no single system of classification that would satisfy the heterogeneous group of vasculitides. In practical terms, it is best to classify the vasculitides using a combination of blood vessel size and underlying pathogenic mechanism(s), where these are known (Fig. 68).

2.5.1 Giant-cell arteritis and polymyalgia rheumatica

Aetiology/pathophysiology/pathology

Giant-cell arteritis (GCA) and polymyalgia rheumatica (PMR) are related disorders with common epidemiological, clinical and serological features. Although GCA is a large-vessel vasculitis, PMR is a clinical syndrome characterised by prolonged proximal girdle pain and stiffness.

The aetiology of GCA and PMR is unknown. The clear preponderance of both disorders in elderly people remains unexplained. An increased frequency of human leucocyte antigen

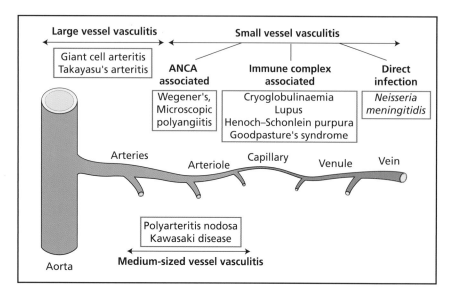

▲ **Fig. 68** Classification of vasculitides according to vessel size and underlying mechanisms. (Modified with permission from Jennette JC and Falk RJ. Small vessel vasculitis. *N. Engl. J. Med.* 1997; 337: 1512–23.)

(HLA)-DR4 and polymorphisms of the HLA-DRB1 genes suggests a genetic predisposition.

The cellular infiltrate in the synovium in PMR is very similar to the infiltrate found in the vascular lesions of GCA:

- CD68+ macrophages;
- CD4+ T cells;
- giant cells.

A striking feature is the strong expression of HLA class II antigens on synovial and inflammatory cells. GCA affects all layers of the vessel wall but particularly the internal elastic lamina, where a granulomatous giant-cell reaction is prominent. The thoracic aorta and its branches are commonly affected. Many of the characteristic clinical manifestations are the result of involvement of branches of the external carotid artery.

Epidemiology

The great majority (90%) of patients are over 60 years of age, with a female preponderance. GCA is the most common of the primary systemic vasculitides in white people (incidence 178 per 10 million).

Clinical presentation

Common

Mild or severe headache occurs in two-thirds of patients, often on a background of fatigue, fever and weight loss. PMR, with its characteristic proximal girdle pain and stiffness, occurs in 50% of patients with GCA and is the presenting feature in 25%. Claudication of the jaw muscles, which produces pain on chewing, occurs in 40%, whereas visual symptoms resulting from

ophthalmic artery involvement occur in 20% of patients.

Uncommon/rare

Occasionally, patients may present with a pyrexia of unknown origin or dissecting aneurysms of the aorta.

Physical signs

Common

Scalp tenderness, frequently over the superficial temporal and occipital arteries, is highly suggestive of GCA and occurs in 40% of patients.

Uncommon

These include arterial bruits, asymmetrical BP and absent pulses in extremities, and ophthalmoscopic evidence of ischaemic optic neuritis.

Investigations

There is no specific serological test. Elevated acute-phase markers, particularly erythrocyte sedimentation rate (ESR) (>40 mm/hour) and C-reactive protein (CRP), occur in 80% of patients and are useful indices for monitoring treatment. Arterial biopsy is recommended for diagnostic confirmation of GCA (Fig. 69) but, in practice, some clinicians reserve biopsy for patients who fail to respond to steroids. Arterial biopsy

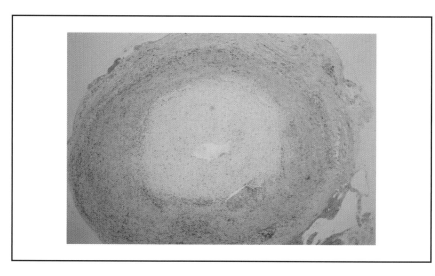

▲ **Fig. 69** Occluded temporal artery in a patient with GCA showing thickening and lymphocytic infiltration throughout the vessel wall. (Courtesy of Dr L. Bridges, Leeds General Infirmary.)

is not required in PMR, although it is positive in 10–20% of patients.

Differential diagnosis

A wide range of disorders may occasionally mimic PMR. Consider the alternative diagnoses listed in the Key point below in cases of diagnostic doubt or where the patient fails to respond promptly to steroid therapy.

Differential diagnosis of PMR

- Infection: tuberculosis and endocarditis.
- Autoimmune rheumatic disease: rheumatoid arthritis, inflammatory muscle disease and systemic lupus.
- Neoplasia.
- Parkinsonism.
- Hypothyroidism.
- Chronic fatigue syndrome.

Treatment

Both GCA and PMR are exquisitely sensitive to steroids. Indeed, failure to respond to steroids is sufficient cause for the original diagnosis to be questioned. The dose of steroids required to suppress inflammation is higher in GCA (40–60 mg/day), whereas 10–20 mg is sufficient in PMR. The response to treatment is monitored using a combination of clinical and acute-phase end-points (ESR and CRP). As most patients require treatment for 1–2 years, it is essential to be alert to the problems of long-term corticosteroid therapy.

Complications

Permanent visual loss occurs in 15–20% of patients with GCA. A smaller percentage develop strokes and aortic aneurysms.

Prognosis

The overall prognosis for PMR is good, with 75% of patients stopping steroids by 2 years. The prognosis in GCA is determined by visual involvement (see above).

FURTHER READING

Bird HA, Leeb BF, Montecucco CM, *et al*. A comparison of diagnostic criteria for polymyalgia rheumatica. *Ann. Rheum. Dis*. 2005; 64: 626–9.

Gonzalez-Gay MA. The diagnosis and management of patients with giant cell arteritis. *J. Rheumatol*. 2005; 32: 1186–8.

Salvarani C, Cantini F, Niccoli L, *et al*. Acute phase reactants and the risk of relapse/recurrence in polymyalgia rheumatica: a prospective follow-up study. *Arthritis Rheum*. 2005; 53: 33–8.

2.5.2 Wegener's granulomatosis

Aetiology/pathophysiology/pathology

Wegener's granulomatosis and microscopic polyangiitis (MPA) represent a spectrum of small-vessel vasculitides associated with antineutrophil cytoplasmic antibodies (ANCAs; see *Nephrology*, Sections 1.4.3, 1.4.5 and 2.7.6).

The aetiology is unknown. Wegener's granulomatosis is characterised by necrotising granulomatous vasculitis with little or no immune deposits. Kidney biopsies typically show a pauci-immune glomerulonephritis.

Epidemiology

Wegener's granulomatosis affects both sexes equally. The peak incidence is in the fourth decade. The incidence of ANCA-associated vasculitis in the UK is estimated to be 20 per 10 million population annually.

Clinical presentation

Common

Most patients present with a pulmonary–renal syndrome (Fig. 70) on a background of upper respiratory tract involvement (haemoptysis, sinusitis, destruction of the nasal septum and epistaxis); 50% have ocular involvement in the form of conjunctivitis, scleritis and uveitis.

Uncommon

An uncommon presentation is cutaneous vasculitis with nail-fold infarcts and purpura.

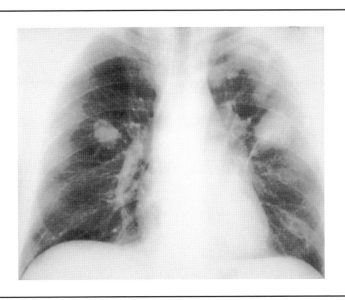

▲**Fig. 70** CXR depicting bilateral lung nodules caused by pulmonary vasculitis in a patient with Wegener's granulomatosis.

Physical signs

Common

Despite the severity of systemic vasculitis, overt physical signs may be limited to a red eye in early disease. A collapsed nasal septum leading to a saddle nose is characteristic of established disease.

Uncommon/rare

- Proptosis caused by retro-orbital granulomas (Fig. 71).

- Cranial nerve deficits resulting from the spread of inflammation from the sinuses.

Investigations

ANCAs directed against proteinase-3 in high titre that appear in this clinical setting are highly suggestive of Wegener's granulomatosis (see Section 3.2.5). Histological confirmation of vasculitis on tissue biopsy (of kidneys, nose or lung) is essential. Approximately 10% of patients are ANCA negative. The severity of inflammation is established by measuring serum C-reactive protein.

Differential diagnosis

The diagnosis is clear-cut in patients presenting with ANCA-positive granulomatous vasculitis on a background of sinus, lung and kidney disease. Other disorders that present with a pulmonary–renal syndrome (Table 33) may occasionally pose problems.

Treatment

Emergency/short term

Combined treatment with steroids and cyclophosphamide induces remission in 90% of patients. In patients without critical organ involvement, low-dose methotrexate is a suitable alternative to cyclophosphamide for remission induction.

Long term

Recent evidence from randomised controlled trials shows that remission can be maintained by the early substitution of cyclophosphamide by azathioprine, thus limiting cyclophosphamide-induced toxicity. However, 50% of patients will relapse within 5 years. Note the increased risk of bladder malignancy and acute leukaemia with long-term cyclophosphamide therapy.

> ⚠ Be vigilant for infective problems (eg *Pneumocystis* pneumonia) that are associated with long-term immunosuppression.

The role of co-trimoxazole in preventing infection-induced relapse is controversial.

> 🔑 Consider the use of intravenous immunoglobulin and therapeutic monoclonal antibodies (anti-CD52 and anti-CD20) in patients unresponsive to standard medication. The role of anti-cytokine treatment (anti-tumour necrosis factor) in Wegener's granulomatosis is under debate in view of the mixed results seen in open and randomised trials.

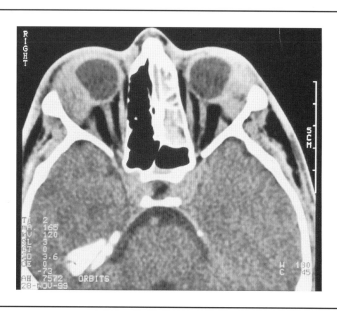

▲ **Fig. 71** Bilateral orbital masses in a patient with Wegener's granulomatosis. (Courtesy of Dr R. Melsom, Bradford Royal Infirmary.)

TABLE 33 DIFFERENTIAL DIAGNOSIS OF THE PULMONARY–RENAL SYNDROME	
Disorder	**Key investigations**
Wegener's granulomatosis/MPA	ANCA and histology
Goodpasture's syndrome	Antiglomerular basement membrane antibody and renal histology
Lupus	Antinuclear antibody and serum complement
Mixed cryoglobulinaemia	Cryoglobulin, rheumatoid factor and serum complement

ANCA, antineutrophil cytoplasma antibodies; MPA, microscopic polyangiitis.

Complications

Common

- Chronic renal failure in 40% of cases.

- Collapsed nasal septum and subglottic stenosis in 30% of cases.

- Iatrogenic infertility in 50% of cases.

Uncommon/rare

- Nasolacrimal duct obstruction.

Prognosis

The 5-year survival rate is >80%. This is largely determined by the patient's renal function at presentation. Significant long-term morbidity is caused by complications of the disease and its treatment.

FURTHER READING

Hellmich B, Lamprecht P and Gross WL. Advances in the treatment of Wegener's granulomatosis. *Curr. Opin. Rheumatol.* 2006; 18: 25–32.

2.5.3 Polyarteritis nodosa

Aetiology/pathophysiology/pathology

This is an immune complex-mediated vasculitis affecting medium-sized blood vessels. The aetiology is unknown. It is associated with hepatitis B antigenaemia in 20% of cases. Vasculitic lesions are triggered by deposition of immune complexes in endothelium with a marked granulocytic infiltration of media, leading to aneurysmal dilatation.

Epidemiology

The peak incidence is in the fourth decade. The estimated annual incidence is 2–9 per 10 million population.

Clinical presentation

Common

Some 40–70% of patients present with a purpuric or urticarial rash, myalgia, arthralgia and peripheral neuropathy, on a background of weight loss, hypertension and renal impairment.

Uncommon/rare

- Bowel perforation.

- Orchitis.

- Congestive heart failure.

Physical signs

Common

- Cutaneous signs.

- 'Glove and stocking' sensory loss.

- Mononeuritis multiplex.

- Areflexia.

Uncommon/rare

- Testicular swelling.

- Papilloedema.

- Retinal detachment.

Investigations

The following are the key diagnostic investigations:

- visceral/renal angiography to demonstrate aneurysms (Fig. 72);

- tissue biopsy (muscle, sural nerve or kidney) for evidence of vasculitis.

Also assess renal function and hepatitis B status. Use C-reactive protein to assess the severity of inflammation.

Differential diagnosis

The absence of glomerulonephritis and negative antineutrophil cytoplasmic antibody in polyarteris nodosa helps differentiate it from microscopic polyangiitis. Consider the possibility of drug-induced vasculitis in young males, eg amphetamine or cocaine abuse may cause aneurysms.

Treatment

Systemic disease requires combined therapy with steroids and cyclophosphamide for about 1 year. Steroids alone are adequate for polyarteritis nodosa confined to the skin.

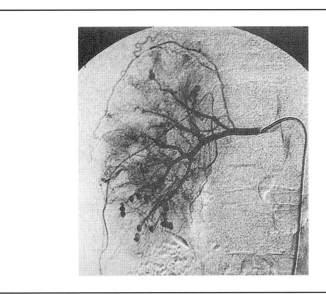

▲**Fig. 72** Multiple aneurysms affecting medium-sized vessels in the right kidney of a patient with hepatitis B-associated polyarteritis nodosa. (Reproduced with permission from Chauveau D and Christophe JL. Renal aneurysms in hepatitis B-associated polyarteritis nodosa. *N. Engl. J. Med.* 1995; 332: 1070.)

Polyarteritis nodosa associated with hepatitis B is best treated with a combination of antiviral agents, ie vidarabine/lamivudine combined with interferon alfa.

Complications

Common

- Chronic renal failure.

- Hypertension.

Uncommon/rare

- Bowel infarction.

- Acute bowel perforation.

Prognosis

Adverse prognostic factors causing increased mortality include proteinuria >1 g/day, raised serum creatinine and visceral involvement. The 5-year mortality rate in patients with all three factors is 46%.

FURTHER READING

Colmagna I and Maldonado-Cocco JA. Polyarteritis nodosa revisited. *Curr. Rheumatol. Rep.* 2005; 7: 288–96.

2.5.4 Cryoglobulinaemic vasculitis

Aetiology/pathophysiology/pathology

This is an immune complex-mediated small-vessel vasculitis associated with mixed cryoglobulinaemia (MC) types II and III (see Table 7). The precise reasons why immunoglobulins cryoprecipitate is not known. Of cases of MC, 60–80% are driven by an underlying hepatitis C virus (HCV) infection. Conversely, up to 50% of patients with HCV infections have MC, although only a small minority develop vasculitis.

Type I cryoglobulins are associated with lymphoproliferative disease and rarely cause vasculitis.

Epidemiology

- Female preponderance.

- Estimated incidence 1 in 100,000.

- Higher incidence in southern Europe, reflecting the prevalence of HCV.

Clinical presentation

Common

- Triad of cutaneous vasculitis, glomerulonephritis and arthralgia (see Fig. 7).

- Skin involvement occurs in almost all cases.

Uncommon/rare

- Mononeuritis multiplex.

- Abdominal pain.

Physical signs

Common

- Purpuric skin rash.

- Raynaud's phenomenon.

Uncommon/rare

- Sensory deficits.

- Areflexia.

Investigations

Important serological clues to the presence of MC are a markedly low C4 and a positive rheumatoid factor. Ensure that a blood sample for cryoglobulins is collected correctly at 37°C and transported immediately to the laboratory (Fig. 73).

Check HCV serology, including HCV RNA in the cyroprecipitate. A routine investigation for other infective triggers (endocarditis, syphilis, Lyme disease, malaria and HIV) reportedly associated with MC is not warranted in the absence of suggestive clinical clues. Perform a renal biopsy to assess renal damage.

Differential diagnosis

See Table 6.

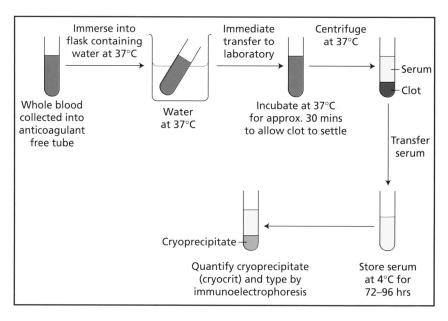

▲ **Fig. 73** Steps in the detection of cryoglobulins in the laboratory.

Treatment

HCV-associated MC
Interferon alfa is the treatment of choice, although rapidly progressive disease may require immunosuppressive therapy (mycophenolate mofetil may be particularly indicated).

Idiopathic MC with progressive renal or hepatic disease
Immunosuppressive therapy using steroids and cyclophosphamide or azathioprine. Plasmapheresis is a useful adjunct for the treatment of acute exacerbations, irrespective of the underlying aetiology. Rituximab, an anti-CD20 monoclonal antibody, appears to be an effective alternative therapeutic option in both HCV-associated and idiopathic MC.

Complications

Common
- Chronic renal failure in 50% of patients.
- Hypertension.
- Leg ulcers.

Uncommon/rare
- Liver failure.
- B-cell lymphoma.

Prognosis
The long-term outcome is determined by the extent of renal disease.

2.5.5 Behçet's disease

Aetiology/pathophysiology/pathology
Behçet's disease is a syndrome of unknown aetiology, with vasculitis of veins and arteries of all sizes, hypercoagulability and neutrophil hyperfunction. It is diagnosed on clinical grounds, after the exclusion of similar diseases.

Epidemiology
It is most common in populations living along the 'Silk Road': Japan, Korea and China through the Middle East to Turkey. The incidence and severity of the disease are associated with human leucocyte antigen (HLA)-B51 in these populations, but not in white populations.

Clinical presentation
The disease typically presents with exacerbations and remissions.

> **Criteria for Behçet's disease**
>
> Defined by the International Study Group for Behçet's Disease as follows.
>
> - Oral ulceration (at least three times per year).
> - At least two of the following: genital ulceration (95% of cases), eye lesions (50–70% of cases), skin lesions (70–90% of cases) and pathergy.
> - Absence of other diagnosis.

Common
Skin There will usually be:

- aphthous ulcers;
- genital ulcers;
- erythema nodosum;
- vasculitic and acneiform lesions;
- superficial thrombophlebitis at venepuncture sites;
- pathergy, ie pustules at sites of skin puncture or minor trauma (eg bra straps, see Fig. 74).

Eye Look for the following.

- Anterior or posterior uveitis: red painful eye, loss of visual acuity and hypopyon.
- Retinal vasculitis: loss of visual acuity.

Urgent ophthalmological opinion is necessary, even in patients who are asymptomatic, because uveitis and retinal vasculitis are common causes of blindness in Behçet's disease.

Joints These are involved in 50–60% of cases by arthralgia or arthritis, which usually affects large joints and which is non-erosive.

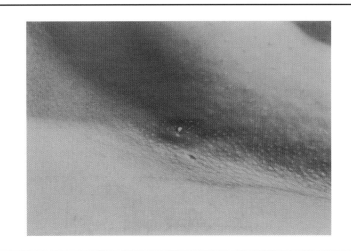

▲**Fig. 74** Pathergy: pustular/acneiform lesions occurring along the line of the bra strap in a woman with Behçet's disease.

Uncommon

- Nervous system (affected in 10–20% of cases): cerebral vasculitis (transient ischaemic attacks, stroke, fits, progressive dementia and meningoencephalitis).

- Respiratory system: pulmonary vasculitis (episodes of dyspnoea and haemoptysis) and pulmonary embolism.

- Gastrointestinal system: intestinal vasculitis (abdominal pain, constipation, mesenteric angina and occasionally infarction with bloody diarrhoea).

- Cardiac: myocardial ischaemia or infarction.

Investigation

- Erythrocyte sedimentation rate and C-reactive protein are sometimes elevated in active disease.

- Biopsies show vasculitis, with neutrophil infiltration of small and medium-sized vessels.

- In cerebral disease CT is usually normal, but MRI may show multiple high-signal white matter lesions (Fig. 75).

- Lumbar puncture may show raised protein, cells (lymphocytes and neutrophils) or neither.

- There is no diagnostic test: most investigations are conducted to exclude other diseases. The presence of raised serum angiotensin-converting enzyme and strongly positive antinuclear antibody, rheumatoid factor or antineutrophil cytoplasmic antibody should prompt you to consider an alternative diagnosis.

Differential diagnosis

- Herpes simplex (recurrent oral and genital lesions).

- Inflammatory bowel disease (gastrointestinal lesions).

- Multiple sclerosis (central nervous system lesions).

- Seronegative arthritis (arthritis and uveitis).

- Sarcoidosis (erythema nodosum, arthritis and uveitis).

- Sweet's syndrome (pathergy).

Treatment

'There are some remedies worse than the disease.' (Publicus Syrus, 42 BC)

Behçet's disease is rare and evidence that demonstrates the effectiveness of many of the standard treatments is lacking. The following have been shown to be effective:

- azathioprine and ciclosporin for eye disease;

- thalidomide for aphthous ulcers;

- benzathine benzylpenicillin for joint disease.

High-dose steroids are used for the initial control of acute severe exacerbations. In addition to the agents listed above, the following have been used for long-term treatment: cytotoxics (methotrexate, cyclophosphamide and chlorambucil), colchicine and interferon alfa. Biological agents such as anti-tumour necrosis factor, anti-CD52 or anti-CD18 have shown promise in small groups of patients.

Whatever the therapy chosen, you will need to monitor clinical and laboratory indices for side effects. Remember that Behçet's disease is a relapsing–remitting disease and the patient may be able to enjoy periods of little or no drug therapy.

- Methotrexate and thalidomide cause severe teratogenicity and are contraindicated in pregnancy, which must be avoided for at least 6 months after stopping methotrexate.

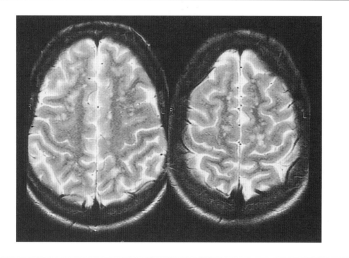

▲**Fig. 75** MRI of the brain of a woman with Behçet's disease, who was suffering from transient ischaemic attacks. Note multiple high-signal lesions.

- Cyclophosphamide and chlorambucil are teratogenic and may cause premature ovarian failure, particularly at high doses.
- These drugs are best avoided in a young female patient but, if considered essential, it is important that she is willing to use reliable contraception and accept the risk of infertility.

Complications

Common

- Venous (including sagittal sinus) thrombosis and pulmonary embolism.

- Pulmonary haemorrhage.

Venous thrombosis is common and presents a management dilemma because anticoagulation, the common treatment, may precipitate life-threatening bleeding from the vasculitic lesions present from Behçet's disease. In practice most patients are anticoagulated without problems, although you would be wise to make a careful risk–benefit assessment and to distinguish pulmonary embolism from pulmonary vasculitis before commencing therapy.

Prognosis

This depends on the site and severity of the disease. HLA-B51 is associated with a worse prognosis.

Morbidity

Blindness occurs in 25% of those with ocular lesions.

Mortality

Death is from thrombosis, haemorrhage or organ failure as a result of the vasculitis.

FURTHER READING

International Study Group for Behçet's Disease. Criteria for diagnosis of Behçet's disease. *Lancet* 1990; 335: 1078–80.

Pipitone N, Olivieri I and Cantini F. New approaches in the treatment of Adamantiades–Behçet's disease. *Curr. Opin. Rheumatol.* 2006; 18: 3–9.

Sansonno D and Dammacco F. Hepatitis C virus, cryoglobulinaemia and vasculitis: immune complex relations. *Lancet Infect. Dis.* 2005; 5: 227–36.

2.5.6 Takayasu's arteritis

Aetiology/pathology

The cause of this arteritis is unknown; the pathology of the arterial lesion is similar to that of giant-cell arteritis (GCA), with focal granulomatous panarteritis associated with infiltration of CD4$^+$ and CD8$^+$ T cells. Fibrosis is a feature of advanced disease.

Epidemiology

It predominantly affects young females of Asian and South American origin. The precise incidence rates in these countries are unknown. The annual incidence in the USA is 2.6 per 10 million population.

Clinical features

Early manifestations include:

- malaise;

- arthralgia;

- myalgia;

- elevated erythrocyte sedimentation rate (ESR).

Later in the course of the disease patients often present with claudication or hypertension, but only a few have inflammatory symptoms. Bruits and an absence of peripheral pulses are noted on physical examination (hence the term 'pulseless disease').

Pattern of disease

The disease primarily affects the aorta and its major branches (subclavian and carotid). A triphasic pattern of disease progression is seen.

- Stage I (pre-pulseless stage): fever, arthralgia and weight loss.
- Stage II (vessel inflammation): vessel pain and tenderness (carotodynia).
- Stage III (burnt-out stage): bruits and ischaemia predominate.

Differential diagnosis

Other disorders that may cause diagnostic confusion (Table 34) should be considered and distinguished on the basis of their distinctive features.

Investigation

Investigations should be aimed at documenting a patient's acute-phase response as an indirect measure of disease activity, excluding other possible diagnoses and performing the appropriate imaging to document the extent of vascular involvement.

Serology

Both C-reactive protein (CRP) and ESR are elevated in 50–70% of cases. Autoantibodies (eg antinuclear antibodies and antineutrophil cytoplasmic antibodies) are not a feature of Takayasu's arteritis.

Aortic arch angiography

The procedure of choice for detecting arterial obstruction is angiography (Fig. 76). This is also helpful in differentiating congenital aortic coarctation from Takayasu's arteritis.

TABLE 34 DIFFERENTIAL DIAGNOSIS OF FEVER AND ABSENT RADIAL PULSES

Disorder	Comments
Takayasu's arteritis	See text
GCA	May be difficult to differentiate in women >40 years old Oriental background, and subclavian and renal artery involvement favour Takayasu's arteritis
Polyarteritis nodosa	Multisystem involvement and aneurysms of visceral/renal circulation (see Section 1.1.16 and 2.5.3)
Connective tissue disorders (sytemic lupus erythematosus, rheumatoid arthritis, scleroderma)	Characteristic clinical picture accompanied by positive serology (see Sections 2.3.3, 2.4.1 and 2.4.3)
Tuberculous aortitis	Causes aneurysms rather than stenoses Look for evidence of tuberculosis elsewhere: CXR, Mantoux test and sputum for acid-fast bacilli
Syphilitic aortitis	Very rare but worth considering Causes aneurysms rather than stenoses Check treponemal serology
Fibromuscular dysplasia	Proliferation of fibrous tissue in the media of large arteries Probably congenital in origin but produces progressive stenoses in young adulthood May be multifocal Non-inflammatory: unresponsive to steroids
Atherosclerosis	Rare cause of absent pulses in young people Consider in the presence of hyperlipidaemia

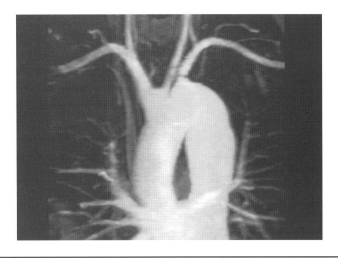

▲**Fig. 76** Magnetic resonance angiogram of aortic arch in a young woman with Takayasu's arteritis showing occlusion of the left subclavian artery at its origin. (Courtesy of Dr H. Marzo-Orteza.)

Non-invasive imaging techniques
Ultrasonography, CT and MRI all provide useful information regarding aortic wall thickness.

MRI is increasingly the imaging modality of choice for the serial evaluation of lesions.

Arterial biopsy
Such a biopsy is seldom required for the diagnosis.

> The usual biopsy finding in Takayasu's arteritis is a granulomatous panarteritis, underlining the difficulty in differentiating this condition from GCA.

Treatment
The following are the important principles:

- medical suppression of inflammation;
- control of hypertension;
- intervention to correct stenotic lesions (in selected cases).

Inflammation
Corticosteroids are the treatment of choice for active Takayasu's arteritis; additional immunosuppressive therapy (azathioprine, cyclophosphamide or methotrexate) is required for patients who fail to respond to steroids. Monitor response to therapy using CRP/ESR.

Hypertension
Management is with aggressive antihypertensive therapy.

Surgery
Surgery may be required in up to 50% of patients. Indications include:

- critical renal artery stenosis causing hypertension;
- severe carotid stenosis;
- significant aortic regurgitation.

Prognosis
For all patients, the 20-year survival rate is about 80%. In patients with one or more complications (retinopathy, hypertension,

aortic valve disease and arterial aneurysms), this is reduced to 65%. Major causes of disability and/or mortality are heart failure, strokes and blindness.

FURTHER READING

Liang P and Hoffman GS. Advances in the medical and surgical treatment of Takayasu arteritis. *Curr. Opin. Rheumatol.* 2005; 17: 16–24.

2.5.7 Systemic Still's disease

Aetiology/pathology

Adult-onset Still's disease (AOSD) is an acute systemic inflammatory disorder of unknown aetiology that frequently poses a diagnostic challenge because of the lack of pathognomonic clinical or laboratory features exhibited by those suffering from it.

Epidemiology

The disorder affects males and females approximately equally, with a slight preponderance of females. Three-quarters of patients are aged between 16 and 35 years at disease onset.

Clinical presentation

Typically presents as a pyrexia of unknown origin with spiking fever, arthralgia, an evanescent rash and multiorgan involvement.

Common

A fleeting maculopapular rash is characteristic and frequently mistaken for drug allergy because penicillin is often given for the sore throat associated with the disease prodrome. The other features usually present include:

- sore throat;

- generalised myalgia without objective evidence of myositis;

- arthralgia;

- polyarthralgia affecting the knees, wrists and fingers is common, with some patients developing frank arthritis with effusions;

- weight loss is a non-specific reflection of a persistent acute-phase response;

- lymphadenopathy and splenomegaly;

- pleuritis and pericarditis is associated with effusions in some patients.

Uncommon

- Renal failure.

- Disseminated intravascular coagulation.

Investigation

In the absence of a specific marker, the diagnosis of AOSD is entirely based on clinical grounds (Table 35). Detailed laboratory investigations and appropriate imaging are essential to exclude infections, autoimmune rheumatic disease (see Section 2.4) and haematological malignancy. Neutrophil counts and inflammatory markers are raised: marked hyperferritinaemia (1,500–10,000 µg/L, normal <300 µg/L) is a feature in >90% of patients and correlates with disease activity. Although ferritin is a non-specific acute-phase protein, the magnitude of its rise in this clinical setting is a useful pointer to AOSD.

The 'classic triad' occurs in <50% of patients with AOSD:

- arthritis;
- persistent spiking fever;
- fleeting maculopapular rash.

Virtually all patients with AOSD have markedly elevated erthrocyte sedimentation rate, C-reactive protein and neutrophil counts. Serum ferritin levels are usually very high.

Differential diagnosis

Prolonged fever with joint pains has a wide differential diagnosis covering a range of disorders (Table 36). A thorough history is therefore crucial.

The crucial clue in AOSD is the long list of negative investigations, which in a systemically unwell patient presenting with high fever, rash, arthralgia and myalgia accompanied by a pronounced acute-phase response raises the distinct possibility of this disorder.

TABLE 35 CLASSIFICATION CRITERIA FOR AOSD. A DEFINITE DIAGNOSIS REQUIRES A PATIENT TO HAVE FIVE OR MORE CRITERIA, INCLUDING TWO OR MORE MAJOR CRITERIA	
Major criteria	Fever of 39°C or higher, lasting for 1 week or longer Arthralgia lasting 2 weeks or longer Typical rash Leucocytosis (>10 × 10⁹/L) including >80% granulocytes
Minor criteria	Sore throat Lymphadenopathy and/or splenomegaly Liver dysfunction Negative rheumatoid factor and antinuclear antibodies
Exclusions	Infections (especially sepsis and infectious mononucleosis) Malignancies (especially malignant lymphoma) Rheumatic diseases (especially polyarteritis nodosa and rheumatoid vasculitis with extra-articular features)

TABLE 36 DIFFERENTIAL DIAGNOSIS OF FEVER AND ARTHRITIS

Condition	Diagnosis
Infection	Direct invasion: bacterial (mycobacteria), fungal and Whipple's disease Indirect: bacterial (acute rheumatic fever) and reactive arthritis
Crystal arthropathy	Urate
Inflammatory disorders	Calcium pyrophosphate Lupus and lupus overlap disorders Necrotising vasculitis AOSD Rheumatoid arthritis Sarcoidosis
Haematological malignancies	Arthritis associated with inflammatory bowel disease

Modified from Van De Putte LBA and Wouters JM. Adult-onset Still's disease. *Bailiére's Clin Rheumatol* 1991; 2: 263275.

Management

Aspirin and other NSAIDs have traditionally been considered first-line therapy, but are successful in only 20% of cases. Over 50% of patients require long-term steroid treatment. Patients with persistent arthropathy require treatment with disease-modifying antirheumatic drugs. A minority of patients who are unresponsive to such conventional immunosuppressive treatment may benefit from anti-tumour necrosis factor therapy.

RHEUMATOLOGY AND CLINICAL IMMUNOLOGY: SECTION 3
INVESTIGATIONS AND PRACTICAL PROCEDURES

3.1 Assessment of acute-phase response

3.1.1 Erythrocyte sedimentation rate

Principle

> The erythrocyte sedimentation rate (ESR), plasma viscosity (PV) and C-reactive protein (CRP) are well-established markers of the acute-phase response (Tables 37 and 38).

The ESR is a measure of the rate of fall of red blood cells in a calibrated vertical tube.

> ESR measures the acute-phase response indirectly by reflecting changes in plasma proteins, particularly:
>
> - fibrinogen;
> - α_2-macroglobulin;
> - immunoglobulins.
>
> The ESR is also significantly influenced by changes in the number, shape and deformability of red blood cells, causing the ESR to rise with a fall in haematocrit.

Indications

As it is influenced by plasma proteins of varying half-lives, the ESR represents, at best, a relatively crude way of assessing a persistent acute-phase response. The PV mirrors changes in the same plasma proteins that influence the ESR, but it is not altered by changes in haematocrit or red cell aggregability.

For this reason and the ease of performing automated assays, there is an increasing tendency to substitute PV for ESR. However, the traditional role of both ESR and PV in monitoring chronic inflammatory disorders is being supplanted by CRP, a highly sensitive marker of the acute-phase response.

3.1.2 C-reactive protein

Principle

C-reactive protein (CRP) is a member of the pentraxin family of proteins and is synthesised in the liver in response to pro-inflammatory cytokines, ie interleukin (IL)-1, IL-6 and tumour necrosis factor, during an acute-phase response. Circulating CRP is easily and accurately measured using nephelometry, a technique that measures the amount of light scattered by immune complexes of

---

TABLE 37 COMPARATIVE UTILITY OF CRP, ESR AND PV AS MARKERS OF TISSUE DAMAGE: I

	CRP	ESR	PV
Change driven by	Cytokines: IL-1, IL-6 and TNF Not dependent on changes in plasma proteins or red cells	Dependent on changes in plasma proteins and red cells	Dependent on changes in plasma proteins; unaffected by changes in red cells
Rapidity of change	Increase within 6 hours of onset of tissue damage; returns to normal within 48 hours of resolution of inflammation/infection	Increase within 24–48 hours of onset of tissue damage; returns to normal over 4–6 days	Kinetics of response similar to ESR
Clinical utility	Highly sensitive and reproducible marker of inflammation, bacterial infection and tissue necrosis Levels correlate with severity	Marker of chronic inflammation/infection Poor correlation with severity	Marker of chronic inflammation/infection

IL, interleukin; TNF, tumour necrosis factor.

TABLE 38 COMPARATIVE UTILITY OF CRP, ESR AND PV AS MARKERS OF TISSUE DAMAGE: II

	CRP	ESR	PV
Disorders characterised by major elevation	Inflammatory disease: rheumatoid arthritis, systemic vasculitis Infection: septicaemia and pyogenic abscesses	Systemic vasculitis Hyperglobulinaemic state: plasma cell dyscrasias, SLE, Sjögren's syndrome Systemic bacterial infection, eg infective endocarditis	As for ESR
Clinical situations associated with discordant responses	Raised ESR with normal CRP. Consider hyperglobulinaemia as in SLE, Sjögren's syndrome (without infection), anaemia and hyperlipidaemia		

SLE, systemic lupus erythematosus.

analyte (in this case CRP) and exogenous antibody. Given a constant antibody concentration, the amount of light scattered reflects the concentration of the analyte.

Indications

Its rapid rise within 6 hours of the onset of tissue damage (peak at 48–72 hours) makes CRP the most useful marker for monitoring inflammatory disease and systemic bacterial infection. Unlike the erythrocyte sedimentation rate or plasma viscosity, CRP is not influenced by changes in plasma proteins or erythrocytes. Recent evidence suggests that CRP concentrations in patients with angina in excess of 2.5 mg/L within the conventional normal range of 0–6 mg/L is predictive of future coronary events.

FURTHER READING

Ng T. Erythrocyte sedimentation rate, plasma viscosity and C-reactive protein in clinical practice. *Br. J. Hosp. Med.* 1999; 58: 521–3.

- - - - - - - - - - - - - - -

Pepys MB. The acute phase response and C-reactive protein. In: Warrell DA, Cox TM and Firth J, eds. *Oxford Textbook of Medicine*, Vol. 2, 4th edn. Oxford: Oxford University Press, 2003: 150–6.

3.2 Serological investigation of autoimmune rheumatic disease

3.2.1 Antibodies to nuclear antigens

Principle

Antibodies to nuclear antigens are detected by indirect immunofluorescence (IIF). Human epithelial cells (HEp-2) are used as a source of antigen. HEp-2 cells are incubated with the patient's serum which contains autoantibodies. IgG antibodies reacting with antigens within the HEp-2 cells are recognised by adding a second anti-IgG antibody (conjugate) that contains a fluorochrome tagged to its Fc end (Fig. 77). Fluorescent microscopy is used to visualise the pattern of immunofluorescence produced by the autoantibody. Recently some laboratories have started using enzyme-linked immunosorbent assays to detect antinuclear antibodies (ANAs).

Indications

A search for ANAs is the key initial investigation (Fig. 78) in patients with suspected systemic lupus erythematosus (SLE), lupus overlap disorders, Sjögren's syndrome and scleroderma (Table 39). Using HEp-2 cells as antigenic substrate, virtually all patients with untreated SLE are ANA positive.

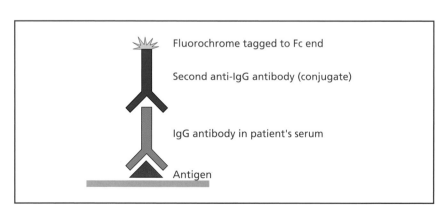

▲**Fig. 77** Diagrammatic representation of IIF for the detection of circulating antibodies.

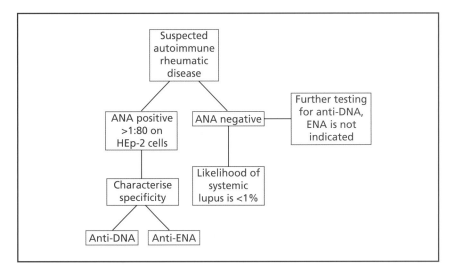

▲**Fig. 78** Algorithm for the use of antibodies to nuclear antigens. ENA, extractable nuclear antigens. (Reproduced with permission from Kavanaugh A, Tomar R, Reveille J, Solomon DH and Homburger HA. Guidelines for clinical use of the antinuclear antibody test and tests for specific autoantibodies to nuclear antigens. *Arch. Pathol. Lab. Med.* 2000; 124: 71–81.)

> Previous reports of rare patients with ANA-negative lupus were based on studies using rodent tissue.

ANAs are not specific for lupus and related disorders; they occur in normal people and in a wide range of inflammatory and infective disorders.

Variants of ANA

Anticentromere antibodies
Antibodies directed against centromere antigens are easily detected by their characteristic pattern on HEp-2 cells by IIF (Fig. 79). Anticentromere antibodies are markers of the limited form of scleroderma, also known as the CREST syndrome (*c*alcinosis, *R*aynaud's, *o*esophageal dysfunction,

sclerodactyly, *t*elangiectasia). Diffuse disease in scleroderma is associated with antibodies to the enzyme DNA topoisomerase (anti-Scl-70). Anti-Scl-70 is associated with more severe disease, especially pulmonary fibrosis.

Antihistone antibodies
Antibodies directed against histones, a group of highly conserved basic proteins in the nucleus, are associated with drug-induced lupus.

3.2.2 Antibodies to double-stranded DNA

Principle
These are detected by a variety of techniques:

- Farr radioisotope assay;
- enzyme-linked immunoassay;
- indirect immunofluorescence using the haemoflagellate *Crithidia luciliae* (Fig. 80).

In practice, enzyme-linked immunoassays are increasingly used in view of their high sensitivity, ease of automation and ability to quantify results reliably (Table 40).

TABLE 39 PREVALENCE OF AUTOANTIBODIES IN AUTOIMMUNE RHEUMATIC DISEASE

Disorder	ANA (%)	DNA (%)	Ro (%)	La (%)	Sm (%)	RNP (%)	ANCA (%)	Centromere (%)	Histones (%)	Jo-1 (%)	Scl-70 (%)
SLE	99–100	60–90	35–60	Accompanies anti-Ro; rare in isolation	30	30–40	25 (p-ANCA)	Rare	50–70 of idiopathic SLE; 90–100 of drug-induced SLE	0	0
Scleroderma	60–90	0–5	0	0	0	0	Not known	60	20	0	20–40
Primary Sjögren's syndrome	40–70	10	40–90	40–90	0	0	Not known	Rare	Not known	0	0
MCTD	100	0–5	0	0	0	100	Not known	Rare	Not known	Variable	Variable
Inflammatory myositis	40–70	0–5	0	0	0	0	Not known	0	Not known	30	0
Wegener's granulomatosis	?5	0	0	0	0	0	80–95 (c-ANCA directed against PR3)	0	Not known	Not known	0
Microscopic polyangiitis	?5	0	0	0	0	0	<80 (p-ANCA directed against MPO)		Not known	Not known	0

ANCA, antineutrophil cytoplasmic antibody; MCTD, mixed connective tissue disease; MPO, myeloperoxidase; PR3, proteinase-3; RNP, ribonucleoprotein.

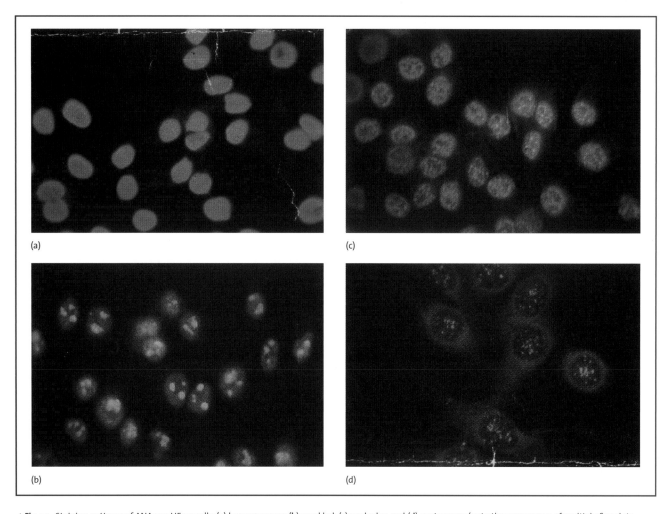

(a)

(c)

(b)

(d)

▲ **Fig. 79** Staining patterns of ANAs on HEp-2 cells: (**a**) homogeneous; (**b**) speckled; (**c**) nucleolar; and (**d**) centromere (note the appearance of multiple fine dots representing staining of the kinetochores of 23 pairs of chromosomes). (Courtesy of Mr K. Taylor, Leeds General Infirmary.)

3.2.3 Antibodies to extractable nuclear antigens

Principle

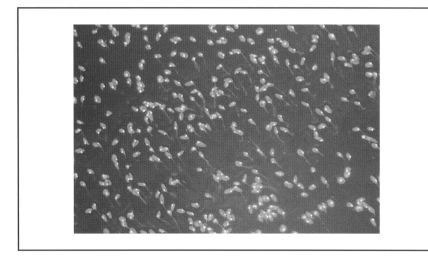

▲ **Fig. 80** Fluorescence confined to the kinetoplast of *Crithidia luciliae* in a serum sample containing high concentrations of anti-DNA antibodies in a patient with active systemic lupus erythematosus.

> Extractable nuclear antigens are a group of saline-extractable antigens known individually as Ro, La, Sm and U1-RNP (uridine ribonucleoprotein). Ro, La and Sm were named after the patients in whom they were first characterised: Robert, Lane and Smith. In conjunction with U1-RNP, these proteins are responsible for splicing and processing mRNA.

Indications

Antibodies to double-stranded DNA are a specific marker of systemic lupus erythematosus (SLE) and are useful for the diagnosis and monitoring of disease activity in SLE. A steady rise in anti-DNA antibody levels heralds a lupus flare in many patients.

These antibodies are detected by a range of techniques:

TABLE 40 COMPARISON OF THREE COMMONLY USED ANTI-DOUBLE-STRANDED DNA ASSAYS IN SLE

	Farr	*Crithidia*	ELISA
Sensitivity	High	High	High
Specificity	High	High	Moderate
Detection of high-avidity antibodies	+++	++	++
Detection of low-avidity antibodies	+	++	+++
Ability to identify individual antibody isotypes (IgG, IgA and IgM)	No	Yes	Yes
Suitability for monitoring disease activity	Yes	No	Yes

ELISA, enzyme-linked immunosorbent assay.

- immunoprecipitation assays such as countercurrent immunoelectrophoresis or double diffusion;

- immunoblotting.

These techniques are specific, but are not suitable for handling large numbers of samples. Enzyme immunoassay is increasingly the method of choice, but this may produce false-positive results in hypergammaglobulinaemic sera.

Indications

- Investigation of systemic lupus erythematosus (SLE).

- Lupus overlap disorders.

- Sjögren's syndrome.

Anti-Ro antibodies

Anti-Ro antibodies correlate with cutaneous disease and vasculitis in SLE. In pregnant women with lupus, anti-Ro antibodies may cross the placenta to cause transient cutaneous lupus in the neonate (5–25% of babies) or permanent congenital heart block (1–3% of babies). Antinuclear antibody-negative, anti-Ro-positive lupus is extremely rare (<1% of lupus patients). Consider primary complement deficiency in such

patients. Anti-La antibodies tend to accompany anti-Ro.

Anti-Sm and anti-U1-RNP antibodies

Anti-Sm antibodies are highly specific for SLE; their prevalence varies with the ethnic background of the patient. Anti-Sm and anti-U1-RNP antibodies tend to occur together because of the shared peptide sequences between Sm and U1-RNP. The presence of anti-U1-RNP antibodies in isolation was thought to identify a group of patients with mixed connective tissue disease, a group of lupus overlap disorders with additional features of polymyositis and scleroderma. Long-term follow-up of the original cohort has raised questions about the existence of mixed connective tissue disease as a distinct entity.

3.2.4 Rheumatoid factor

Principle

Traditional sheep cell agglutination assays have been replaced by latex-enhanced turbidimetry or nephelometry (see Section 3.1.2).

Indications

- Prognostic marker in rheumatoid arthritis (RA).

- IgM rheumatoid factor occurs in 50–90% of patients with RA and in a wide range of other inflammatory and infective disorders. The role of rheumatoid factor as a marker of RA is increasingly being supplanted by antibodies to cyclic citrullinated peptide, which have recently been shown to be highly specific for RA and are predictive of aggressive disease.

3.2.5 Antineutrophil cytoplasmic antibody

Principle

Indirect immunofluorescence using human neutrophil as substrate is used to define patterns of antineutrophil cytoplasmic antibodies (ANCA). A cytoplasmic pattern of fluorescence (c-ANCA) is associated with antibodies directed against proteinase-3 (PR-3-ANCA), whereas a perinuclear pattern (p-ANCA) is associated predominantly with antibodies directed against myeloperoxidase (MPO-ANCA) (Fig. 81). Antigenic specificity is confirmed by enzyme immunoassay.

Indications

PR-3-ANCA and MPO-ANCA are sensitive markers of Wegener's granulomatosis and microscopic polyangiitis, respectively. False positives may occur with infection, malignancy and other inflammatory disorders. In a routine clinical setting, the positive predictive value of ANCA is less than 50%, ie the majority of ANCA-positive patients do not have small-vessel vasculitis.

3.2.6 Serum complement concentrations

Principle

C3 and C4 are assayed by nephelometry (see Section 3.1.2).

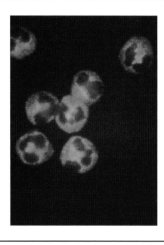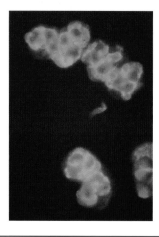

▲ **Fig. 81** ANCA: (**a**) granular cytoplasmic fluorescence with interlobular accentuation characteristic of c-ANCA; (**b**) perinuclear immunofluorescence characteristic of p-ANCA.

Indications

For the investigation of suspected systemic immune-complex disease. Hypocomplementaemia is a characteristic feature of systemic lupus erythematosus and mixed cryoglobulinaemia, but it may also occur as a transient feature with infection, eg bacterial endocarditis.

FURTHER READING

Reveille JD, Solomon DH and the American College of Rheumatology Ad Hoc Committee on immunologic testing guidelines. Evidence-based guidelines for the use of immunologic tests: anticentromere, Scl-70 and nucleolar antibodies. *Arthritis Rheum.* 2003; 49: 399–412.

Savige J, Dimech W, Fritzler M, *et al.* Addendum to the International Consensus Statement on testing and reporting of antineutrophil cytoplasmic antibodies. *Am. J. Clin. Pathol.* 2003; 120: 312–18.

Solomon DH, Kavanaugh AJ, Schur P and the American College of Rheumatology Ad Hoc Committee on immunologic testing guidelines. Evidence-based guidelines for the use of immunologic tests: antinuclear antibody testing. *Arthritis Rheum.* 2002; 47: 434–44.

3.3 Suspected immune deficiency in adults

Principle

Immune deficiency

Suspect immune deficiency when:

- infections are severe, frequent or prolonged;
- unusual (opportunistic) organisms are isolated;
- in relatives of patients with known or suspected hereditary immunodeficiencies.

Antibody deficiency

Antibodies are most important for extracellular organisms and for secondary protection against some viruses. Ask about the following:

- bacterial infections;
- *Giardia* spp.;
- enteroviruses.

Phagocyte defect

Phagocytes (neutrophils and macrophages) are scavengers, engulfing foreign material. They are important in the early response to infection (before the specific immune responses are under way) and, later, they are the effectors against organisms targeted by the specific immune response. Ask about the following:

- septicaemia, periodontitis or deep abscesses with Gram-negative bacteria or staphylococci, or invasive *Candida* or *Aspergillus* spp.;
- poor wound healing.

Screening for ciliary dysfunction

Ciliary dysfunction may masquerade as antibody deficiency. Test for this by placing a piece of saccharine tablet in the nose on the inferior turbinate. The patient should taste sweetness within 20 minutes if their ciliary function is normal.

T-lymphocyte defect

T lymphocytes activate macrophages to kill organisms that they have phagocytosed, kill virus-infected cells and help B cells produce antibodies. Severe cellular defects present in infancy but milder forms may be diagnosed only in adulthood. Ask about the following.

- Viral infections: herpes simplex and zoster, cytomegalovirus (CMV), Kaposi's sarcoma and warts (including cervical intraepithelial neoplasia).
- Intracellular bacterial infections: *Salmonella* infection and mycobacteria, including tuberculosis.
- Mucocutaneous candidiasis.
- Invasive cryptococci (meningitis).
- *Pneumocystis* spp. (pneumonia).

TABLE 41 COMMON CAUSES OF SECONDARY IMMUNODEFICIENCY

Cause	Deficiency
Drugs	
Steroids and cytotoxics	Cellular deficiency or neutropenia (quantitative/functional)
Antiepileptics	Antibody deficiency
Penicillamine, gold and sulfasalazine	Antibody deficiency
Carbimazole	Idiopathic neutropenia
Antibiotics	Disruption of normal bacterial flora
Smoking	Impaired mucociliary clearance
Viral respiratory tract infections	Impaired mucociliary clearance
HIV	Cellular deficiency
Haematological malignancy	Cellular, antibody or complement deficiency
Burns, wounds (skin) and severe eczema	Breach of protective barrier

Consider secondary immunodeficiencies (Table 41).

Complement defects

An intact complement pathway is essential for the opsonisation of microorganisms and solubilisation of immune complexes. Patients with terminal complement component deficiencies are prone to neisserial infection (see Sections 1.1.2 and 2.1.5), whereas early component deficiencies predispose to systemic lupus erythematosus (SLE) and a broader range of bacterial infections.

Practical details

> Detailed immunological investigations should be undertaken in conjunction with a clinical immunologist in order to ensure appropriate test selection.

Your investigations will depend on your clinical assessment. Your aim is to:

- define the immunodeficiency (if any);

- assess your patient's individual risk of opportunistic infection with a view to avoidance, prophylaxis or early treatment.

Basic investigations

For most patients, a sensible starting point would be to check the following.

- FBC and a differential white cell count: lymphopenia is a feature of many cellular defects whereas a marked persistent neutrophilia (even in the absence of sepsis) would point to an adhesion molecule deficiency.

- Serum immunoglobulins as a basic screen of B-cell function. Exclude urinary loss of IgG by performing urine electrophoresis in patients with an isolated low IgG.

- Lymphocyte surface markers (eg CD3, CD4, CD8 for total, helper and cytotoxic T cells; CD19 for B cells; and CD16 for natural killer cells) to quantify numbers of circulating lymphocytes. Close liaison with the clinical immunology laboratory is essential for selection of appropriate markers.

Antibody deficiency

Diagnosing antibody deficiency is relatively straightforward in patients with marked hypogammaglobulinaemia. If serum immunoglobulins are normal or moderately low, or if there is isolated IgA deficiency, check baseline antibody levels to common pathogens (*Streptococcus pneumoniae*) and routine immunisations (tetanus, diphtheria and *Haemophilus influenzae* type b).

> A normal serum immunoglobulin profile does not exclude significant antibody deficiency.

If antibody levels are low, proceed to test immunisation with appropriate killed vaccines or toxoid [tetanus toxoid, Pneumovax (pneumococcal polysaccharide) and *Haemophilus influenzae* type b conjugate] and recheck antibody levels 3–4 weeks later. IgG subclass measurements are of limited value and are meaningless without information about specific antibody production.

> Live vaccines should be avoided in cases of suspected immunodeficiency because of the risk of vaccine-induced disease, eg paralytic poliomyelitis caused by oral polio vaccine.

Establishing the cause If B cells are absent, consider checking for mutations in the following:

- Bruton tyrosine kinase gene (X-linked);

- μ heavy chain gene (autosomal recessive);

- λ5 light chain gene (autosomal recessive);

- Igα (CD79a) gene, a component of the pre-B cell receptor.

> Severe hypogammaglobulinaemia accompanied by lack of circulating B cells is suggestive of a defect in B-cell differentiation.

In male patients with hypogammaglobulinaemia and a normal or high serum IgM, exclude CD40 ligand deficiency.

Complement deficiency

Check the integrity of complement pathways by testing haemolytic activity of the classic and alternate pathways (CH50 and AP50, see Section 2.1.5). Also consider secondary causes:

- C3 nephritic factor, an IgG autoantibody that stabilises the alternate pathway C3 convertase causing consumption of C3 (associated with mesangiocapillary glomerulonephritis);
- immune complex diseases, such as endocarditis or SLE.

T-lymphocyte defect

Total lymphocyte and individual lymphocyte subset numbers are usually low. Check additionally for human leucocyte antigen class I and II expression by flow cytometry. Check lymphocyte proliferation to mitogens such as phytohaemagglutinin (stimulates all lymphocytes) and to antigens such as PPD or tetanus toxoid (stimulate only lymphocytes with appropriate T-cell receptors). Consider *in vivo* intradermal testing to a range of antigens (PPD, *Candida* spp. and tetanus, streptokinase).

Establishing the underlying causes Delineate aetiology in appropriate cases by the following.

- Chromosomal analysis (22q11 associated with absent thymus in DiGeorge syndrome).
- Enzyme assays: adenosine deaminase and purine nucleoside phosphorylase (PNP) deficiency is associated with progressive combined deficiencies.

> A useful clue to PNP deficiency is the presence of marked hypouricaemia, reflecting the key role of PNP in urate production.

Phagocyte defect

Check for cyclical neutropenia. Perform neutrophil counts three times weekly for 1 month. Carry out a nitroblue tetrazolium test (see Fig. 5).

Check for leucocyte adhesion defects: use flow cytometry to check for the presence of adhesion molecules, especially CD18. Assess neutrophil chemotaxis.

Determining risk of infection

Knowledge of the patient's individual immune defect, combined with his or her probable exposure to pathogens, will help determine the likelihood of infection (Table 42). Take a thorough history, including details of any travel or immunisation. Serological tests based on antibody detection are

TABLE 42 PATTERNS OF INFECTION IN IMMUNODEFICIENCY

	Antibody/complement	Cell mediated	Phagocyte
Bacterial	Streptococcus *pneumoniae*	*Salmonella* spp.	*Staphylococcus aureus* *Staphylococcus epidermidis*
	Haemophilus influenzae *Neisseria meningitidis* *Mycoplasma* spp.	*Listeria* spp. *Nocardia* spp. Mycobacteria (TB and aytpical)	*Escherichia coli* *Klebsiella* spp. *Pseudomonas* spp.
Viral	Enteroviruses, including invasive echovirus and polio*	Herpesviruses, including HSV-1 and HSV-2, invasive CMV, lymphomas (EBV) and Kaposi's sarcoma (human herpesvirus 8) Papillomavirus (warts, cervical and anal neoplasia) JC virus (progressive multifocal leucoencephalopathy)	
Fungal		*Candida* spp. (mucocutaneous) *Pneumocystis* spp. Cryptococci	*Candida* spp. (invasive) *Aspergillus* spp.
Protozoal	*Giardia* spp.*	*Toxoplasma* spp. *Cryptosporidium* spp. *Microsporidium* spp.	

* *Giardia* and enteroviral infections are not a feature of complement deficiency.
CMV, cytomegalovirus; EBV, Epstein–Barr virus; HSV, herpes simplex virus.

likely to be unreliable in the presence of immunodeficiency, but may give information about previous exposure (risk of reactivation) or immunity (risk of severe disease if non-immune). Cultures, biopsy and antigen-detection techniques (immunofluoresence or polymerase chain reaction) will usually be necessary to diagnose active infections because clinical features may be atypical in immunodeficient individuals. Invasive investigations may be required.

FURTHER READING

Chapel HM, Misbah S and Webster D. Assessment of the immune system. In: Ochs HD, Smith CIE and Puck JM, eds. *Primary Immunodeficiency Diseases. A Molecular and Cellular Approach*, 2nd edn. Oxford: Oxford University Press, 2006: 611–32.

3.4 Imaging in rheumatological disease

3.4.1 Plain radiology

Principle

The primary use of radiography is to detect changes in bony structure. It is much less useful in soft-tissue pathology.

Indications

Diagnostic

- Differential diagnosis of chronic arthritis: inflammatory and erosive arthritis can be distinguished from osteoarthritis (OA). Distinct forms of inflammatory arthritis can be further differentiated (Fig. 82).

- Back pain: plain radiographs are greatly overused in the assessment of back pain. However, in 'red flag' back pain (see Section 1.1.13) plain radiographs may provide definitive diagnostic information (eg of osteoporotic fracture or ankylosing spondylitis) or provide pointers to appropriate further investigation (eg in cases of suspected malignancy or septic discitis). Plain radiographs hardly ever help in the assessment of neurological problems.

- Metabolic bone disease: diagnostic in Paget's disease (increased trabecular markings; see Fig. 33), supportive in osteomalacia and unhelpful in osteoporosis (unless a fracture is present).

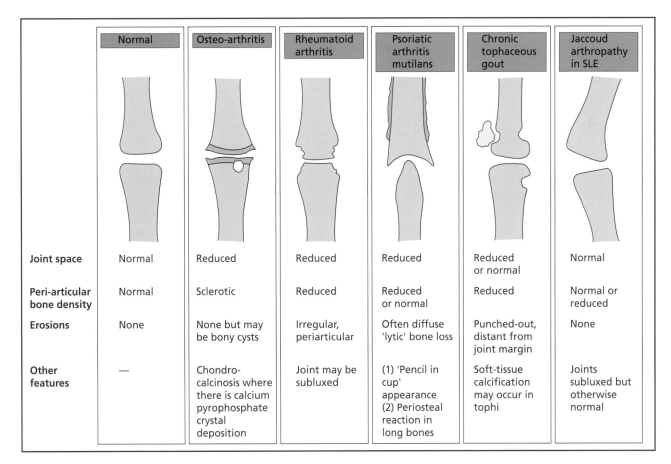

	Normal	Osteo-arthritis	Rheumatoid arthritis	Psoriatic arthritis mutilans	Chronic tophaceous gout	Jaccoud arthropathy in SLE
Joint space	Normal	Reduced	Reduced	Reduced	Reduced or normal	Normal
Peri-articular bone density	Normal	Sclerotic	Reduced	Reduced or normal	Reduced	Normal or reduced
Erosions	None	None but may be bony cysts	Irregular, periarticular	Often diffuse 'lytic' bone loss	Punched-out, distant from joint margin	None
Other features	—	Chondro-calcinosis where there is calcium pyrophosphate crystal deposition	Joint may be subluxed	(1) 'Pencil in cup' appearance (2) Periosteal reaction in long bones	Soft-tissue calcification may occur in tophi	Joints subluxed but otherwise normal

▲**Fig. 82** Schematic representation of radiological changes in major arthritides. These changes are found in advanced, long-standing disease. Radiographs may be normal in early disease.

- Malignancy: gives few definitive diagnostic findings, but often provides strong supportive evidence for both primary and metastatic bone tumours.

Prognosis/disease outcome

Plain radiographs play a major role in assessing the progress of inflammatory arthritis. The development of bony erosions, the progression of erosive changes and the development of secondary osteoarthritic changes are the most robust methods for assessing articular damage, prognosis and response to treatment (see Sections 1.1.14, 1.1.17 and 2.3.3).

In rheumatoid arthritis (RA), annual or biannual serial radiographs of the hands (Fig. 83) and wrists are the most useful means of monitoring the rate of joint damage and assessing the effects of treatment. The early development of erosions is one of the best predictors of aggressive disease. Radiographs of larger joints in RA are only useful in documenting the development of secondary OA. Neck pain or neurological signs in the limbs should provoke radiography of the cervical spine, particularly to look for atlantoaxial subluxation. Views in cervical flexion and extension are required.

Limitations of plain radiographs

- Radiation exposure.
- Failure to detect soft-tissue pathology.
- Changes only appear late in the disease process; neoplastic and inflammatory bone destruction is usually well advanced before it is evident on a plain film.

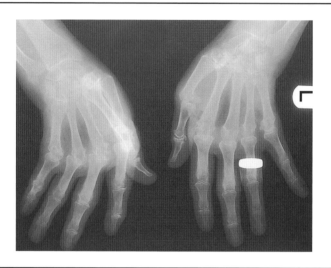

▲ **Fig. 83** Radiograph of the hands in a patient with advanced RA showing deforming, erosive arthropathy.

3.4.2 Bone densitometry

Principle

Plain radiographs cannot provide a reliable assessment of bone mineral density (BMD). Several techniques exist for quantitating the absorption of radiation by bone while simultaneously compensating for any absorption by soft tissues. Dual-energy X-ray absorptiometry (DEXA) scanning is the most widely used technique, because it is highly accurate and involves low radiation exposure. BMD is usually measured at the hip and lumbar spine and results expressed as the following.

- Standard deviations above (+) or below (–) the mean for the patient's sex and age (Z score).

- Standard deviation from the mean BMD for a young adult (T score).

- Fracture risk varies continuously with a reduction in BMD, and approximately doubles with each standard deviation below the mean. However, osteoporosis is usually defined as BMD T score <–2.5.

Indications

BMD measurement should be used only where the result will influence treatment. If a decision has been made to treat on clinical grounds (eg with hormone-replacement therapy in a woman with an early menopause, maternal history of hip fracture and a vertebral crush fracture), then DEXA scanning is unlikely to add anything useful.

When to use DEXA

DEXA scanning should be considered in the following circumstances.

- Plain radiographs suggest osteopenia or vertebral deformity.
- Previous fragility fractures have occurred.
- Patient has been on prednisolone therapy (or equivalent other corticosteroids) for >6 months at doses >7.5 mg.
- Gonadal failure (early menopause, prolonged amenorrhoea and hypogonadism in men).
- Chronic systemic ill-health, especially if it involves weight loss, malabsorption or metabolic bone disease.
- Serial monitoring of BMD in response to treatment or risk factors such as corticosteroid treatment.

3.4.3 Magnetic resonance imaging

Principle

MRI utilises the changes in magnetic field induced by excitation of the protons in hydrogen atoms to produce cross-sectional imaging; these can powerfully differentiate types of soft tissue, largely on the basis of water content. Cross-sectional images can be constructed in any plane. Scans are usually performed to detect two different patterns of change in magnetic field, known as T1-weighted (T1w) and T2-weighted (T2w) scans. T1w scans show high signal from fat but not fluid, whereas T2w scans show both fat and fluid as high signal. The signal from fat can be suppressed on a T2w scan to give selective imaging of the fluid content.

Tissues with a low fluid and fat content (eg bone, ligament and tendon) appear dark on MRI, whereas pathological processes such as inflammation or neoplasia appear bright on T2w scans because of their rich blood supply.

Indications

⚠️ MRI is an extremely sensitive technique. Minor pathologies of doubtful significance are frequently demonstrated, eg scans of the lumbar spine are rarely 'normal' in patients over the age of 40. Great care needs to be exercised when requesting and interpreting MRI scans. Scans performed as a 'screening' exercise, without a sound diagnostic hypothesis, are more likely to confuse than to inform.

🔑 **When to use MRI**

MRI may provide diagnostic information in the following circumstances.

- 'Red flag' pattern back pain: suspected malignancy, discitis or serious neurological involvement (see Section 1.1.13).
- Cervical and lumbar pain with neurological involvement, particularly spinal cord pathology.
- Central nervous system disease in systemic lupus or systemic vasculitis.
- Suspected avascular necrosis of bone: changes may pre-date plain radiographs by several weeks, and surgical intervention is unlikely to be helpful once changes are seen on a plain radiograph.
- Polymyositis: useful in patchy disease, both diagnostically and to identify sites for biopsy.
- Mechanical knee pain: as useful as arthroscopy in demonstrating meniscal or ligament pathology.
- Shoulder pain: assessment of the rotator cuff.
- Suspected soft-tissue tumours: malignant and benign tumours can usually be distinguished, and pointers to histology can be found (eg haemangioma, neurofibroma, lipoma or synovial cyst).
- MRI of inflammatory arthritis can be used to detect synovitis and early erosive changes, but currently it is largely a research tool.

Contraindications

⚠️ MRI is free from radiation hazards, although scanning anatomically fragile sites where mobile pieces of metal are present can have disastrous consequences: intracranial aneurysm clips, foreign bodies in the eye and permanent pacemakers all rule out the use of MRI. Imaging can be performed with fixed non-mobile metal such as joint prostheses, although the quality of imaging may be poor near the metal object.

3.4.4 Nuclear medicine

Principle

A short-lived radioisotope that emits gamma radiation is attached to either a pharmacologically active molecule or whole cells. After injection, localisation of the isotope is visualised with a gamma camera. In general, scintigraphic techniques are strong at providing information on function, but relatively weak on anatomical definition. Radioisotope bone scanning is the most commonly used technique in rheumatology: this uses technetium-99m-labelled bisphosphonates, which are taken up at sites of bone turnover.

Indications

Bone scintigraphy

- Suspected stress fracture: scintigraphic changes may pre-date changes visible on a plain radiograph by two or more weeks.

- Suspected osteomyelitis: again, scintigraphy precedes changes on a plain radiograph.

- Metabolic bone disease: may strongly support a diagnosis of Paget's disease (Fig. 84) or of osteomalacia.

- Peripheral joint disease: limited utility in defining the distribution of an arthritic process.

- Suspected bony malignancy: sensitive but low specificity.

🔑 Bone scintigraphy is usually normal in multiple myeloma.

Inflammation or infection

This is most commonly performed using radiolabelled autologous leucocytes. This is of particular use in locating occult sepsis (eg in pyrexia of unknown origin).

Amyloid

The diagnosis and response to treatment of all forms of amyloidosis is facilitated by scintigraphy, using

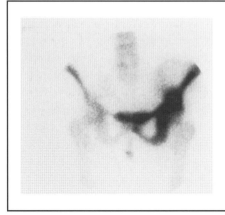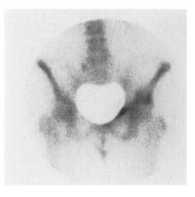

▲ **Fig. 84** Isotope bone scan showing Paget's disease of the pelvis (**a**) before and (**b**) after treatment with pamidronate infusions.

radiolabelled serum amyloid P protein. Unfortunately this technique is restricted to a small number of centres.

3.4.5 Ultrasound

Principle

Modern high-frequency ultrasound machines can be used to provide high-definition dynamic imaging of the soft tissues. Although heavily dependent on the skill of the operator, ultrasound can be used in the clinic to supplement information derived from conventional clinical assessment.

Indications

Ultrasound can be used to make accurate anatomical diagnoses of regional pathology involving tendons, entheses and joints (for example to differentiate causes of shoulder pain); to guide accurate aspiration and injection of joints; and to identify damage (such as erosions in early rheumatoid arthritis) with greater sensitivity than conventional radiology.

FURTHER READING

Wakefield RJ, Kong KO, Conaghan PG, *et al.* The role of ultrasonography and magnetic resonance imaging in early rheumatoid arthritis. *Clin. Exp. Rheumatol.* 2003; 21: S42–S49.

3.5 Arthrocentesis

Principle

Aspiration of synovial fluid is a useful diagnostic procedure in the differential diagnosis of joint disease (see Section 1.4.4). Macroscopic examination of synovial fluid may demonstrate the clear viscous synovial fluid found in osteoarthritis and other non-inflammatory disorders, and also the turbid fluid of inflammatory arthritis or haemarthrosis. The use of Gram stain, culture and polarised light microscopy will differentiate between septic arthritis, crystal arthritis and other inflammatory arthritides.

Indications

- Any inflammatory arthritis or joint effusion of uncertain cause.

- Any established inflammatory arthritis that behaves in an unexpected fashion, for example a severe monoarticular flare in otherwise stable rheumatoid disease – this may be the result of septic arthritis.

Lack of experience in the technique is not an excuse: if you can't do it, find someone who can!

Contraindications

There are very few contraindications.

- Probable periarticular sepsis (eg cellulitis overlying an inflamed joint) may lead to the introduction of sepsis into the joint.

- Prosthetic joints should usually be left to the orthopaedic surgeons.

- Warfarin treatment with INR in the therapeutic range is not a contraindication, but severe bleeding tendencies (eg severe haemophilia or thrombocytopenia severe enough to cause spontaneous bleeding) should usually be corrected before aspiration.

⚠ Prosthetic joint problems should be referred to the orthopaedic surgeons. Never aspirate a prosthetic joint without at least discussing this with your orthopaedic colleagues.

Practical details

Before the procedure

Arthrocentesis can be performed in the outpatient clinic or at the bedside. No equipment is needed other than something to clean the skin and a needle and syringe. In general, use a green 21G needle for large joints such as the knee or shoulder, and a blue or orange needle for smaller joints. Use of an excessively small needle may prevent aspiration of viscous fluid. Choose a size of syringe appropriate to the size of the effusion: you are unlikely to aspirate more than 1–2 mL from the wrist, but an acutely swollen knee may contain >200 mL of fluid.

Most rheumatologists use a 'no-touch' technique, whereby the site of aspiration is identified and marked before skin preparation and aspiration are performed, often without the use of gloves.

Most experienced aspirators do not use local anaesthetic because its infiltration can be as uncomfortable as the procedure itself. However it may be useful when aspirating the knee.

> Virtually all extraspinal joints can be aspirated at the bedside, guided by surface anatomy. The exception is the hip, which is so deep seated that aspiration under radiological or ultrasonic control is recommended. Radiological help can also be invaluable with effusions that are difficult to aspirate but clinically important.

The procedure

Detailed instructions for individual joints cannot be given here. However, some general points apply.

1. Palpate the inflamed joint.

2. Decide whether a fluctuant effusion is present.

3. Mark the point of entry and clean the skin with alcohol or iodine.

4. Insert the needle at the point of maximum fluctuation, taking care to avoid major neurovascular structures (eg the ulnar nerve at the elbow).

5. Entry to the joint cavity will usually be with a palpable 'give'.

6. Draw back on the syringe at intervals during the advance of the needle until fluid is obtained.

7. Aspirate as much fluid as possible without causing undue discomfort.

8. If no obvious effusion is present, fluid is less likely to be obtained. However, in some deep-seated joints such as the hip, shoulder and elbow, significant effusions may be present even when not palpable at the surface.

After the procedure

Samples for microbiological examination should be placed in a clean sterile container. Some laboratories prefer an anticoagulant sample for polarised light microscopy and cytology, so check with your local laboratory first. Samples should arrive at the laboratory within the same working day, although samples stored overnight may be suitable for culture and detection of crystals (see Sections 1.4.4, 2.3.6 and 2.3.7).

Diagnostic microscopy and culture can be performed on samples of <0.5 mL. Also, crystals can sometimes be seen in the flushings from the needle of an apparently dry tap, so it may be worth taking the needle and syringe to the laboratory.

Complications

Complications are rare but include the following.

- Major: infection may be introduced into the joint on rare occasions, but the risk is less than 1 in 30,000.

- Minor: some discomfort is inevitable, but this is usually minor.

3.6 Corticosteroid injection techniques

Principle

A suspension of poorly soluble corticosteroid crystals is injected into an inflamed joint or soft-tissue lesion. This produces a prolonged, potent, local anti-inflammatory effect with minimal systemic corticosteroid action.

Indications

This technique is one of the most useful therapeutic manoeuvres in rheumatology and is useful in the following:

- non-septic inflammatory arthritis in any joint;

- selected cases of non-inflammatory arthritis;

- soft-tissue rheumatic disorders (tennis elbow, plantar fasciitis and trochanteric bursitis);

- carpal tunnel syndrome, especially resulting from an inflammatory cause.

Contraindications

Absolute

- Septic or suspected septic arthritis.

- Septicaemia.

- Allergy to any component of the corticosteroid preparation.

- Prosthetic joints.

- Infected skin overlying joint.

Relative

- Peritendinous injection may predispose the patient to subsequent rupture of the tendon, especially the Achilles tendon and the long head of biceps. Injection at these sites should be at the discretion of a senior colleague.

- Bleeding tendency.

Practical details

The preparation and techniques for the introduction of a needle into a joint are described in Section 3.5. Aspiration of the joint before injection is not always required

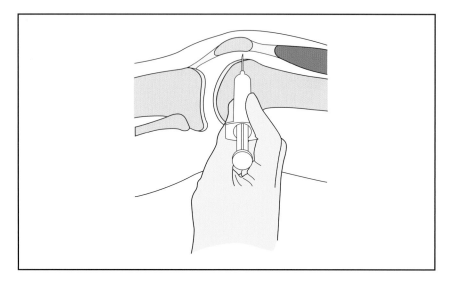

▲ **Fig. 85** Injection of the medial aspect of the knee joint in extension. (Reproduced with permission from the Arthritis and Rheumatism Council.)

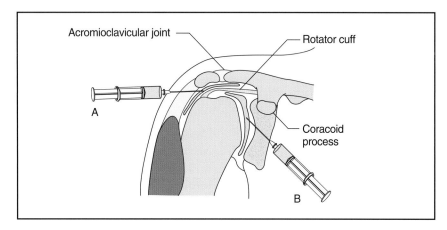

Acromioclavicular joint

Rotator cuff

A

Coracoid process

B

▲ **Fig. 86** Injection of (**a**) subdeltoid and (**b**) glenohumeral joints. (Reproduced with permission from the Arthritis and Rheumatism Council.)

(if you do not know the diagnosis, you should not be injecting) and may not be possible if no effusion is present. However, large or tense effusions should be aspirated because this will make the joint less uncomfortable. Some rheumatologists recommend that any fluid that can be aspirated should be sent for culture to exclude unrecognised infection. Figures 85 and 86 show the landmarks for injection of the knee and shoulder.

If aspiration is being performed before injection, the syringe for aspiration should be removed leaving the needle *in situ*. Then the syringe containing the corticosteroid preparation should be carefully placed in the hub of the needle, taking care not to touch any sterile area. Even if aspiration is not performed before injection, gentle suction should be placed on the syringe containing the preparation as it aspirates the joint upon entry; reflux of synovial fluid confirms that you are in the joint space.

- Injection into the joint space should meet almost no resistance and be almost pain-free.
- Accurate intra-articular placement gives a better response than periarticular injection.

Individual soft-tissue injection techniques cannot be described here. In general, the corticosteroid is injected directly at the site of pathology, into the most tender area. Soft-tissue injections are therefore usually more painful than intra-articular injections.

The steroid preparations used most commonly are poorly soluble salts of methylprednisolone, triamcinolone and hydrocortisone. Hydrocortisone preparations are the least potent and shortest acting, and are often preferred for use in superficial soft tissue or peritendinous injections to reduce the risk of skin atrophy and tendon rupture. The differences between the other preparations are not great. The amount of steroid injected depends on the size of the joint, eg 40–80 mg (1–2 mL) methylprednisolone is appropriate for a large joint such as a knee, but only 5–10 mg (0.25–0.5 mL) is required for a small finger joint. Many rheumatologists use a mixture of steroids and local anaesthetic for injection. The evidence for any beneficial effect of mixtures of local anaesthetic and steroid is small, but they may reduce discomfort after injection, particularly soft-tissue injections. Only methylprednisolone and lidocaine (lignocaine) are available in a premixed form.

In theory, any number of joints may be injected in a single session, but in practice this is limited by discomfort and the cumulative dose of steroids. In practice, it is recommended that no more than three or four joints are injected in one session. Sometimes intramuscular steroid injections are considered in patients with multiple swollen joints, eg methylprednisolone 8–120 mg or triamcinolone 40–80 mg.

Outcome

Improvement usually occurs within 24–48 hours. Historically, most rheumatologists recommended 24–48 hours bed-rest after receiving an injection in a weight-bearing joint, but this is no longer practical or necessary. However, advice to minimise the weight borne by the affected joint does seem to be associated with a modest increase in efficacy.

> 🔑 The duration of response after injection depends on the severity of synovitis, with improvement usually occurring over a period of weeks to months. A rapid relapse of inflammation in a patient with a chronic arthritis should lead you, first, to question the diagnosis (Could this be sepsis? Is there an atypical infection?) and, second, to question whether the patient's systemic medication needs modification. The need for repeated injections should also lead to a review of the patient's disease-modifying therapy.

Complications

- Intra-articular infection is rare, occurring in around 1 in 30,000 procedures.

- Short-term increases in pain and inflammation after an injection are common, particularly with soft-tissue injections. Patients should be warned about this, although it usually settles within 48 hours and can be managed with analgesics. Rarely, a very florid flare in arthritis is seen, which must be differentiated from sepsis by re-aspiration.

- Tendon rupture.

- Skin atrophy and depigmentation: this is more common after a superficial injection, particularly with the use of potent steroids and with repeat injections.

- Facial flushing may be experienced in the hour after injection.

- Exacerbation of diabetes mellitus: changes in diabetic medication are not usually required because the effect is generally mild and transient, but patients should be warned that their glucose readings may increase temporarily.

- Systemic side effects of corticosteroids: adrenal suppression and iatrogenic Cushing's syndrome may occur if frequent injections are used, or if there is concurrent use of oral steroids.

> 🔑 Local corticosteroid injections are generally used to minimise the systemic side effects associated with this class of drugs. However, some systemic absorption does occur and this can sometimes be therapeutically useful in the patient with a florid polyarthritis. Injection of the two to four worst affected joints will often enable sufficient systemic anti-inflammatory action to reduce more widespread joint inflammation and improve well-being, without resorting to oral steroids (which are often difficult to stop once started).

3.7 Immunoglobulin replacement

Principle

Intravenous immunoglobulin (IVIg) therapy has two roles: replacement of IgG in patients with defective B-cell function and as an immunomodulator in autoimmune disease. Immunoglobulin replacement may also be given subcutaneously.

Indications

Antibody deficiency

IVIg is the treatment of choice for severe antibody deficiencies (Fig. 87). For milder antibody deficiencies, such as IgG subclass deficiency, antibiotic prophylaxis is usually sufficient. Immunoglobulin replacement should be reserved for cases with objective evidence of specific antibody deficiency, failure to respond to proven infection or test vaccination, or where antibiotic prophylaxis has failed.

Immunomodulation

IVIg therapy has been enthusiastically tried in a wide range of diseases, but proof of its efficacy has been demonstrated in relatively few.

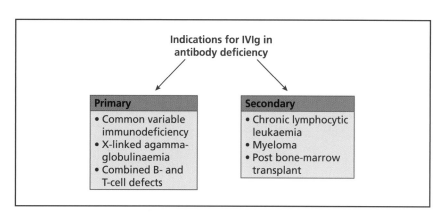

Indications for IVIg in antibody deficiency

Primary	Secondary
• Common variable immunodeficiency • X-linked agamma-globulinaemia • Combined B- and T-cell defects	• Chronic lymphocytic leukaemia • Myeloma • Post bone-marrow transplant

▲ **Fig. 87** Indications for IVIg in antibody deficiency.

> **IVIg as an immunomodulatory agent**
>
> Efficacy proven in randomised controlled trials (RCT):
> - Immune thrombocytopenia.
> - Guillain–Barré syndrome.
> - Chronic inflammatory demyelinating polyneuropathy.
> - Kawasaki's disease.
> - Dermatomyositis.
> - Lambert–Eaton syndrome.
> - Multifocal motor neuropathy.
>
> Ineffective in RCT:
> - Postviral fatigue (chronic fatigue syndrome).
> - Rheumatoid arthritis.
> - Juvenile rheumatoid arthritis.

Contraindications

There are no absolute contraindications, but caution should be exercised in the following.

- Patients with total IgA deficiency and anti-IgA antibodies, in view of the risk of anaphylaxis. Use an IVIg product containing low levels of IgA for such patients.

- Patients with pre-existing renal impairment: infusion of high-dose IVIg may precipitate reversible renal failure in this situation.

- Untreated bacterial infection: defer immunoglobulin for 24–48 hours and initiate antibiotic treatment.

> ⚠️ Infusion of IVIg in the presence of bacterial sepsis may result in exogenous IgG complexing with bacterial antigen to cause an immune complex reaction.

Practical details

Before procedure

It is important to counsel patients on the risks and benefits of treatment with a blood product derivative. Measure hepatitis B surface antigen, hepatitis C RNA and save serum before the first infusion and annually. Measure liver function and trough IgG every 3 months. Ensure the availability of a trained assistant and a telephone if the patient is self-infusing at home.

The procedure

Intravenous immunoglobulin

The usual dose is 0.4 g/kg every 2–3 weeks, and this should be sufficient to keep trough IgG well within the normal range. Higher levels may be required in established bronchiectasis or if granulomatous disease is present. Infuse at 0.01–0.07 mL/kg per minute. Slower rates are used when initiating treatment.

> 🔑 The dose of IVIg used for immunomodulation is five times higher (2 g/kg) than that used for antibody replacement.

Subcutaneous immunoglobulin

The usual dose is 0.1–0.2 g/kg every 1–2 weeks. Concentrated solutions formulated for subcutaneous use are used. Infusions are given via infusion pumps in the abdomen or thighs, providing 15–20 mL at each site. Local reactions are common but improve with time. Systemic and delayed reactions are much less common via this route.

Whichever administration route is used, observe for adverse effects. Reduce the infusion rate if mild side effects occur. Discontinue if moderate or severe side effects occur. Flu-like symptoms occurring after 24–48 hours will respond to paracetamol.

After the procedure

Note batch number of IVIg and any adverse events.

Complications

Complications may be divided into immediate infusion-related events, those related to infusing high doses of IgG, and transmission of infections as a result of infusing a blood product.

Infusion-related events

Serious anaphylactoid or immune complex-mediated reactions are rare. Milder infusion-related reactions, eg headache, flushing, low backache, nausea, chills and abdominal pain, occur in 2–6% of cases and respond rapidly to a reduction in the rate of infusion.

Sudden rise in serum IgG

These complications are seen only with high-dose IVIg.

- Aseptic meningitis: aetiology unknown, occurs in approximately 10% of patients.

- Haemolysis caused by anti-blood group antibodies: this is exceptional but may occur if IVIg contains high titres of blood group antibodies.

- Reversible renal failure: a result of osmotic tubular injury caused by the carbohydrate component of IVIg.

- Arterial or venous thrombosis: occurs in patients with pre-existing hyperviscosity, cardiovascular disease or thrombophilia.

Blood-borne viral transmission

Stringent precautions in donor selection, plasma screening and the inclusion of antiviral steps in immunoglobulin preparation has minimised the risk of infection. Emerging pathogens such as prions remain a theoretical concern. Minimise risk by monitoring batch numbers, thus enabling a swift recall in case of an infected batch. Do not change the IVIg preparation except for strong clinical reasons.

> HIV and hepatitis B have not been transmitted by IVIg, presumably because these viruses do not survive Cohn ethanol fractionation, the manufacturing process for IVIg.

FURTHER READING

Association of British Neurologists. *Guidelines for the use of intravenous immunoglobulin in neurological diseases*, July 2005. Available at www.theabn.org

Jolles S, Sewell WA and Misbah SA. Clinical uses of intravenous immunoglobulin. *Clin. Exp. Immunol.* 2005; 142: 1–11.

UK Primary Immune Deficiency Network. *Guidelines*. Available at http://www.ukpin.org.uk/

RHEUMATOLOGY AND CLINICAL IMMUNOLOGY: **SECTION 4**
SELF-ASSESSMENT

4.1 Self-assessment questions

Question 1

Clinical scenario

A previously well 55-year-old man is rushed to the Emergency Department of a London hospital following a sudden collapse at work. He has no past medical history, excepting splenectomy for a ruptured spleen following a road traffic accident 10 years previously. On examination he is febrile (39.8°C) with evidence of cardiovascular compromise (pulse 150 bpm and BP 70/40 mmHg). In taking his history it emerges that he was bitten by a dog 4 days previously. Given his asplenia, it is thought that he is septicaemic and urgent antibiotic treatment is commenced pending results of his blood cultures.

Question

Which of the following pathogens is likely to be responsible for his symptoms?

Answers

A *Capnocytophaga canimorsus* (DF-2)

B *Streptococcus suis*

C *Pseudomonas aeruginosa*

D *Clostridium difficile*

E *Staphylococcus aureus*

Question 2

Clinical scenario

A 65-year-old woman with primary Sjögren's syndrome, which was diagnosed 1 year previously, is noted to have a persistently elevated erythrocyte sedimentation rate (ESR) of 90–100 mm/hour and a normal C-reactive protein (CRP). At a routine outpatient visit it is noted that her sicca symptoms are still troublesome, but there are no other abnormalities on clinical examination. The following investigations are performed: haemoglobin 12.5 g/dL (normal range 12–16), white cell count 6.4×10^9/L (normal range 4–11), platelet count 320×10^9/L (normal range 150–400), ESR 98 mm/hour, CRP <6 mg/dL (normal <6), serum IgG 42 g/L (normal range 6–13), IgA 8.4 g/L (normal range 0.8–4.0) and IgM 3.6 g/L (normal range 0.4–2.0), and serum electrophoresis shows polyclonal hypergammaglobulinaemia.

Question

Her persistently elevated ESR is best explained by which of the following?

Answers

A Development of lymphoma

B Poorly controlled sicca symptoms

C Positive antinuclear antibody

D Positive antibodies to Ro and La antigens

E Polyclonal hypergammaglobulinaemia

Question 3

Clinical scenario

An 18-year-old student with known asthma and peanut allergy collapses following a meal in the hospital canteen. Strenuous attempts at resuscitation are tragically unsuccessful. It is thought that the most likely cause of his collapse was an anaphylactic reaction to 'hidden' nuts contained in the meal.

Question

Which of the following mast cell-derived mediators is it most useful to measure to confirm the clinical suspicion of anaphylaxis?

Answers

A Platelet-derived factor

B Chymase

C Interleukin-6

D Tryptase

E Transforming growth factor-β

Question 4

Clinical scenario

A 70-year-old woman with a history of blood transfusion in the early 1980s presents with a 10-month history of malaise and is noted to have impaired renal function. Her urine sediment reveals red cell casts. The results of immunological investigations are as follows: serum IgG 6.5 g/L (normal range 6–13), IgA 1.5 g/L (normal range 0.8–4.0), IgM 5.7 g/L (normal range 0.4–2.0), serum electrophoresis shows faint band in gamma region, complement C3 1.02 g/L (normal range 0.75–1.65), complement C4 <0.02 g/L (normal range 0.20–0.65) and rheumatoid factor 894 IU/L (normal range <40).

Question

Which of the following investigations is likely to be most important in making a definitive diagnosis?

Answers

A Antineutrophil cytoplasmic antibodies

B Antinuclear antibodies

C Antiglomerular basement membrane antibodies

D Antimyeloperoxidase antibodies

E Cryoglobulins

Question 5

Clinical scenario

A 30-year-old carpenter notices increasing weakness of his dominant right hand accompanied by fasciculations in both arms and legs. On examination he is noted to have a right wrist drop but preserved muscle power in his legs. A clinical diagnosis of multifocal motor neuropathy is made following a detailed electrophysiological assessment.

Question

Which two of the following treatments are likely to be most efficacious in improving his wrist drop?

Answers

A Corticosteroids

B Colchicine

C Plasmapheresis

D Azathioprine

E Intravenous immunoglobulin

F Antithymocyte globulin

G Ciclosporin

H Bone marrow transplantation

I Dapsone

J Cyclophosphamide

Question 6

Clinical scenario

A 75-year-old woman presents to the Emergency Department with a hot swollen left knee and difficulty in weight-bearing. She has mild heart failure and is on treatment.

Question

Which one of the following tests will be most useful in determining how best to manage her condition?

Answers

A Aspiration, microscopy and culture of synovial fluid

B Plain radiograph of knee

C FBC

D C-reactive protein

E Serum uric acid

Question 7

Clinical scenario

A 45-year-old woman developed Raynaud's 2 years ago. She now complains of breathlessness and skin tightness affecting her fingers. A high-resolution CT scan shows evidence of pulmonary fibrosis.

Question

Which of the following tests is most likely to be positive?

Answers

A Anticentromere antibody

B Anti-double-stranded DNA antibody

C Anti-Ro antibody

D Anti-Scl-70 antibody

E Anti-Jo-1 antibody

Question 8

Clinical scenario

A 70-year-old woman presents with inflammatory joint pain, fatigue and a dry mouth. She is found to have marked hypergammaglobulinaemia and a raised erythrocyte sedimentation rate with a normal C-reactive protein.

Question

What is the most likely diagnosis?

Answers

A Rheumatoid arthritis

B Pyrophosphate arthropathy

C Primary Sjögren's syndrome

D Systemic lupus erythematosus

E Fibromyalgia

Question 9

Clinical scenario

A 35-year-old woman has polymyositis and the Jo-1 antibody.

Question

Which manifestation is typically associated with this profile?

Answers

A Photosensitive rash

B Sicca symptoms

C Dysphagia

D Inflammatory arthritis

E Inflammatory lung disease

Question 10

Clinical scenario

A 68-year-old man has lost weight. His alkaline phosphatase is raised at 290 U/L (normal range 35–120). Plain radiographs show sclerotic lesions of bone.

Question

What is the likely diagnosis?

Answers

A Stomach cancer

B Prostate cancer

C Multiple myeloma

D Lung cancer

E Osteomalacia

Question 11

Clinical scenario

A 56-year-old man presents with recurrent attacks of polyarticular gout despite treatment with allopurinol 300 mg daily for the last year. He is adamant that his compliance with his drug treatment regimen is good.

Question

Which of the following factors is most likely to explain his poor response to allopurinol?

Answers

A Concurrent treatment with colchicine

B Fast metabolism of allopurinol

C High alcohol intake

D Poor urate clearance via the kidney

E High dietary purine intake

Question 12

Clinical scenario

A 56-year-old man presents with a 2-month history of progressive mid-thoracic spinal pain that disturbs his sleep. A CXR is normal. His erythrocyte sedimentation rate is 60 mm/hour (normal <10 mm).

Question

Which of the following investigations is most likely to clarify the cause of his pain?

Answers

A Isotope bone scan

B MRI scan of the thoracic spine

C CT scan of the thoracic spine

D Myeloma screen

E Plain radiograph of the thoracic spine

Question 13

Clinical scenario

A 23-year-old woman is brought by ambulance to the Emergency Department having collapsed in a restaurant while eating a curry. Her friends have given a history of previous allergic reactions to nuts. On admission she is flushed, breathless and wheezy, has a pulse rate of 140 bpm and a BP of 84/40 mmHg.

Question

What is the most appropriate first line of treatment?

Answers

A High-flow oxygen, intravenous hydrocortisone and chlorpheniramine

B High-flow oxygen and intravenous epinephrine 500 μg

C 24% oxygen and intramuscular epinephrine 500 μg

D 1 litre intravenous saline and intravenous chlorpheniramine

E High-flow oxygen and intramuscular epinephrine 500 μg

Question 14

Clinical scenario

A 38-year-old man presents with 4 months of pain, stiffness and swelling of the small joints of his hands and feet. He has a past history of mild psoriasis. His GP has found his erythrocyte sedimentation rate to be elevated at 65 mm/hour.

Question

Which of the following clinical features would be *least* likely to suggest a diagnosis of psoriatic arthritis?

Answers

A Involvement of the distal interphalangeal joints

B Subcutaneous nodules

C Dactylitis

D Nail involvement

E Asymmetrical arthritis

Question 15

Clinical scenario

A 33-year-old woman presents with a 6-month history of Raynaud's phenomenon affecting her hands and feet. She is previously well and takes no medication.

Question

Which two of the following clinical features or investigation results are the strongest predictors that she will develop a connective tissue disease in the future?

Answers

A Age >25 years

B Abnormal nail-fold capillary microscopy

C Elevated erythrocyte sedimentation rate

D History of recurrent miscarriage

E Family history of Raynaud's

F Anaemia

G Strongly positive antinuclear antibody

H History of chilblains

I Raised platelet count

J Dry eyes and dry mouth

Question 16

Clinical scenario

A 57-year-old woman is admitted to the Emergency Department at 5 a.m. with orofacial angio-oedema. She has a past history of hypertension and hypothyroidism, and has recently been treated for a chest infection. Her medication includes bendroflumethiazide, lisinopril and levothyroxine. She has a history of penicillin allergy. The previous evening she ate a prawn curry. On admission she is comfortable at rest and has no urticaria. Observations are as follows: temperature 37°C, pulse 80 bpm, respiratory rate 16/minute and BP 170/100 mmHg.

Question

What is the most likely diagnosis?

Answers

A Angiotensin-converting enzyme inhibitor-induced angio-oedema.

B Anaphylaxis due to prawns

C Penicillin allergy

D Idiopathic anaphylaxis

E Diuretic allergy

Question 17

Clinical scenario

A 74-year-old man presents with new-onset angio-oedema. Investigations show complement C3 0.74 g/L (normal range 0.75–1.65) and C4 0.01 g/L (normal range 0.14–0.54).

Question

Which one of the following statements is *not* true?

Answers

A This man is likely to have C1 inhibitor deficiency

B The diagnosis is almost certainly hereditary angio-oedema

C There may be an underlying lymphoma

D The angio-oedema will not respond to antihistamines

E There may be associated autoimmune disease

Question 18

Clinical scenario

A 41-year-old woman is undergoing a course of chemotherapy for non-Hodgkin's lymphoma. Eleven days after her second treatment with doxorubicin, cyclophosphamide, vindesine, bleomycin and prednisolone, she presents with fever, headache and faintness. On admission to your unit, her observations are as follows: temperature 38.6°C, pulse 96 bpm, respiratory rate 28/minute and BP 85/40 mmHg.

Question

Which one of the following options is the most likely diagnosis?

Answers

A Pneumonia as a result of antibody deficiency secondary to her lymphoma

B Urinary tract infection as a result of antibody deficiency secondary to her lymphoma

C Meningitis as a result of central nervous system involvement of her lymphoma

D Meningitis as a result of neutropenia secondary to chemotherapy

E Urinary tract infection as a result of neutropenia secondary to chemotherapy

Question 19

Clinical scenario

A 49-year-old plumber is recovering from his third episode of pneumonia. He has no significant personal or family history other than mild asthma, for which he takes inhaled salbutamol as required and inhaled budesonide 200 mg twice daily. He is on no other medication. He smokes 10 cigarettes per day.

Question

Which two underlying conditions are most likely?

Answers

A Combined immune deficiency

B Carcinoma of the lung

C Antibody deficiency

D Immunosuppression caused by corticosteroids

E Complement deficiency

F *Legionella* pneumonia

G Chronic granulomatous disease

H Wegener's granulomatosis

I Neutropenia

J HIV infection

Question 20

Clinical scenario

A 76-year-old man with chronic lymphatic leukaemia (CLL) is admitted to the general medical ward with fever and chest pain. His leukaemia was diagnosed 14 months previously and, other than fatigue, he has had no symptoms and has required no specific treatment. On admission his temperature is 39°C, respiratory rate 26/minute and oxygen saturation 92% (breathing air). There are fine crackles in his left upper zone. His CXR shows pneumonia of the left upper lobe. His blood count reveals haemoglobin 11.2 g/dL (normal range 13.5–17.5), white cell count 37.6×10^9/L (normal range 4–11) with neutrophils 2.0×10^9/L (normal range 2–7.5) and lymphocytes 35.1×10^9/L (normal range 1.5–4), and platelets 135×10^9/L (normal range 150–400). His creatinine, electrolytes and liver function are normal. He is treated with penicillin and erythromycin and makes a slow recovery.

Question

Which of the following statements regarding his immediate management is true?

Answers

A Chemotherapy for CLL is indicated

B Lymphocyte phenotyping is indicated

C Granulocyte colony-stimulating factor treatment should be considered

D Immunoglobulin replacement is unlikely to be helpful

E Antibody levels should be checked during the acute admission

4.2 Self-assessment answers

Answer to Question 1

A

In addition to the well-known risk of overwhelming pneumococcal sepsis, asplenic patients are also prone to fulminant septicaemia with other organisms such as *Capnocytophaga canimorsus* (previously known as dysgonic fermenter, DF) and *Streptococcus suis*. Given that *Capnocytophaga canimorsus* is found abundantly in canine saliva and that this patient recently suffered a dog bite, this organism is most likely to be responsible for this patient's septicaemia.

Answer to Question 2

E

Together with fibrinogen, serum immunoglobulins are the major driving force causing an elevation in erythrocyte sedimentation rate

(ESR). Any disorder associated with a persistently elevated polyclonal hypergammaglobulinaemia, such as primary Sjögren's syndrome, is likely to be linked with a persistently elevated ESR. Note that her C-reactive protein (CRP) is normal, which reflects the fact that CRP production is not influenced by changes in serum immunoglobulin levels.

Answer to Question 3

D

Amongst the array of mediators released by mast cells during anaphylaxis, tryptase has proven to be a reliable marker of mast cell degranulation on account of its stability, relatively long half-life and ease of measurement. Consequently, an elevated tryptase in the correct clinical context is a useful surrogate marker of an anaphylactic /anaphylactoid reaction.

Answer to Question 4

E

The combination of a markedly low C4 (with normal C3), elevated rheumatoid factor, elevated serum IgM on a background of active urinary sediment and a history of blood transfusion is highly suggestive of hepatitis C-associated cryoglobulinaemic vasculitis. Of the investigations listed, cryoglobulins are the single most important test in establishing a definitive diagnosis in this patient.

Answer to Question 5

E and J

Evidence from double-blind, randomised, placebo-controlled trials attests to the efficacy of high-dose intravenous immunoglobulin in multifocal motor neuropathy (MMN). Although cyclophosphamide is also efficacious, its adverse effect profile has led to intravenous immunoglobulin being increasingly considered the treatment of choice in MMN.

Answer to Question 6

A

In a patient presenting with a monoarthritis, the most important diagnosis to consider/exclude is a septic arthritis. This is best diagnosed by microscopy and culture of the synovial fluid. Radiography will be helpful in determining if the patient has pre-existing osteoarthritis or chondrocalcinosis. A raised white cell count might suggest infection. A raised C-reactive protein would indicate inflammation or infection. This patient has mild heart failure and so may be taking bendroflumethiazide or loop diuretics, which may cause hyperuricaemia and gout and hence a monoarthritis.

Answer to Question 7

D

This patient has clinical symptoms suggestive of diffuse cutaneous systemic sclerosis. Pulmonary fibrosis and anti-Scl-70 are more common in patients with diffuse disease. Anticentromere antibody is associated with limited cutaneous systemic sclerosis. Anti-double-stranded DNA antibody is associated with systemic lupus erythematosus. Anti-Ro antibody is associated with lupus and primary Sjögren's syndrome. Anti-Jo-1 is associated with polymyositis, particularly in patients with inflammatory lung disease.

Answer to Question 8

C

Sicca symptoms, a raised erythrocyte sedimentation rate but normal C-reactive protein (CRP) and hypergammaglobulinaemia are classic features of primary Sjögren's syndrome. This syndrome tends to begin in the fifth and sixth decades compared with lupus, which typically begins between the second and fourth decades. This patient could have rheumatoid arthritis but this is unlikely since the CRP is normal. Blood tests are usually normal in patients with primary fibromyalgia.

Answer to Question 9

E

The Jo-1 antibody is associated with the anti-synthetase syndrome, which includes inflammatory myositis, inflammatory lung disease, Raynaud's phenomenon and symmetrical non-erosive arthritis. A photosensitive rash typically occurs in systemic lupus erythematosus. Sicca symptoms can occur with primary or secondary Sjögren's syndrome in relation to the underlying connective tissue disease. Dysphagia may occur in polymyositis or scleroderma. Inflammatory arthritis is non-specific and can occur in many connective tissue diseases.

Answer to Question 10

B

Cancer of the prostate is typically associated with sclerotic bone lesions in contrast to the lytic lesions seen in multiple myeloma. Osteomalacia is associated with Looser's zones.

Answer to Question 11

C

Persistently high alcohol consumption is a common cause of poor response to allopurinol, although the underlying mechanism of this is unclear. B, D and E are plausible answers, but are less important in practice. Most adults will respond to allopurinol 300 mg daily, although a small proportion will require 600 or even 900 mg daily. The aim of treatment should be to suppress the serum urate level to the lower end of the normal range or just below.

Answer to Question 12

B
The clinical picture suggests malignancy or chronic infection, although sometimes osteoarthritis may produce severe pain. Osteoporotic crush fractures usually cause pain of sudden onset. An isotope bone scan may reveal the site of the painful lesion but is unlikely to reveal the cause, and may be normal in myeloma. Plain radiographs and CT scans will show evidence of advanced disease but may be normal in early malignancy and infection. MRI scanning is the most sensitive technique, and will also give information about associated soft tissues.

Answer to Question 13

E
Intramuscular epinephrine is the key treatment in anaphylaxis. Intravenous epinephrine may occasionally be used with extreme caution in patients with cardiovascular collapse, but it is more likely to cause ventricular arrhythmias when administered by this route. Antihistamines and corticosteroids (without epinephrine) are inadequate immediate treatments for anaphylaxis, but may be administered in milder allergic reactions and also to prevent late deterioration in the event of anaphylaxis.

Answer to Question 14

B
Subcutaneous nodule formation is very strongly suggestive of rheumatoid factor-positive rheumatoid arthritis. All the other features occur in psoriatic arthritis. Nail involvement is a feature of skin psoriasis, but is also strongly associated with distal interphalangeal joint involvement in psoriatic arthritis.

Answer to Question 15

B and G
These factors are strongly predictive of a future connective tissue disease (CTD), particularly abnormal nail-fold capillaries. The likelihood of developing a CTD also increases with age of onset of Raynaud's, with a particularly high risk in those aged over 35 years. All the other features apart from a family history (which suggests primary Raynaud's) are associated with CTD, but have not been shown to have the same predictive value as B and G.

Answer to Question 16

A
Angio-oedema may be related to use of an angiotensin-converting enzyme inhibitor and may occur even after apparent tolerance of the drug for many months; in this case, the drug should be stopped or substituted. Allergic angio-oedema is usually obvious by its fast onset: it usually occurs within a few minutes of contact with the allergen.

Answer to Question 17

B
Although the symptoms and the low C4 are highly suggestive of C1 inhibitor deficiency, it would be unusual for hereditary angio-oedema to initially manifest at such an

advanced age. This case is more likely to be acquired angio-oedema (acquired C1 inhibitor deficiency), which is often associated with lymphoma or autoimmune disease.

Answer to Question 18

E
Although all the above are possible diagnoses, by far the most likely is E. Bone-marrow suppression after chemotherapy reaches its nadir after around 10 days. Neutropenia is common and Gram-negative septicaemia is the commonest clinical manifestation. The commonest source is the urinary tract.

Answer to Question 19

B and C
Carcinoma of the lung is common and causes infection secondary to obstruction of the normal airway clearance mechanisms. Smoking, even in the absence of any other pathology, dramatically increases the risk of infection because it reduces ciliary activity, thus impairing the mucociliary escalator. Antibody deficiencies, although much less common, are also typically associated with respiratory tract infection.

Answer to Question 20

E
Antibody deficiency is a common complication of chronic lymphatic leukaemia. Where this occurs, replacement immunoglobulin therapy may reduce the chance of recurrent pneumonia and improve the chance of survival. In this situation, serum immunoglobulin concentrations are unlikely to increase significantly during infections, so testing should not be delayed.

THE MEDICAL MASTERCLASS SERIES

Scientific Background to Medicine 1

GENETICS AND MOLECULAR MEDICINE

Nucleic Acids and Chromosomes 3

Techniques in Molecular Biology 11

Molecular Basis of Simple Genetic Traits 17

More Complex Issues 23

Self-assessment 30

BIOCHEMISTRY AND METABOLISM

Requirement for Energy 35

Carbohydrates 41

Fatty Acids and Lipids 45

3.1 Fatty acids 45
3.2 Lipids 48

Cholesterol and Steroid Hormones 51

Amino Acids and Proteins 53

5.1 Amino acids 53
5.2 Proteins 56

Haem 59

Nucleotides 61

Self-assessment 66

CELL BIOLOGY

Ion Transport 71

1.1 Ion channels 72
1.2 Ion carriers 79

Receptors and Intracellular Signalling 82

Cell Cycle and Apoptosis 88

Haematopoiesis 94

Self-assessment 97

IMMUNOLOGY AND IMMUNOSUPPRESSION

Overview of the Immune System 103

The Major Histocompatibility Complex, Antigen Presentation and Transplantation 106

T Cells 109

B Cells 112

Tolerance and Autoimmunity 115

Complement 117

Inflammation 120

Immunosuppressive Therapy 125

Self-assessment 130

ANATOMY

Heart and Major Vessels 135

Lungs 138

Liver and Biliary Tract 140

Spleen 142

Kidney 143

Endocrine Glands 144

Gastrointestinal Tract 147

Eye 150

Nervous System 152

Self-assessment 167

PHYSIOLOGY

Cardiovascular System 171

1.1 The heart as a pump 171
1.2 The systemic and pulmonary circulations 176
1.3 Blood vessels 177
1.4 Endocrine function of the heart 180

Respiratory System 182

2.1 The lungs 182

Gastrointestinal System 187

3.1 The gut 187
3.2 The liver 190
3.3 The exocrine pancreas 193

Brain and Nerves 194

4.1 The action potential 194
4.2 Synaptic transmission 196
4.3 Neuromuscular transmission 199

Endocrine Physiology 200

5.1 The growth hormone–insulin-like growth factor 1 axis 200
5.2 The hypothalamic–pituitary–adrenal axis 200
5.3 Thyroid hormones 201
5.4 The endocrine pancreas 203
5.5 The ovary and testis 204
5.6 The breast 206
5.7 The posterior pituitary 207

Renal Physiology 209

6.1 Blood flow and glomerular filtration 209
6.2 Function of the renal tubules 211
6.3 Endocrine function of the kidney 217

Self-assessment 220

Scientific Background to Medicine 2

CLINICAL PHARMACOLOGY

Introducing Clinical Pharmacology 3

1.1 Risks versus benefits 4
1.2 Safe prescribing 4
1.3 Rational prescribing 5
1.4 The role of clinical pharmacology 5

Pharmacokinetics 7

2.1 Introduction 7
2.2 Drug absorption 7
2.3 Drug distribution 11
2.4 Drug metabolism 12
2.5 Drug elimination 17
2.6 Plasma half-life and steady-state plasma concentrations 19
2.7 Drug monitoring 20

Pharmacodynamics 22

3.1 How drugs exert their effects 22
3.2 Selectivity is the key to the therapeutic utility of an agent 25
3.3 Basic aspects of the interaction of a drug with its target 27
3.4 Heterogeneity of drug responses, pharmacogenetics and pharmacogenomics 31

Prescribing in Special Circumstances 33

4.1 Introduction 33
4.2 Prescribing and liver disease 33
4.3 Prescribing in pregnancy 36
4.4 Prescribing for women of childbearing potential 39
4.5 Prescribing to lactating mothers 39
4.6 Prescribing in renal disease 41
4.7 Prescribing in the elderly 44

Adverse Drug Reactions 46

5.1 Introduction and definition 46
5.2 Classification of adverse drug reactions 46
5.3 Clinical approach to adverse drug reactions 47
5.4 Dose-related adverse drug reactions (type A) 48
5.5 Non-dose-related adverse drug reactions (type B) 51
5.6 Adverse reactions caused by long-term effects of drugs (type C) 56
5.7 Adverse reactions caused by delayed effects of drugs (type D) 57
5.8 Withdrawal reactions (type E) 58
5.9 Drugs in overdose and use of illicit drugs 59

Drug Development and Rational Prescribing 60

6.1 Drug development 60
6.2 Rational prescribing 65
6.3 Clinical governance and rational prescribing 66
6.4 Rational prescribing: evaluating the evidence for yourself 68
6.5 Rational prescribing, irrational patients 68

Self-assessment 70

STATISTICS, EPIDEMIOLOGY, CLINICAL TRIALS AND META-ANALYSES

Statistics 79

Epidemiology 86

2.1 Observational studies 87

Clinical Trials and Meta-Analyses 92

Self-assessment 103

Clinical Skills

CLINICAL SKILLS FOR PACES

Introduction 3

History-taking for PACES (Station 2) 6

Communication Skills and Ethics for PACES (Station 4) 11

Examination for PACES Stations 1, 3 and 5: General Considerations 13

Station 1: Respiratory System 16

Station 1: Abdominal System 21

Station 3: Cardiovascular System 27

Station 3: Central Nervous System 36

Station 5: Skin, Locomotor System, Endocrine System and Eyes 54

PAIN RELIEF AND PALLIATIVE CARE

PACES Stations and Acute Scenarios 61

1.1 **History-taking 61**
  1.1.1 Pain 61
  1.1.2 Constipation/bowel obstruction 63

1.2 **Communication skills and ethics 65**
  1.2.1 Pain 65
  1.2.2 Breathlessness 66
  1.2.3 Nausea and vomiting 67
  1.2.4 Bowel obstruction 69
  1.2.5 End of life 70

1.3 **Acute scenarios 71**
  1.3.1 Pain 71
  1.3.2 Breathlessness 74
  1.3.3 Nausea and vomiting 76
  1.3.4 Bowel obstruction 79

Diseases and Treatments 82

2.1 **Pain 82**
2.2 **Breathlessness 87**
2.3 **Nausea and vomiting 88**
2.4 **Constipation 89**
2.5 **Bowel obstruction 90**
2.6 **Anxiety and depression 91**
2.7 **Confusion 93**
2.8 **End-of-life care: the dying patient 94**
2.9 **Specialist palliative care services 96**

Self-assessment 98

MEDICINE FOR THE ELDERLY

PACES Stations and Acute Scenarios 107

1.1 **History-taking 107**
  1.1.1 Frequent falls 107
  1.1.2 Recent onset of confusion 110
  1.1.3 Urinary incontinence and immobility 114
  1.1.4 Collapse 116
  1.1.5 Vague aches and pains 119
  1.1.6 Swollen legs and back pain 121
  1.1.7 Failure to thrive: gradual decline and weight loss 127

1.2 **Clinical examination 129**
  1.2.1 Confusion (respiratory) 129
  1.2.2 Confusion (abdominal) 130
  1.2.3 Failure to thrive (abdominal) 131
  1.2.4 Frequent falls (cardiovascular) 131
  1.2.5 Confusion (cardiovascular) 132
  1.2.6 Frequent falls (neurological) 132
  1.2.7 Confusion (neurological) 134
  1.2.8 Impaired mobility (neurological) 135
  1.2.9 Confusion (skin) 135
  1.2.10 Frequent falls (locomotor) 136
  1.2.11 Confusion (endocrine) 136
  1.2.12 Confusion (eye) 136

1.3 **Communication skills and ethics 137**
  1.3.1 Frequent falls 137
  1.3.2 Confusion 138
  1.3.3 Collapse 139

1.4 **Acute scenarios 141**
  1.4.1 Sudden onset of confusion 141
  1.4.2 Collapse 143

Diseases and Treatments 147

2.1 **Why elderly patients are different 147**
2.2 **General approach to management 149**
2.3 **Falls 151**
2.4 **Urinary and faecal incontinence 155**
  2.4.1 Urinary incontinence 155
  2.4.2 Faecal incontinence 157
2.5 **Hypothermia 158**
2.6 **Drugs in elderly people 161**
2.7 **Dementia 162**
2.8 **Rehabilitation 165**
2.9 **Aids, appliances and assistive technology 166**
2.10 **Hearing impairment 168**
2.11 **Nutrition 170**

2.12 Benefits 174
2.13 Legal aspects of elderly care
175

Investigations and Practical Procedures 178

3.1 Diagnosis vs common sense
178
3.2 Assessment of cognition,
mood and function 178

Self-assessment 181

Acute Medicine

ACUTE MEDICINE

PACES Stations and Acute Scenarios 3

1.1 Communication skills and
ethics 3
  1.1.1 Cardiac arrest 3
  1.1.2 Stroke 4
  1.1.3 Congestive cardiac
failure 5
  1.1.4 Lumbar back pain 6
  1.1.5 Community-acquired
pneumonia 7
  1.1.6 Acute pneumothorax 7
1.2 Acute scenarios 8
  1.2.1 Cardiac arrest 8
  1.2.2 Chest pain and
hypotension 12
  1.2.3 Should he be
thrombolysed? 15
  1.2.4 Hypotension in acute
coronary syndrome 20
  1.2.5 Postoperative
breathlessness 21
  1.2.6 Two patients with
tachyarrhythmia 23
  1.2.7 Bradyarrhythmia 27
  1.2.8 Collapse of unknown
cause 30
  1.2.9 Asthma 33
  1.2.10 Pleurisy 36

  1.2.11 Chest infection/
pneumonia 39
  1.2.12 Acute-on-chronic
airways obstruction 42
  1.2.13 Stridor 44
  1.2.14 Pneumothorax 46
  1.2.15 Upper gastrointestinal
haemorrhage 48
  1.2.16 Bloody diarrhoea 51
  1.2.17 Abdominal pain 54
  1.2.18 Hepatic encephalopathy/
alcohol withdrawal 56
  1.2.19 Renal failure, fluid
overload and
hyperkalaemia 59
  1.2.20 Diabetic ketoacidosis 62
  1.2.21 Hypoglycaemia 65
  1.2.22 Hypercalcaemia 67
  1.2.23 Hyponatraemia 69
  1.2.24 Addisonian crisis 71
  1.2.25 Thyrotoxic crisis 74
  1.2.26 Sudden onset of severe
headache 75
  1.2.27 Severe headache with
fever 77
  1.2.28 Acute spastic paraparesis
79
  1.2.29 Status epilepticus 81
  1.2.30 Stroke 83
  1.2.31 Coma 86
  1.2.32 Fever in a returning
traveller 89
  1.2.33 Anaphylaxis 90
  1.2.34 A painful joint 91
  1.2.35 Back pain 94
  1.2.36 Self-harm 96
  1.2.37 Violence and aggression
97

Diseases and Treatments 100

2.1 Overdoses 100
  2.1.1 Prevention of drug
absorption from the
gut 100
  2.1.2 Management of overdoses
of specific drugs 100

Investigations and Practical Procedures 103

3.1 Central venous lines 103
  3.1.1 Indications,
contraindications, consent
and preparation 103

  3.1.2 Specific techniques for
insertion of central lines
104
  3.1.3 Interpretation of central
venous pressure
measurements 106
3.2 Lumbar puncture 106
3.3 Cardiac pacing 107
3.4 Elective DC cardioversion 109
3.5 Intercostal chest drain
insertion 109
3.6 Arterial blood gases 112
  3.6.1 Measurement of arterial
blood gases 112
  3.6.2 Interpretation of arterial
blood gases 113
3.7 Airway management 113
  3.7.1 Basic airway
management 113
  3.7.2 Tracheostomy 116
3.8 Ventilatory support 117
  3.8.1 Controlled oxygen
therapy 117
  3.8.2 Continuous positive
airway pressure 117
  3.8.3 Non-invasive ventilation
118
  3.8.4 Invasive ventilation 118

Self-assessment 120

Infectious Diseases and Dermatology

INFECTIOUS DISEASES

PACES Stations and Acute Scenarios 3

1.1 History-taking 3
  1.1.1 A cavitating lung lesion 3
  1.1.2 Fever and
lymphadenopathy 5
  1.1.3 Still feverish after
6 weeks 7
  1.1.4 Chronic fatigue 10

1.1.5 A spot on the penis 12

1.1.6 Penile discharge 15

1.1.7 Woman with a genital sore 17

1.2 Communication skills and ethics 20

1.2.1 Fever, hypotension and confusion 20

1.2.2 A swollen red foot 21

1.2.3 Still feverish after 6 weeks 22

1.2.4 Chronic fatigue 23

1.2.5 Malaise, mouth ulcers and fever 24

1.2.6 Don't tell my wife 25

1.3 Acute scenarios 27

1.3.1 Fever 27

1.3.2 Fever, hypotension and confusion 30

1.3.3 A swollen red foot 33

1.3.4 Fever and cough 34

1.3.5 Fever, back pain and weak legs 37

1.3.6 Drug user with fever and a murmur 40

1.3.7 Fever and heart failure 44

1.3.8 Persistent fever in the intensive care unit 47

1.3.9 Pyelonephritis 49

1.3.10 A sore throat 52

1.3.11 Fever and headache 55

1.3.12 Fever with reduced conscious level 60

1.3.13 Fever in the neutropenic patient 62

1.3.14 Fever after renal transplant 65

1.3.15 Varicella in pregnancy 68

1.3.16 Imported fever 70

1.3.17 Eosinophilia 74

1.3.18 Jaundice and fever after travelling 76

1.3.19 A traveller with diarrhoea 78

1.3.20 Malaise, mouth ulcers and fever 81

1.3.21 Breathlessness in a HIV-positive patient 83

1.3.22 HIV positive and blurred vision 86

1.3.23 Abdominal pain and vaginal discharge 88

1.3.24 Penicillin allergy 91

Pathogens and Management 94

2.1 Antimicrobial prophylaxis 94

2.2 Immunisation 95

2.3 Infection control 97

2.4 Travel advice 99

2.5 Bacteria 100

2.5.1 Gram-positive bacteria 101

2.5.2 Gram-negative bacteria 104

2.6 Mycobacteria 108

2.6.1 Mycobacterium tuberculosis 108

2.6.2 Mycobacterium leprae 113

2.6.3 Opportunistic mycobacteria 114

2.7 Spirochaetes 115

2.7.1 Syphilis 115

2.7.2 Lyme disease 117

2.7.3 Relapsing fever 118

2.7.4 Leptospirosis 118

2.8 Miscellaneous bacteria 119

2.8.1 *Mycoplasma* and *Ureaplasma* 119

2.8.2 Rickettsiae 120

2.8.3 *Coxiella burnetii* (Q fever) 120

2.8.4 Chlamydiae 121

2.9 Fungi 121

2.9.1 *Candida* spp. 121

2.9.2 *Aspergillus* 123

2.9.3 *Cryptococcus neoformans* 124

2.9.4 Dimorphic fungi 125

2.9.5 Miscellaneous fungi 126

2.10 Viruses 126

2.10.1 Herpes simplex viruses 127

2.10.2 Varicella-zoster virus 128

2.10.3 Cytomegalovirus 130

2.10.4 Epstein–Barr virus 130

2.10.5 Human herpesviruses 6 and 7 130

2.10.6 Human herpesvirus 8 131

2.10.7 Parvovirus 131

2.10.8 Hepatitis viruses 132

2.10.9 Influenza virus 133

2.10.10 Paramyxoviruses 134

2.10.11 Enteroviruses 134

2.10.12 Coronaviruses and SARS 135

2.11 Human immunodeficiency virus 135

2.11.1 Prevention following sharps injury 140

2.12 Travel-related viruses 142

2.12.1 Rabies 142

2.12.2 Dengue 143

2.12.3 Arbovirus infections 143

2.13 Protozoan parasites 144

2.13.1 Malaria 144

2.13.2 Leishmaniasis 145

2.13.3 Amoebiasis 146

2.13.4 Toxoplasmosis 147

2.14 Metazoan parasites 148

2.14.1 Schistosomiasis 148

2.14.2 Strongyloidiasis 149

2.14.3 Cysticercosis 150

2.14.4 Filariasis 151

2.14.5 Trichinosis 151

2.14.6 Toxocariasis 152

2.14.7 Hydatid disease 152

Investigations and Practical Procedures 154

3.1 Getting the best from the laboratory 154

3.2 Specific investigations 154

Self-assessment 159

DERMATOLOGY

PACES Stations and Acute Scenarios 175

1.1 History taking 175

1.1.1 Blistering disorders 175

1.1.2 Chronic red facial rash 177

1.1.3 Pruritus 178
1.1.4 Alopecia 180
1.1.5 Hyperpigmentation 181
1.1.6 Hypopigmentation 183
1.1.7 Red legs 185
1.1.8 Leg ulcers 187
1.2 Clinical examination 189
  1.2.1 Blistering disorder 189
  1.2.2 A chronic red facial rash 193
  1.2.3 Pruritus 198
  1.2.4 Alopecia 200
  1.2.5 Hyperpigmentation 202
  1.2.6 Hypopigmentation 205
  1.2.7 Red legs 207
  1.2.8 Lumps and bumps 210
  1.2.9 Telangiectases 212
  1.2.10 Purpura 214
  1.2.11 Lesion on the shin 216
  1.2.12 Non-pigmented lesion on the face 217
  1.2.13 A pigmented lesion on the face 219
  1.2.14 Leg ulcers 221
  1.2.15 Examine these hands 223
1.3 Communication skills and ethics 225
  1.3.1 Consenting a patient to enter a dermatological trial 225
  1.3.2 A steroid-phobic patient 227
  1.3.3 An anxious woman with a family history of melanoma who wants all her moles removed 228
  1.3.4 Prescribing isotretinoin to a woman of reproductive age 229
1.4 Acute scenarios 231
  1.4.1 Acute generalised rashes 231
  1.4.2 Erythroderma 238

Diseases and Treatments 243

2.1 Acne vulgaris 243
2.2 Acanthosis nigricans 245
2.3 Alopecia areata 245

2.4 Bullous pemphigoid 246
2.5 Dermatomyositis 248
2.6 Dermatitis herpetiformis 249
2.7 Drug eruptions 249
2.8 Atopic eczema 251
2.9 Contact dermatitis 252
2.10 Erythema multiforme, Stevens–Johnson syndrome and toxic epidermal necrolysis 253
2.11 Erythema nodosum 254
2.12 Fungal infections of skin, hair and nails (superficial fungal infections) 255
2.13 HIV and the skin 257
2.14 Lichen planus 258
2.15 Lymphoma of the skin: mycosis fungoides and Sézary syndrome 260
2.16 Pemphigus vulgaris 261
2.17 Psoriasis 263
2.18 Pyoderma gangrenosum 265
2.19 Scabies 266
2.20 Basal cell carcinoma 268
2.21 Squamous cell carcinoma 270
2.22 Malignant melanoma 271
2.23 Urticaria and angio-oedema 274
2.24 Vitiligo 275
2.25 Cutaneous vasculitis 276
2.26 Topical therapy: corticosteroids and immunosuppressants 277
2.27 Phototherapy 278
2.28 Retinoids 279

Investigations and Practical Procedures 281

3.1 Skin biopsy 281
3.2 Direct and indirect immunofluorescence 282
3.3 Patch tests 282
3.4 Obtaining specimens for mycological analysis 284

Self-assessment 285

Haematology and Oncology

HAEMATOLOGY

PACES Stations and Acute Scenarios 1

1.1 History-taking 3
  1.1.1 Microcytic hypochromic anaemia 3
  1.1.2 Macrocytic anaemia 5
  1.1.3 Lymphocytosis and anaemia 8
  1.1.4 Thromboembolism and fetal loss 11
  1.1.5 Weight loss and thrombocytosis 12
1.2 Clinical examination 14
  1.2.1 Normocytic anaemia 14
  1.2.2 Thrombocytopenia and purpura 14
  1.2.3 Jaundice and anaemia 16
  1.2.4 Polycythaemia 17
  1.2.5 Splenomegaly 18
1.3 Communication skills and ethics 19
  1.3.1 Persuading a patient to accept HIV testing 19
  1.3.2 Talking to a distressed relative 20
  1.3.3 Explaining a medical error 22
  1.3.4 Breaking bad news 23
1.4 Acute scenarios 25
  1.4.1 Chest syndrome in sickle cell disease 25
  1.4.2 Neutropenia 27
  1.4.3 Leucocytosis 29
  1.4.4 Spontaneous bleeding and weight loss 31
  1.4.5 Cervical lymphadenopathy and difficulty breathing 32
  1.4.6 Swelling of the leg 35

Diseases and Treatments 37

2.1 **Causes of anaemia 37**
  2.1.1 Thalassaemia syndromes 38
  2.1.2 Sickle cell syndromes 39
  2.1.3 Enzyme defects 41
  2.1.4 Membrane defects 41
  2.1.5 Iron metabolism and iron-deficiency anaemia 43
  2.1.6 Vitamin B_{12} and folate metabolism and deficiency 44
  2.1.7 Acquired haemolytic anaemia 44
  2.1.8 Bone-marrow failure and infiltration 46
2.2 **Haematological malignancy 46**
  2.2.1 Multiple myeloma 46
  2.2.2 Acute leukaemia: acute lymphoblastic leukaemia and acute myeloid leukaemia 49
  2.2.3 Chronic lymphocytic leukaemia 52
  2.2.4 Chronic myeloid leukaemia 54
  2.2.5 Malignant lymphomas: non-Hodgkin's lymphoma and Hodgkin's lymphoma 55
  2.2.6 Myelodysplastic syndromes 58
  2.2.7 Non-leukaemic myeloproliferative disorders (including polycythaemia vera, essential thrombocythaemia and myelofibrosis) 60
  2.2.8 Amyloidosis 62
2.3 **Bleeding disorders 64**
  2.3.1 Inherited bleeding disorders 64
  2.3.2 Aquired bleeding disorders 67
  2.3.3 Idiopathic throbocytopenic purpura 68
2.4 **Thrombotic disorders 69**
  2.4.1 Inherited thrombotic disease 69
  2.4.2 Acquired thrombotic disease 72
2.5 **Clinical use of blood products 74**
2.6 **Haematological features of systemic disease 76**
2.7 **Haematology of pregnancy 79**
2.8 **Iron overload 80**
2.9 **Chemotherapy and related therapies 82**
2.10 **Principles of bone-marrow and peripheral blood stem-cell transplantation 85**

Investigations and Practical Procedures 87

3.1 **The full blood count and film 87**
3.2 **Bone-marrow examination 89**
3.3 **Clotting screen 91**
3.4 **Coombs' test (direct antiglobulin test) 91**
3.5 **Erythrocyte sedimentation rate versus plasma viscosity 92**
3.6 **Therapeutic anticoagulation 92**

Self-assessment 94

ONCOLOGY

PACES Stations and Acute Scenarios 109

1.1 **History-taking 109**
  1.1.1 A dark spot 109
1.2 **Clinical examination 110**
  1.2.1 A lump in the neck 110
1.3 **Communication skills and ethics 111**
  1.3.1 Am I at risk of cancer? 111
  1.3.2 Consent for chemotherapy (1) 113
  1.3.3 Consent for chemotherapy (2) 114
  1.3.4 Don't tell him the diagnosis 116
1.4 **Acute scenarios 117**
  1.4.1 Acute deterioration after starting chemotherapy 117
  1.4.2 Back pain and weak legs 119
  1.4.3 Breathless, hoarse, dizzy and swollen 121

Diseases and Treatments 124

2.1 **Breast cancer 124**
2.2 **Central nervous system cancers 126**
2.3 **Digestive tract cancers 129**
2.4 **Genitourinary cancer 132**
2.5 **Gynaecological cancer 136**
2.6 **Head and neck cancer 139**
2.7 **Skin tumours 140**
2.8 **Paediatric solid tumours 144**
2.9 **Lung cancer 146**
2.10 **Liver and biliary tree cancer 149**
2.11 **Bone cancer and sarcoma 151**
2.12 **Endocrine tumours 157**
2.13 **The causes of cancer 159**
2.14 **Paraneoplastic conditions 162**

Investigations and Practical Procedures 167

3.1 **Investigation of unknown primary cancers 167**
3.2 **Investigation and management of metastatic disease 169**
3.3 **Tumour markers 171**
3.4 **Screening 173**
3.5 **Radiotherapy 175**
3.6 **Chemotherapy 176**
3.7 **Immunotherapy 179**
3.8 **Stem-cell transplantation 180**
3.9 **Oncological emergencies 180**

Self-assessment 185

Cardiology and Respiratory Medicine

CARDIOLOGY

PACES Stations and Acute Scenarios 3

1.1 History-taking 3
- 1.1.1 Paroxysmal palpitations 3
- 1.1.2 Palpitations with dizziness 6
- 1.1.3 Breathlessness and ankle swelling 9
- 1.1.4 Breathlessness and exertional presyncope 12
- 1.1.5 Dyspnoea, ankle oedema and cyanosis 14
- 1.1.6 Chest pain and recurrent syncope 16
- 1.1.7 Hypertension found at routine screening 19
- 1.1.8 Murmur in pregnancy 23

1.2 Clinical examination 25
- 1.2.1 Irregular pulse 25
- 1.2.2 Congestive heart failure 27
- 1.2.3 Hypertension 29
- 1.2.4 Mechanical valve 29
- 1.2.5 Pansystolic murmur 30
- 1.2.6 Mitral stenosis 31
- 1.2.7 Aortic stenosis 32
- 1.2.8 Aortic regurgitation 33
- 1.2.9 Tricuspid regurgitation 34
- 1.2.10 Eisenmenger's syndrome 35
- 1.2.11 Dextrocardia 36

1.3 Communication skills and ethics 37
- 1.3.1 Advising a patient against unnecessary investigations 37
- 1.3.2 Explanation of uncertainty of diagnosis 38
- 1.3.3 Discussion of the need to screen relatives for an inherited condition 38
- 1.3.4 Communicating news of a patient's death to a spouse 39
- 1.3.5 Explanation to a patient of the need for investigations 40
- 1.3.6 Explanation to a patient who is reluctant to receive treatment 41

1.4 Acute scenarios 42
- 1.4.1 Syncope 42
- 1.4.2 Stroke and a murmur 46
- 1.4.3 Acute chest pain 49
- 1.4.4 Hypotension following acute myocardial infarction 52
- 1.4.5 Breathlessness and collapse 54
- 1.4.6 Pleuritic chest pain 57
- 1.4.7 Fever, weight loss and a murmur 60
- 1.4.8 Chest pain following a 'flu-like illness 64

Diseases and Treatments 69

2.1 Coronary artery disease 69
- 2.1.1 Stable angina 69
- 2.1.2 Unstable angina and non-ST-elevation myocardial infarction 71
- 2.1.3 ST-elevation myocardial infarction 72

2.2 Cardiac arrhythmia 76
- 2.2.1 Bradycardia 76
- 2.2.2 Tachycardia 78

2.3 Cardiac failure 82

2.4 Diseases of heart muscle 86
- 2.4.1 Hypertrophic cardiomyopathy 86
- 2.4.2 Dilated cardiomyopathy 89
- 2.4.3 Restrictive cardiomyopathy 89
- 2.4.4 Arrhythmogenic right ventricular cardiomyopathy 90
- 2.4.5 Left ventricular non-compaction 90

2.5 Valvular heart disease 90
- 2.5.1 Aortic stenosis 90
- 2.5.2 Aortic regurgitation 92
- 2.5.3 Mitral stenosis 93
- 2.5.4 Mitral regurgitation 95
- 2.5.5 Tricuspid valve disease 97
- 2.5.6 Pulmonary valve disease 98

2.6 Pericardial disease 98
- 2.6.1 Acute pericarditis 98
- 2.6.2 Pericardial effusion 100
- 2.6.3 Constrictive pericarditis 102

2.7 Congenital heart disease 104
- 2.7.1 Acyanotic congenital heart disease 105
  - 2.7.1.1 Atrial septal defect 105
  - 2.7.1.2 Isolated ventricular septal defect 107
  - 2.7.1.3 Patent ductus arteriosus 107
  - 2.7.1.4 Coarctation of the aorta 108
- 2.7.2 Cyanotic congenital heart disease 109
  - 2.7.2.1 Tetralogy of Fallot 109
  - 2.7.2.2 Complete transposition of great arteries 111
  - 2.7.2.3 Ebstein's anomaly 112
- 2.7.3 Eisenmenger's syndrome 113

2.8 Infective diseases of the heart 114
- 2.8.1 Infective endocarditis 114
- 2.8.2 Rheumatic fever 119

2.9 Cardiac tumours 120

2.10 Traumatic heart disease 122

2.11 Disease of systemic arteries 124
    2.11.1 Aortic dissection 124
2.12 Diseases of pulmonary arteries 126
    2.12.1 Primary pulmonary hypertension 126
    2.12.2 Secondary pulmonary hypertension 129
2.13 Cardiac complications of systemic disease 130
    2.13.1 Thyroid disease 130
    2.13.2 Diabetes 131
    2.13.3 Autoimmune rheumatic diseases 131
    2.13.4 Renal disease 132
2.14 Systemic complications of cardiac disease 133
    2.14.1 Stroke 133
2.15 Pregnancy and the heart 134
2.16 General anaesthesia in heart disease 136
2.17 Hypertension 136
    2.17.1 Hypertensive emergencies 140
2.18 Venous thromboembolism 141
    2.18.1 Pulmonary embolism 141
2.19 Driving restrictions in cardiology 145

Investigations and Practical Procedures 147

3.1 ECG 147
    3.1.1 Exercise ECGs 151
3.2 Basic electrophysiology studies 152
3.3 Ambulatory monitoring 154
3.4 Radiofrequency ablation and implantable cardioverter defibrillators 156
    3.4.1 Radiofrequency ablation 156
    3.4.2 Implantable cardioverter defibrillator 157
    3.4.3 Cardiac resynchronisation therapy 158
3.5 Pacemakers 159

3.6 Chest radiograph in cardiac disease 161
3.7 Cardiac biochemical markers 163
3.8 CT and MRI 164
    3.8.1 Multislice spiral CT 164
    3.8.2 MRI 165
3.9 Ventilation–perfusion imaging 166
3.10 Echocardiography 167
3.11 Nuclear cardiology 170
    3.11.1 Myocardial perfusion imaging 170
    3.11.2 Radionuclide ventriculography 170
    3.11.3 Positron emission tomography 171
3.12 Cardiac catheterisation 171
    3.12.1 Percutaneous coronary intervention 172
    3.12.2 Percutaneous valvuloplasty 173**

Self-assessment 176

RESPIRATORY MEDICINE

PACES Stations and Acute Scenarios 191

1.1 History-taking 191
    1.1.1 New breathlessness 191
    1.1.2 Solitary pulmonary nodule 193
    1.1.3 Exertional dyspnoea with daily sputum 195
    1.1.4 Dyspnoea and fine inspiratory crackles 197
    1.1.5 Nocturnal cough 199
    1.1.6 Daytime sleepiness and morning headache 202
    1.1.7 Lung cancer with asbestos exposure 204
    1.1.8 Breathlessness with a normal chest radiograph 206

1.2 Clinical examination 209
    1.2.1 Coarse crackles: bronchiectasis 209
    1.2.2 Fine crackles: interstitial lung disease 210
    1.2.3 Stridor 212
    1.2.4 Pleural effusion 213
    1.2.5 Wheeze and crackles: chronic obstructive pulmonary disease 215
    1.2.6 Cor pulmonale 216
    1.2.7 Pneumonectomy/lobectomy 217
    1.2.8 Apical signs: old tuberculosis 218
    1.2.9 Cystic fibrosis 219
1.3 Communication skills and ethics 220
    1.3.1 Lifestyle modification 220
    1.3.2 Possible cancer 221
    1.3.3 Potentially life-threatening illness 222
    1.3.4 Sudden unexplained death 224
    1.3.5 Intubation for ventilation 225
    1.3.6 Patient refusing ventilation 226
1.4 Acute scenarios 228
    1.4.1 Pleuritic chest pain 228
    1.4.2 Unexplained hypoxia 232
    1.4.3 Haemoptysis and weight loss 234
    1.4.4 Pleural effusion and fever 237
    1.4.5 Lobar collapse in non-smoker 239
    1.4.6 Upper airway obstruction 241

Diseases and Treatments 243

2.1 Upper airway 243
    2.1.1 Sleep apnoea 243
2.2 Atopy and asthma 245
    2.2.1 Allergic rhinitis 245
    2.2.2 Asthma 246
2.3 Chronic obstructive pulmonary disease 251
2.4 Bronchiectasis 253

2.5 **Cystic fibrosis** 256
2.6 **Occupational lung disease 258**
   2.6.1 Asbestosis and the pneumoconioses 258
2.7 **Diffuse parenchymal lung disease 261**
   2.7.1 Usual interstitial pneumonia 261
   2.7.2 Cryptogenic organising pneumonia 262
   2.7.3 Bronchiolitis obliterans 263
2.8 **Miscellaneous conditions 264**
   2.8.1 Extrinsic allergic alveolitis 264
   2.8.2 Sarcoidosis 265
   2.8.3 Respiratory complications of rheumatoid arthritis 267
   2.8.4 Pulmonary vasculitis 269
   2.8.5 Pulmonary eosinophilia 270
   2.8.6 Iatrogenic lung disease 272
   2.8.7 Smoke inhalation 274
   2.8.8 Sickle cell disease and the lung 276
   2.8.9 Human immunodeficiency virus and the lung 278
2.9 **Malignancy 279**
   2.9.1 Lung cancer 279
   2.9.2 Mesothelioma 283
   2.9.3 Mediastinal tumours 285
2.10 **Disorders of the chest wall and diaphragm 287**
2.11 **Complications of respiratory disease 288**
   2.11.1 Chronic respiratory failure 288
   2.11.2 Cor pulmonale 289
2.12 **Treatments in respiratory disease 290**
   2.12.1 Domiciliary oxygen therapy 290
   2.12.2 Continuous positive airways pressure 292

2.12.3 Non-invasive ventilation 292
2.13 **Lung transplantation 294**

Investigations and Practical Procedures 297

3.1 **Arterial blood gas sampling 297**
3.2 **Aspiration of pleural effusion or pneumothorax 298**
3.3 **Pleural biopsy 298**
3.4 **Intercostal tube insertion 300**
3.5 **Fibreoptic bronchoscopy and transbronchial biopsy 302**
   3.5.1 Fibreoptic bronchoscopy 302
   3.5.2 Transbronchial biopsy 302
3.6 **Interpretation of clinical data 302**
   3.6.1 Arterial blood gases 302
   3.6.2 Lung function tests 304
   3.6.3 Overnight oximetry 306
   3.6.4 Chest radiograph 306
   3.6.5 Computed tomography scan of the thorax 307

Self-assessment 312

Gastroenterology and Hepatology

GASTROENTEROLOGY AND HEPATOLOGY

PACES Stations and Acute Scenarios 3

1.1 **History-taking 3**
   1.1.1 Heartburn and dyspepsia 3
   1.1.2 Dysphagia and feeding difficulties 5
   1.1.3 Chronic diarrhoea 8
   1.1.4 Rectal bleeding 10

1.1.5 Weight loss 14
1.1.6 Chronic abdominal pain 16
1.1.7 Abnormal liver function tests 18
1.1.8 Abdominal swelling 21
1.2 **Clinical examination 24**
   1.2.1 Inflammatory bowel disease 24
   1.2.2 Chronic liver disease 24
   1.2.3 Splenomegaly 25
   1.2.4 Abdominal swelling 26
1.3 **Communication skills and ethics 27**
   1.3.1 A decision about feeding 27
   1.3.2 Limitation of management 29
   1.3.3 Limitation of investigation 30
   1.3.4 A patient who does not want to give a history 31
1.4 **Acute scenarios 32**
   1.4.1 Nausea and vomiting 32
   1.4.2 Acute diarrhoea 36
   1.4.3 Haematemesis and melaena 39
   1.4.4 Acute abdominal pain 46
   1.4.5 Jaundice 50
   1.4.6 Acute liver failure 54

Diseases and Treatments 60

2.1 **Oesophageal disease 60**
   2.1.1 Gastro-oesophageal reflux disease 60
   2.1.2 Achalasia and oesophageal dysmotility 62
   2.1.3 Oesophageal cancer and Barrett's oesophagus 63
2.2 **Gastric disease 66**
   2.2.1 Peptic ulceration and *Helicobacter pylori* 66
   2.2.2 Gastric carcinoma 68
   2.2.3 Rare gastric tumours 69
   2.2.4 Rare causes of gastrointestinal haemorrhage 70

2.3 Small bowel disease 71
- **2.3.1** Malabsorption 71
  - **2.3.1.1** Bacterial overgrowth 71
  - **2.3.1.2** Other causes of malabsorption 72
- **2.3.2** Coeliac disease 73

2.4 Pancreatic disease 75
- **2.4.1** Acute pancreatitis 75
- **2.4.2** Chronic pancreatitis 78
- **2.4.3** Pancreatic cancer 80
- **2.4.4** Neuroendocrine tumours 82

2.5 Biliary disease 83
- **2.5.1** Choledocholithiasis 83
- **2.5.2** Primary biliary cirrhosis 85
- **2.5.3** Primary sclerosing cholangitis 87
- **2.5.4** Intrahepatic cholestasis 89
- **2.5.5** Cholangiocarcinoma 89

2.6 Infectious diseases 92
- **2.6.1** Food poisoning and gastroenteritis 92
- **2.6.2** Bacterial dysentery 93
- **2.6.3** Antibiotic-associated diarrhoea 94
- **2.6.4** Parasitic infestations of the intestine 94
- **2.6.5** Intestinal and liver amoebiasis 95
- **2.6.6** Intestinal features of HIV infection 95

2.7 Inflammatory bowel disease 95
- **2.7.1** Crohn's disease 95
- **2.7.2** Ulcerative colitis 98
- **2.7.3** Microscopic colitis 101

2.8 Functional bowel disorders 101

2.9 Large bowel disorders 103
- **2.9.1** Adenomatous polyps of the colon 103
- **2.9.2** Colorectal carcinoma 104
- **2.9.3** Diverticular disease 107
- **2.9.4** Intestinal ischaemia 108
- **2.9.5** Anorectal diseases 109

2.10 Liver disease 109
- **2.10.1** Acute viral hepatitis 109
  - **2.10.1.1** Hepatitis A 109
  - **2.10.1.2** Other acute viral hepatitis 112
- **2.10.2** Chronic viral hepatitis 113
  - **2.10.2.1** Hepatitis B 113
  - **2.10.2.2** Hepatitis C 114
- **2.10.3** Acute liver failure 115
- **2.10.4** Alcohol-related liver disease 116
- **2.10.5** Drugs and the liver 118
  - **2.10.5.1** Hepatic drug toxicity 118
  - **2.10.5.2** Drugs and chronic liver disease 120
- **2.10.6** Chronic liver disease and cirrhosis 120
- **2.10.7** Focal liver lesion 124
- **2.10.8** Liver transplantation 127

2.11 Nutrition 129
- **2.11.1** Defining nutrition 129
- **2.11.2** Protein–calorie malnutrition 133
- **2.11.3** Obesity 133
- **2.11.4** Enteral and parenteral nutrition and special diets 134

Investigations and Practical Procedures 136

3.1 General investigations 136
3.2 Tests of gastrointestinal and liver function 137
3.3 Diagnostic and therapeutic endoscopy 138
3.4 Diagnostic and therapeutic radiology 139
3.5 Rigid sigmoidoscopy and rectal biopsy 140
3.6 Paracentesis 143
3.7 Liver biopsy 144

Self-assessment 147

Neurology, Ophthalmology and Psychiatry

NEUROLOGY

PACES Stations and Acute Scenarios 3

1.1 History-taking 3
- **1.1.1** Episodic headache 3
- **1.1.2** Facial pain 6
- **1.1.3** Funny turns/blackouts 8
- **1.1.4** Increasing seizure frequency 11
- **1.1.5** Numb toes 12
- **1.1.6** Tremor 15
- **1.1.7** Memory problems 17
- **1.1.8** Chorea 19
- **1.1.9** Muscle weakness and pain 20
- **1.1.10** Sleep disorders 21
- **1.1.11** Dysphagia 24
- **1.1.12** Visual hallucinations 26

1.2 Clinical examination 27
- **1.2.1** Numb toes and foot drop 27
- **1.2.2** Weakness in one leg 28
- **1.2.3** Spastic legs 32
- **1.2.4** Gait disturbance 33
- **1.2.5** Cerebellar syndrome 36
- **1.2.6** Weak arm/hand 37
- **1.2.7** Proximal muscle weakness 40
- **1.2.8** Muscle wasting 41
- **1.2.9** Hemiplegia 42
- **1.2.10** Tremor 44
- **1.2.11** Visual field defect 45
- **1.2.12** Unequal pupils 47
- **1.2.13** Ptosis 48
- **1.2.14** Abnormal ocular movements 51
- **1.2.15** Facial weakness 53
- **1.2.16** Lower cranial nerve assessment 55
- **1.2.17** Speech disturbance 57

1.3 Communication skills and ethics 60

1.3.1 Genetic implications 60
1.3.2 Explanation of the diagnosis of Alzheimer's disease 61
1.3.3 Prognosis after stroke 62
1.3.4 Conversion disorder 63
1.3.5 Explaining the diagnosis of multiple sclerosis 64
1.4 Acute scenarios 65
1.4.1 Acute weakness of legs 65
1.4.2 Acute ischaemic stroke 67
1.4.3 Subarachnoid haemorrhage 71
1.4.4 Status epilepticus 73
1.4.5 Encephalopathy/coma 78

Diseases and Treatments 81

2.1 Peripheral neuropathies and diseases of the lower motor neuron 81
2.1.1 Peripheral neuropathies 81
2.1.2 Guillain–Barré syndrome 85
2.1.3 Motor neuron disease 87
2.2 Diseases of muscle 89
2.2.1 Metabolic muscle disease 89
2.2.2 Inflammatory muscle disease 91
2.2.3 Inherited dystrophies (myopathies) 91
2.2.4 Channelopathies 93
2.2.5 Myasthenia gravis 93
2.3 Extrapyramidal disorders 95
2.3.1 Parkinson's disease 95
2.4 Dementia 99
2.4.1 Alzheimer's disease 99
2.5 Multiple sclerosis 101
2.6 Headache 104
2.6.1 Migraine 104
2.6.2 Trigeminal neuralgia 107
2.6.3 Cluster headache 108
2.6.4 Tension-type headache 109

2.7 Epilepsy 110
2.8 Cerebrovascular disease 116
2.8.1 Stroke 116
2.8.2 Transient ischaemic attacks 120
2.8.3 Intracerebral haemorrhage 122
2.8.4 Subarachnoid haemorrhage 125
2.9 Brain tumours 127
2.10 Neurological complications of infection 131
2.10.1 New variant Creutzfeldt–Jakob disease 131
2.11 Neurological complications of systemic disease 132
2.11.1 Paraneoplastic conditions 132
2.12 Neuropharmacology 133

Investigations and Practical Procedures 139

3.1 Neuropsychometry 139
3.2 Lumbar puncture 140
3.3 Neurophysiology 142
3.3.1 Electroencephalography 142
3.3.2 Evoked potentials 142
3.3.3 Electromyography 142
3.3.4 Nerve conduction studies 143
3.4 Neuroimaging 143
3.4.1 Computed tomography and computed tomography angiography 143
3.4.2 Magnetic resonance imaging and magnetic resonance angiography 144
3.4.3 Angiography 145
3.5 Single-photon emission computed tomography and positron emission tomography 145
3.6 Carotid Dopplers 147

Self-assessment 148

OPHTHALMOLOGY

PACES Stations and Acute Scenarios 161

1.1 Clinical scenarios 161
1.1.1 Examination of the eye 161
1.2 Acute scenarios 164
1.2.1 An acutely painful red eye 164
1.2.2 Two painful red eyes and a systemic disorder 166
1.2.3 Acute painless loss of vision in one eye 168
1.2.4 Acute painful loss of vision in a young woman 170
1.2.5 Acute loss of vision in an elderly man 171

Diseases and Treatments 173

2.1 Iritis 173
2.2 Scleritis 174
2.3 Retinal artery occlusion 175
2.4 Retinal vein occlusion 178
2.5 Optic neuritis 179
2.6 Ischaemic optic neuropathy in giant-cell arteritis 180
2.7 Diabetic retinopathy 181

Investigations and Practical Procedures 186

3.1 Fluorescein angiography 186
3.2 Temporal artery biopsy 186

Self-assessment 188

PSYCHIATRY

PACES Stations and Acute Scenarios 195

1.1 History-taking 195
1.1.1 Eating disorders 195
1.1.2 Medically unexplained symptoms 197

1.2 Communication skills and ethics 199
- **1.2.1** Panic attack and hyperventilation 199
- **1.2.2** Deliberate self-harm 200
- **1.2.3** Medically unexplained symptoms 201

1.3 Acute scenarios 202
- **1.3.1** Acute confusional state 202
- **1.3.2** Panic attack and hyperventilation 205
- **1.3.3** Deliberate self-harm 207
- **1.3.4** The alcoholic in hospital 208
- **1.3.5** Drug abuser in hospital 210
- **1.3.6** The frightening patient 212

Diseases and Treatments 215

2.1 Dissociative disorders 215
2.2 Dementia 215
2.3 Schizophrenia and antipsychotic drugs 217
- **2.3.1** Schizophrenia 217
- **2.3.2** Antipsychotics 218

2.4 Personality disorder 220
2.5 Psychiatric presentation of physical disease 221
2.6 Psychological reactions to physical illness (adjustment disorders) 222
2.7 Anxiety disorders 223
- **2.7.1** Generalised anxiety disorder 225
- **2.7.2** Panic disorder 226
- **2.7.3** Phobic anxiety disorders 228

2.8 Obsessive–compulsive disorder 229
2.9 Acute stress reactions and post-traumatic stress disorder 231
- **2.9.1** Acute stress reaction 231
- **2.9.2** Post-traumatic stress disorder 231

2.10 Puerperal disorders 233
- **2.10.1** Maternity blues 233
- **2.10.2** Postnatal depressive disorder 233
- **2.10.3** Puerperal psychosis 233

2.11 Depression 235
2.12 Bipolar affective disorder 237
2.13 Delusional disorder 238
2.14 The Mental Health Act 1983 239

Self-assessment 241

Endocrinology

ENDOCRINOLOGY

PACES Stations and Acute Scenarios 3

1.1 History-taking 3
- **1.1.1** Hypercalcaemia 3
- **1.1.2** Polyuria 5
- **1.1.3** Faints, sweats and palpitations 8
- **1.1.4** Gynaecomastia 12
- **1.1.5** Hirsutism 14
- **1.1.6** Post-pill amenorrhoea 16
- **1.1.7** A short girl with no periods 17
- **1.1.8** Young man who has 'not developed' 20
- **1.1.9** Depression and diabetes 21
- **1.1.10** Acromegaly 23
- **1.1.11** Relentless weight gain 24
- **1.1.12** Weight loss 26
- **1.1.13** Tiredness and lethargy 29
- **1.1.14** Flushing and diarrhoea 32
- **1.1.15** Avoiding another coronary 34
- **1.1.16** High blood pressure and low serum potassium 37
- **1.1.17** Tiredness, weight loss and amenorrhoea 39

1.2 Clinical examination 42
- **1.2.1** Amenorrhoea and low blood pressure 42
- **1.2.2** Young man who has 'not developed' 43
- **1.2.3** Depression and diabetes 45
- **1.2.4** Acromegaly 45
- **1.2.5** Weight loss and gritty eyes 47
- **1.2.6** Tiredness and lethargy 48
- **1.2.7** Hypertension and a lump in the neck 48

1.3 Communication skills and ethics 50
- **1.3.1** Explaining an uncertain outcome 50
- **1.3.2** The possibility of cancer 51
- **1.3.3** No medical cause for hirsutism 52
- **1.3.4** A short girl with no periods 53
- **1.3.5** Simple obesity, not a problem with 'the glands' 54
- **1.3.6** I don't want to take the tablets 55

1.4 Acute scenarios 56
- **1.4.1** Coma with hyponatraemia 56
- **1.4.2** Hypercalcaemic and confused 60
- **1.4.3** Thyrotoxic crisis 61
- **1.4.4** Addisonian crisis 63
- **1.4.5** 'Off legs' 65

Diseases and Treatments 68

2.1 Hypothalamic and pituitary diseases 68
- **2.1.1** Cushing's syndrome 68
- **2.1.2** Acromegaly 71
- **2.1.3** Hyperprolactinaemia 73
- **2.1.4** Non-functioning pituitary tumours 76
- **2.1.5** Pituitary apoplexy 77
- **2.1.6** Craniopharyngioma 78
- **2.1.7** Diabetes insipidus 80
- **2.1.8** Hypopituitarism and hormone replacement 83

2.2 Adrenal disease 85
  2.2.1 Cushing's syndrome 85
  2.2.2 Primary hyperaldosteronism 85
  2.2.3 Virilising tumours 87
  2.2.4 Phaeochromocytoma 89
  2.2.5 Congenital adrenal hyperplasia 92
  2.2.6 Primary adrenal insufficiency 94
2.3 Thyroid disease 97
  2.3.1 Hypothyroidism 97
  2.3.2 Thyrotoxicosis 100
  2.3.3 Thyroid nodules and goitre 105
  2.3.4 Thyroid malignancy 107
2.4 Reproductive disorders 107
  2.4.1 Delayed growth and puberty 107
  2.4.2 Male hypogonadism 111
  2.4.3 Oligomenorrhoea/ amenorrhoea and premature menopause 113
  2.4.4 Turner's syndrome 115
  2.4.5 Polycystic ovarian syndrome 116
  2.4.6 Hirsutism 118
  2.4.7 Erectile dysfunction 120
  2.4.8 Infertility 123
2.5 Metabolic and bone diseases 125
  2.5.1 Hyperlipidaemia/ dyslipidaemia 125
  2.5.2 Porphyria 128
  2.5.3 Haemochromatosis 130
  2.5.4 Osteoporosis 131
  2.5.5 Osteomalacia 134
  2.5.6 Paget's disease 136
  2.5.7 Hyperparathyroidism 137
  2.5.8 Hypercalcaemia 140
  2.5.9 Hypocalcaemia 141
2.6 Diabetes mellitus 143
  2.6.1 Management of hyperglycaemic emergencies 145
  2.6.2 Management of hypoglycaemic emergencies 147
  2.6.3 Short- and long-term management of diabetes 147

  2.6.4 Complications 153
  2.6.5 Important information for patients 160
2.7 Other endocrine disorders 162
  2.7.1 Multiple endocrine neoplasia 162
  2.7.2 Autoimmune polyglandular endocrinopathies 163
  2.7.3 Ectopic hormone syndromes 164

Investigations and Practical Procedures 165

3.1 Stimulation tests 165
  3.1.1 Short Synacthen test 165
  3.1.2 Corticotrophin-releasing hormone test 166
  3.1.3 Thyrotrophin-releasing hormone test 166
  3.1.4 Gonadotrophin-releasing hormone test 167
  3.1.5 Insulin tolerance test 167
  3.1.6 Pentagastrin stimulation test 168
  3.1.7 Oral glucose tolerance test 169
3.2 Suppression tests 169
  3.2.1 Overnight dexamethasone suppression test 169
  3.2.2 Low-dose dexamethasone suppression test 170
  3.2.3 High-dose dexamethasone suppression test 170
  3.2.4 Oral glucose tolerance test in acromegaly 171
3.3 Other investigations 171
  3.3.1 Thyroid function tests 171
  3.3.2 Water deprivation test 172

Self-assessment 174

Nephrology

NEPHROLOGY

PACES Stations and Acute Scenarios 3

1.1 History-taking 3
  1.1.1 Dipstick haematuria 3
  1.1.2 Pregnancy with renal disease 5
  1.1.3 A swollen young woman 8
  1.1.4 Rheumatoid arthritis with swollen legs 11
  1.1.5 A blood test shows moderate renal failure 13
  1.1.6 Diabetes with impaired renal function 16
  1.1.7 Atherosclerosis and renal failure 18
  1.1.8 Recurrent loin pain 20
1.2 Clinical examination 22
  1.2.1 Polycystic kidneys 22
  1.2.2 Transplant kidney 23
1.3 Communication skills and ethics 23
  1.3.1 Renal disease in pregnancy 23
  1.3.2 A new diagnosis of amyloidosis 24
  1.3.3 Is dialysis appropriate? 25
1.4 Acute scenarios 26
  1.4.1 A worrying potassium level 26
  1.4.2 Postoperative acute renal failure 30
  1.4.3 Renal impairment and a multisystem disease 33
  1.4.4 Renal impairment and fever 36
  1.4.5 Renal failure and haemoptysis 38
  1.4.6 Renal colic 41
  1.4.7 Backache and renal failure 43
  1.4.8 Renal failure and coma 47

Diseases and Treatments 49

2.1 Major renal syndromes 49
  2.1.1 Acute renal failure 49
  2.1.2 Chronic renal failure 51
  2.1.3 End-stage renal failure 58
  2.1.4 Nephrotic syndromes 60
2.2 Renal replacement therapy 64
  2.2.1 Haemodialysis 64
  2.2.2 Peritoneal dialysis 66
  2.2.3 Renal transplantation 69
2.3 Glomerular diseases 72
  2.3.1 Primary glomerular disease 72
  2.3.2 Secondary glomerular disease 79
2.4 Tubulointerstitial diseases 81
  2.4.1 Acute tubular necrosis 81
  2.4.2 Acute interstitial nephritis 82
  2.4.3 Chronic interstitial nephritis 82
  2.4.4 Specific tubulointerstitial disorders 83
2.5 Diseases of renal vessels 86
  2.5.1 Renovascular disease 86
  2.5.2 Cholesterol atheroembolisation 88
2.6 Postrenal problems 89
  2.6.1 Obstructive uropathy 89
  2.6.2 Stones 90
  2.6.3 Retroperitonal fibrosis or periaortitis 91
  2.6.4 Urinary tract infection 92
2.7 The kidney in systemic disease 92
  2.7.1 Myeloma 92
  2.7.2 Amyloidosis 93
  2.7.3 Thrombotic microangiopathy (haemolytic–uraemic syndrome) 94
  2.7.4 Sickle cell disease 95
  2.7.5 Autoimmune rheumatic disorders 95
  2.7.6 Systemic vasculitis 97
  2.7.7 Diabetic nephropathy 99
  2.7.8 Hypertension 101
  2.7.9 Sarcoidosis 102
  2.7.10 Hepatorenal syndrome 102
  2.7.11 Pregnancy and the kidney 103
2.8 Genetic renal conditions 104
  2.8.1 Autosomal dominant polycystic kidney disease 104
  2.8.2 Alport's syndrome 106
  2.8.3 X-linked hypophosphataemic vitamin-D resistant rickets 106

Investigations and Practical Procedures 108

3.1 Examination of the urine 108
  3.1.1 Urinalysis 108
  3.1.2 Urine microscopy 109
3.2 Estimation of glomerular filtration rate 109
3.3 Imaging the renal tract 110
3.4 Renal biopsy 114

Self-assessment 116

Rheumatology and Clinical Immunology

RHEUMATOLOGY AND CLINICAL IMMUNOLOGY

PACES Stations and Acute Scenarios 3

1.1 History-taking 3
  1.1.1 Recurrent chest infections 3
  1.1.2 Recurrent meningitis 5
  1.1.3 Recurrent facial swelling and abdominal pain 7
  1.1.4 Recurrent skin abscesses 9
  1.1.5 Flushing and skin rash 12
  1.1.6 Drug-induced anaphylaxis 14
  1.1.7 Arthralgia, purpuric rash and renal impairment 16
  1.1.8 Arthralgia and photosensitive rash 19
  1.1.9 Cold fingers and difficulty swallowing 23
  1.1.10 Dry eyes and fatigue 25
  1.1.11 Breathlessness and weakness 27
  1.1.12 Low back pain 30
  1.1.13 Chronic back pain 32
  1.1.14 Recurrent joint pain and stiffness 33
  1.1.15 Foot drop and weight loss in a patient with rheumatoid arthritis 35
  1.1.16 Fever, myalgia, arthralgia and elevated acute-phase indices 38
  1.1.17 Non-rheumatoid pain and stiffness 40
  1.1.18 Widespread pain 42
1.2 Clinical examination 44
  1.2.1 Hands (general) 44
  1.2.2 Non-rheumatoid pain and stiffness: generalised osteoarthritis 45
  1.2.3 Rheumatoid arthritis 46
  1.2.4 Psoriatic arthritis 47
  1.2.5 Systemic sclerosis 49
  1.2.6 Chronic tophaceous gout 49
  1.2.7 Ankylosing spondylitis 50
  1.2.8 Deformity of bone: Paget's disease 51
  1.2.9 Marfan's syndrome 51
1.3 Communication skills and ethics 52
  1.3.1 Collapse during a restaurant meal 52
  1.3.2 Cold fingers and difficulty swallowing 54
  1.3.3 Back pain 55
  1.3.4 Widespread pain 56
  1.3.5 Explain a recommendation to start a disease-modifying antirheumatic drug 57

1.4 Acute scenarios 59

1.4.1 Fulminant septicaemia in an asplenic woman 59

1.4.2 Collapse during a restaurant meal 61

1.4.3 Systemic lupus erythematosus and confusion 64

1.4.4 Acute hot joints 66

1.4.5 A crush fracture 69

Diseases and Treatments 72

2.1 Immunodeficiency 72

2.1.1 Primary antibody deficiency 72

2.1.2 Combined T-cell and B-cell defects 75

2.1.3 Chronic granulomatous disease 77

2.1.4 Cytokine and cytokine-receptor deficiencies 78

2.1.5 Terminal pathway complement deficiency 80

2.1.6 Hyposplenism 81

2.2 Allergy 82

2.2.1 Anaphylaxis 82

2.2.2 Mastocytosis 84

2.2.3 Nut allergy 85

2.2.4 Drug allergy 87

2.3 Rheumatology 88

2.3.1 Carpal tunnel syndrome 88

2.3.2 Osteoarthritis 89

2.3.3 Rheumatoid arthritis 91

2.3.4 Seronegative spondyloarthropathies 94

2.3.5 Idiopathic inflammatory myopathies 98

2.3.6 Crystal arthritis: gout 99

2.3.7 Calcium pyrophosphate deposition disease 101

2.3.8 Fibromyalgia 101

2.4 Autoimmune rheumatic diseases 103

2.4.1 Systemic lupus erythematosus 103

2.4.2 Sjögren's syndrome 105

2.4.3 Systemic sclerosis (scleroderma) 106

2.5 Vasculitides 109

2.5.1 Giant-cell arteritis and polymyalgia rheumatica 109

2.5.2 Wegener's granulomatosis 111

2.5.3 Polyarteritis nodosa 113

2.5.4 Cryoglobulinaemic vasculitis 114

2.5.5 Behçet's disease 115

2.5.6 Takayasu's arteritis 117

2.5.7 Systemic Still's disease 119

Investigations and Practical Procedures 121

3.1 Assessment of acute-phase response 121

3.1.1 Erythrocyte sedimentation rate 121

3.1.2 C-reactive protein 121

3.2 Serological investigation of autoimmune rheumatic disease 122

3.2.1 Antibodies to nuclear antigens 122

3.2.2 Antibodies to double-stranded DNA 123

3.2.3 Antibodies to extractable nuclear antigens 124

3.2.4 Rheumatoid factor 125

3.2.5 Antineutrophil cytoplasmic antibody 125

3.2.6 Serum complement concentrations 125

3.3 Suspected immune deficiency in adults 126

3.4 Imaging in rheumatological disease 129

3.4.1 Plain radiology 129

3.4.2 Bone densitometry 130

3.4.3 Magnetic resonance imaging 131

3.4.4 Nuclear medicine 131

3.4.5 Ultrasound 132

3.5 Arthrocentesis 132

3.6 Corticosteroid injection techniques 133

3.7 Immunoglobulin replacement 135

Self-assessment 138

INDEX

Page numbers in *italics* represent figures, those in **bold** represent tables

A

abdominal pain 7–9
ACE inhibitors
  anaphylaxis **15**
  angio-oedema 8, 9
achlorhydria 74
acute phase response 121–2
  C-reactive protein 22, 35, 37, 40,
    121–2, **121**, **122**
  erythrocyte sedimentation rate 35, 37,
    40, 121, **121**, **122**
adalimumab 94
adenosine deaminase deficiency 75
adult onset Still's disease **39**, 119–20
  aetiology/pathology 119
  clinical presentation 119
  differential diagnosis 119, **120**
  epidemiology 119
  investigation 119, **119**
  management 120
alanine transaminase 29
allergy 82–8, *82*
  anaphylaxis 82–3
  drug allergy 87–8, **87**
  mastocytosis 84–5, *85*
  nut allergy 52–4, 85–6
allopurinol 101
amiodarone hypersensitivity **87**
amitryptyline 32
anaemia 4
anaphylaxis 8, 61–4, 82–3
  aetiology/pathophysiology/pathology
    82
  clinical presentation 82
  differential diagnosis 83
  drug history 63
  drug-induced 14–16
  epidemiology 82
  examination 63
  history 62–3
  idiopathic 16
  immediate management 63
  investigations 63–4, 82–3, *83*
  later management 64
  nut allergy 52–4, 85–6
  physical signs 82
  self-management 53
  treatment 83, *84*
angio-oedema 7–9
  anaphylactic 8
  anaphylactoid 8
  immune complex mediated 8

ankylosing spondylitis 50–1
  clinical presentation 95–6
  epidemiology 95
  prognosis 97
  Schoeber's test *51*
  spinal examination 50–1
anti-B cell therapy 94
anti-IgE antibodies *86*
anti-Ro antibodies 125
anti-Sm antibodies 125
anti-U1-RNP antibodies 125
antibiotic hypersensitivity **87**
antibodies
  ANCA 19, 125
  anti-Ro 125
  anti-Sm 125
  anti-U1-RNP 125
  anticentromere 123
  antihistone 123
  antinuclear 21, 108–9, *109*
  antiphospholipid 22, *22*
  to double-stranded DNA 123–4, *124*,
    125
  to extractable nuclear antigens
    124–5
  to nuclear antigens 122–3, *122*, *123*,
    124
antibody deficiency 4, 126, 127–8
  immunoglobulin replacement 135
anticentromere antibodies 123
antihistamines 14
antihistone antibodies 123
antineutrophil cytoplasmic antibodies
  (ANCAs) 19, 125, *126*
antinuclear antibodies 21, 108–9, *109*
antiphospholipid antibodies 22, *22*
aphthous ulcers 4
arachnodactyly 52
arthralgia 4
  photosensitive rash 19–23
    history 20–1, *20*, *21*
    investigation 21–2, *22*
    referral letter 19
  purpuric rash and renal impairment
    16–19
    differential diagnosis 16, **17**
    history 17–18
    investigation 18–19, **18**
    management 19
arthritis mutilans 48
arthrocentesis 35, 132–3
  complications 133

contraindications 132
indications 132
technique 132–3
aseptic monoarthritis 74
aspartate transaminase 29
Aspergillus spp. 11, **77**
aspirin in anaphylaxis **15**
asthma 8
atherosclerosis **118**
autoantibodies **123**
  see also antibodies
autoimmune blood dyscrasias 74
autoimmune disease 103–9
  autoantibody prevalence **123**
  Sjögren's syndrome 26, **26**, 34, 105–6
  systemic lupus erythematosus 5, *20*,
    34, 64–6, 103–5
  systemic sclerosis 23, 24, 49, 54–5,
    106–9
autoimmunity 72
azithromycin 79

B

Babesia spp. **59**
Behçet's disease 5, 115–17
  aetiology/pathophysiology/pathology
    115
  clinical presentation 115–16, *115*
  complications 117
  differential diagnosis 116
  epidemiology 115
  investigation 116, *116*
  morbidity 117
  mortality 117
  prognosis 117
  treatment 116–17
blepharitis 26
blood count 92
bone densitometry 130
bone scintigraphy 131
Bouchard's nodes 46, 50, 90
boutonnière deformity 47, 50
breathlessness 27–30
  history 27–9, *28*, **28**
  investigation 29
  management 29–30
  referral letter 27
bronchiectasis 4
Bruton's agammaglobulinaemia *see*
  X-linked agammaglobulinaemia
Burkholderia spp. 11, **77**

C

C-reactive protein 22, 35, 37, 40, 121–2, **121**, **122**
C1 inhibitor 8
C1 inhibitor deficiency 8–9
  acquired 8
  congenital 8
  diagnosis 8–9, *9*
  management 9
  precipitating factors 8
  and pregnancy 9
  surgical and dental procedures 9
C1q deficiency 81
C2 deficiency 81
C3 19, 21
C3 deficiency 81
C4 19, 21
C4 deficiency 81
calcinosis cutis 49, *107*
calcium pyrophosphate deposition
    disease 101, *102*
Campylobacter spp. 73
Campylobacter jejuni 94
Candida spp. 76, **77**
candidiasis 4
Capnocytophaga canimorsus 59
carbimazole hypersensitivity **87**
carcinoid syndrome **13**
carcinomatous neuromyopathy **28**
carpal tunnel syndrome 46, 47, 88–9, *88*
  aetiology/pathophysiology/pathology 88
  clinical presentation 88, *88*
  differential diagnosis 89
  investigations 89
  physical signs 88–9
  treatment 89
cauda equina syndrome 32, 33
CD4 deficiency 3
CD117 84
cephalosporins in anaphylaxis **15**
cerebrospinal fluid leak 5, 6
chest infections, recurrent 3–5
  history 3, 4
  investigation 4–5, *5*
  management 5
  referral letter 3
  severity 3–4
chest X-ray *5*
Chlamydia trachomatis 94
chlorambucil, teratogenicity 117
chronic back pain 32–3
  history 32
  infection 32
  investigation 33
  malignancy 32
  management 33
  osteoporosis 32–3
  referral letter 32

chronic granulomatous disease 10, **10**, 77–8
  aetiology/pathophysiology/pathology 77, *77*
  clinical presentation 77, **77**
  complications 78
  differential diagnosis 78
  disease associations 78
  epidemiology 77
  investigation 77
  management 12
  morbidity 78
  mortality 78
  prevention 78
  prevention of infection **12**
  treatment 78
ciclosporin 98
ciprofloxacin 79
circinate balanitis 96
coeliac disease 4
colchicine 100
cold agglutinin disease 23
cold fingers 23–5, 54–5
  diagnosis/prognosis 24–5, *25*
  history 23–4, *24*
  management 25
combined T-cell/B-cell defects 75–7
  aetiology/pathophysiology/ pathology 75, **75**
  clinical presentation 75–6, *76*
  complications 76
  disease associations 76
  epidemiology 75
  morbidity 76
  mortality 76
  physical signs 76
  prevention 76
  prognosis 76
  treatment 76
common cytokine receptor gamma-chain deficiency 75
common variable immunodeficiency 3, 4, 72–5
  aetiology/pathophysiology/pathology 72, *72*
  clinical presentation 72–3, *73*
  complications 74
  consequences 4
  differential diagnosis 73–4
  epidemiology 72
  infectious complications 73
  morbidity 74
  mortality 74
  non-infectious complications *74*
  physical signs 73
  prevention 74
  prognosis 74
  treatment 74
communications skill/ethics 52–8

complement
  deficiency 5, 6, 7, 127, 128
  serum concentrations 125–6
  terminal pathway deficiency *see* terminal pathway complement deficiency
confusion 64–6
'corneal melt' syndrome 36
corticosteroids
  gout 100
  idiopathic inflammatory myopathies 98
  injection 133–5
    complications 135
    contraindications 133
    indications 133
    outcome 134–5
    technique 133–4, *134*
  polyarteritis nodosa 113
  rheumatoid arthritis 93
COX-2 inhibitors 93
coxsackievirus **26**
cracker sign 10
creatine kinase 29
crepitus 41
CREST syndrome 107–8, **107**, *108*
crush fracture 69–71
cryoglobulinaemia 23
cryoglobulinaemic vasculitis 114–15
  aetiology/pathophysiology/ pathology 114
  clinical presentation 114
  complications 115
  differential diagnosis 114
  epidemiology 114
  investigations 114, *114*
  physical signs 114
  prognosis 115
  treatment 115
cryoglobulins, classification **18**
Cryptosporidium spp. 73
crystal arthritis *see* gout
Cushing's syndrome **28**
cyclophosphamide 98, 113
  teratogenicity 117
cytokine and cytokine receptor deficiencies 78–9
  aetiology/pathophysiology/pathology 78–9, *79*
  clinical presentation 79
  complications 79
  differential diagnosis 79
  disease associations 79
  epidemiology 79
  morbidity 79
  mortality 79
  physical signs 79
  prevention 79
  treatment 79
cytomegalovirus **26**, **39**

D

dactylitis 96
Darier's sign 13
depression 43
dermatomyositis 19–20, 27
diabetes mellitus **28**
diffuse cutaneous systemic sclerosis 23
digital gangrene 36, *37*
digital ischaemia *44*, 49
disability 43
discoid lupus erythematosus 20, *21*
disease-modifying antirheumatic drugs 35, 57–8, 93, **93**
diuretics, hypersensitivity **87**
dog bite 59
drug allergy 87–8, **87**
  aetiology/pathophysiology/pathology 87
  clinical presentation 87, **87**
  differential diagnosis 88
  epidemiology 87
  immunological classification **87**
  investigations 87–8
  treatment 88
drug fever **39**
drug-induced anaphylaxis 14–16
  history 15–16
  investigation 16
  management 16
  referral letter 14–15
dry eyes 25–7
  history 26–7, **26**
  investigation 27
  management 27
  referral letter 25–6
dual-energy X-ray absorptiometry (DEXA) 130
Duncan's syndrome 74
dysphagia *see* swallowing difficulties

E

echovirus *73*
eczema, and skin abscesses 9–12
electromyography 29
enteropathic arthritis 96
epinephrine 52–4
EpiPen *64*
Epstein-Barr virus **26**, **39**
erythrocyte sedimentation rate 35, 37, 40, 121, **121**
Escherichia coli 6, 11, **77**
ethambutol 79
extractable nuclear antigens 21

F

facial swelling
  acute **64**
  recurrent 7–9
factor D 6

fatigue 43
femoral nerve root involvement 31
fever 38–40
fibromuscular dysplasia **118**
fibromyalgia 28, 34, 42, 56–7, 101–3
  aetiology/pathophysiology/pathology 101–2
  clinical presentation 102
  epidemiology 102
  fatigue in 43
  investigations 102
  physical signs 102
  prognosis 103
  treatment 102–3
flushing 12–14
  differential diagnosis **13**
foot drop 35–8

G

gabapentin 32
gastric carcinoma *74*
genetic counselling 7
giant-cell arteritis 109–10
  aetiology/pathophysiology/pathology 109–10
  clinical presentation 110
  differential diagnosis 111
  epidemiology 110
  investigations 110–11, *110*
  physical signs 110
  treatment 111
Giardia spp. 3, 4, *73*
Glasgow Coma Scale 60
glomerulonephritis **18**, 36
gluten-sensitive enteropathy *74*
gold salts **93**
  hypersensitivity **87**
gonorrhoea 6
Gottron's papules *29*, 98
gout 34, 99–101
  acute 99–100
  aetiology/pathophysiology/pathology 99
  clinical presentation 99
  epidemiology 99
  investigations 100
  nephrolithiasis 100
  physical signs 100
  risk factors 68
  tophaceous *45*, 49–50, 100
  treatment 100–1
  uric acid nephropathy 100
gouty tophi 50
granuloma 72, *73*, *74*

H

haemolytic complement assays 7, *7*
Haemophilus influenzae 6, **59**, *73*
hairy oral leucoplakia 4

hands 44–5
  ankylosing spondylitis 50–1
  digital ischaemia *44*
  osteoarthritis *44*, 45–6, 90
    nodal *44*
  psoriatic arthritis 47–8
  psoriatic arthropathy 45
  rheumatoid arthritis *44*, 46–7
  systemic sclerosis 49, 109
  tophaceous gout *45*, 49–50
head injuries 6
Heberden's nodes 46, 48, 50, 90
Henoch-Schönlein purpura **17**
heparin hypersensitivity **87**
herpes 4
herpes simplex 5
hip, osteoarthritis 91
history-taking 3–71
HIV **26**
HLA-B27 **95**
hot joints 66–9
  diagnosis 67
  differential diagnosis **67**
  examination 68–9, *69*
  history 67
  infection 68
  management 69
  risk factors for gout 68
  risk factors for sepsis 67
Howell-Jolly bodies *61*, 81
hydralazine hypersensitivity **87**
hyper-IgE syndrome 10
hyper-IgM antibody deficiency *72*
hyper-IgM syndrome 3, 73
hypergryphosis 48
hypogammaglobulinaemia 4
hyposplenism 59–61, 81
  causes of **59**
  red-cell pocks *62*
  vaccination recommendations **61**
hypotension 8

I

idiopathic anaphylaxis 16
idiopathic inflammatory myopathies 98–9
  aetiology/pathophysiology/pathology 98
  clinical presentation 98
  epidemiology 98
  investigations 98
  prognosis 99
  treatment 98–9
IgE-mediated anaphylaxis **15**
IgG deposits *22*
imaging 129–32
  bone densitometry 130
  magnetic resonance imaging 131
  nuclear medicine 131–2, *132*
  plain radiology 129–30, *129*, *130*
  ultrasound 132

imatinib 85
immunisation 7
immunodeficiency 72–82, 126–9
    antibody deficiency 126, 127–8
    chest infections 3
    chronic granulomatous disease 77–8
    combined T-cell/B-cell defects 75–7
    common variable 72–5
    complement deficiency 127, 128
    cytokine and cytokine receptor deficiencies 78–9
    hyposplenism 81
    infection in **128**
    investigations 127
    phagocyte defect 126, 128–9
    secondary **127**
    skin abscesses 10
    T-lymphocyte defect 126–7, 128
    terminal pathway complement deficiency 80–1
    warning signs 3
immunoglobulin replacement 135–7
    complications 136–7
    contraindications 136
    indications 135–6, *135*
    technique 136
immunomodulation 135
infection **39**
    and chronic back pain 32
    reactive arthritis 68
inflammatory bowel disease 4, 97
infliximab 94
interferon alfa 115
interleukin-2 receptor α-chain deficiency 75
isoniazid 79

J

Jaccoud's arthropathy 103, *104*
janus kinase 3 deficiency *75*
Jo-1 antibodies 29
Job's syndrome 10
joint aspiration 68
joint pain/stiffness 16–19, 20, 33–5
    complications 35
    damage/prognosis 35
    diagnosis 35
    history 34
    investigation 34
    management 35
    referral letter 33
joint replacement 94

K

Kell antigens 78
keratoconjunctivitis sicca 27, 105
keratoderma blennorrhagica 96
Klebsiella spp. **77**

Klebsiella pneumoniae **59**
knee, osteoarthritis 91
kyphoscoliosis 52
kyphosis 96

L

lamivudine 114
laryngeal swelling **64**
leflunomide **93**
leucocyte adhesion molecule deficiency 78
Libman-Sacks endocarditis 104
limited cutaneous systemic sclerosis 23
low back pain 30–2, 55–6
    causes **31**
    chronic *see* chronic back pain
    differential diagnosis **30**
    history 30–1, *31*, **31**
    investigation 31
    management 31–2
    nerve root lesions **31**
    psychosocial 'yellow flags' 31
    red flag symptoms 30, 32
    referral letter 30
lower limbs
    dermatomes *31*
    Paget's disease of bone 51
    peripheral nerves *31*
lupus **17**, **39**
lupus band *22*
Lyme disease 20

M

McLeod's syndrome 78
magnetic resonance imaging 131
malignancy
    and chronic back pain 32
    thyroid medullary carcinoma **13**
mannan-binding ligand deficiency 81
Marfan's syndrome 51–2, *52*
mast cell hyperplasia 14
mastocytosis 84–5, *85*
    aetiology/pathophysiology/pathology 84
    clinical presentation 84
    differential diagnosis 84
    epidemiology 84
    investigation 84
    physical signs 84
    prognosis 85
    systemic 13, **13**
    treatment 84–5, *85*
meningitis, recurrent 5–7
    history 6
    immunological cause 6
    investigation 6–7
    management 7
    referral letter 5

meningococcal meningitis 5–7
menopause **13**
methotrexate **93**, 98
    teratogenicity 116
methyldopa hypersensitivity **87**
microscopic polyangiitis **39**
microstomia 49
minocycline hypersensitivity **87**
mixed cryoglobulinaemia *17*, **17**
Mollaret's aseptic meningitis 5
monoarthritis 97
mononeuritis multiplex 36, 37
mouth ulcers *22*
mumps **26**
muscle disease 29
muscle weakness **28**
myalgia 38–40
myasthenia gravis **28**
mycophenolate mofetil 115
Mycoplasma spp. 4, 73
Mycoplasma pneumoniae 73

N

nails 45
    psoriatic arthritis 48
    rheumatoid arthritis 46
    systemic sclerosis 49
nail dystrophy 48
nail-fold capillary microscopy 25, *25*
nail-fold vasculitis 46
Neisseria meningitidis 7, **59**
nephrolithiasis 100
neuromuscular blockers, anaphylaxis **15**
neutropenia 78
neutrophilia 40
nitroblue tetrazolium test 11, *12*, 77
nitrofurantoin hypersensitivity **87**
nodal osteoarthritis *44*
nodular lymphoid hyperplasia *74*
non-inflammatory arthritis 34
non-rheumatoid pain/stiffness 40–2, 45–6
NSAIDs
    anaphylaxis **15**
    gout 100
    hypersensitivity **87**
    low back pain 32
    systemic lupus erythematosus 105
nuclear medicine 131–2, *132*
nut allergy 52–4, 85–6
    aetiology/pathophysiology/pathology 85
    clinical presentation 86
    differential diagnosis 86
    epidemiology 85
    investigations 86
    prevention 86
    prognosis 86
    treatment 86

O

occlusive arterial disease 23, 24
olecranon bursae 50
oligoarthritis 97
omalizumab 86
Omenn syndrome *75*
onycholysis 48
osteoarthritis 34, 40–2, 89–91
  aetiology/pathophysiology/pathology
    89–90, **89**
  clinical presentation 90
  epidemiology 90, *90*
  hand *44*, 45–6, 90
  hip and knee 91
  history 40–1
  investigation *41*
  joint involvement **41**, *46*
  management 41–2
  physical signs 90
  referral letter 40
  treatment/prognosis 90
osteomalacia 28, **28**
osteophytes 41
osteoporosis 71
  causes 70
  and chronic back pain 32–3
  crush fracture 69–71
  diagnosis 71
  management 71
overlap syndromes 104–5, *104*

P

Paget's disease of bone 51, *52*
pain 42–3
  see also chronic back pain; low back
    pain
parotid gland enlargement **26**
parvovirus 19
peanut allergy *see* nut allergy
pectus carinatum 52
pectus excavatum 52
D-penicillamine hypersensitivity **87**
penicillins
  anaphylaxis **15**
  hypersensitivity **87**
periodontal disease 4
phagocyte defect 126, 128–9
Phalen's test 89
phenoxymethylpenicillin 7
phospholipid syndrome 105
photosensitivity 20, *21*
plasma viscosity **121**, **122**
Plasmodium spp. 59
Pneumococcus spp. 73
Pneumocystis carinii 76, *76*
Pneumocystis pneumonia 3
polyarteritis nodosa 38, **38**, 113–14
  aetiology/pathophysiology/pathology
    113

clinical presentation 113
complications 114
differential diagnosis 113, **118**
digital gangrene *37*
epidemiology 113
history 39–40
investigation 40
investigations 113, *113*
management 40
physical signs 113
prognosis 114
rash *39*
treatment 113–14
polyarthralgia *see* joint pain/stiffness
polyarthritis 97
polycythaemia rubra vera 23
polymyalgia rheumatica 5, 34, 109–10
  aetiology/pathophysiology/pathology
    109–10
  clinical presentation 110
  differential diagnosis 111
  investigations 110–11
  physical signs 110
  treatment 111
polymyositis 27
primary antibody deficiency *see* common
    variable immunodeficiency
properdin deficiency 5, 6
pseudogout 101
psoriatic arthritis 20, 34
  clinical presentation 96
  epidemiology 95
  hands 47–8
  prognosis 97
psoriatic arthropathy *45*
purine nucleoside phosphorylase
    deficiency *75*
purpuric rash 16–19, *17*

R

radiology 129–30, *129*, *130*
  diagnostic 129–30
  prognostic 130
rash 12–14
  purpuric 16–19, *17*
Raynaud's phenomenon 18, **23**, 49, 54–5,
    109
reactive arthritis
  epidemiology 95
  prognosis 97
recombinase-activating gene 1/2
    deficiency *75*
renal impairment 18
rheumatic fever 20
rheumatoid arthritis 33, 35, 91–4
  acute-phase indices 92
  aetiology 91
  blood count 92
  clinical presentation 91
  differential diagnosis **39**

epidemiology 91
foot drop and weight loss 35–8
hands *44*, 46–7, *48*
investigations 92
non-articular manifestations **47**
pathology 91, *91*
physical signs 92
prognosis 94
radiology 92
scleromalacia perforans *48*
skin rash *36*
synovial biopsy 92
treatment 92–4, **93**
rheumatoid factor 19, 35, 37, 92, 125
rheumatoid hands 44
rheumatoid vasculitis **17**
rheumatology 88–103
  calcium pyrophosphate deposition
    disease 101
  carpal tunnel syndrome 46, 47, 88–9,
    88
  fibromyalgia 28, 34, 42, 56–7, 101–3
  gout 34, 99–101
  idiopathic inflammatory myopathies
    98–9
  osteoarthritis 34, 40–2, 89–91
  rheumatoid arthritis 33, 35, 91–4
  seronegative spondyloarthropathies
    94–7
rifabutin 79
rituximab 94

S

sacroiliitis 97
Salmonella spp. 11, **77**, 94
Salmonella enteriditis **59**
sarcoidosis **26**
  differential diagnosis **39**
Schirmer's test 27, *106*
Schoeber's test *51*, 96
sciatic nerve root irritation 31
scleritis 36
sclerodactyly 49
scleroderma *see* systemic sclerosis
scleromalacia perforans *48*
sepsis, risk factors 67
septicaemia 59–61
  history 59–60
  investigation 60
  management 60
seronegative spondyloarthropathies
    94–7
  aetiology/pathophysiology/pathology
    94–5, **95**
  blood tests 96
  clinical presentation 95–6, *95*
  differential diagnosis 97
  epidemiology 95
  physical signs 96
  prognosis 97

seronegative spondyloarthropathies (*cont'd*)
  radiology 97
  treatment 97
Serratia spp. 11, **77**
severe combined immunodeficiency
    syndrome 3, 75–7
Shigella spp. 94
Sjögren's syndrome 26, **26**, 34, 105–6
  aetiology/pathology 105
  clinical presentation 105–6, *105*, *106*
  complications 106
  investigations 106
  treatment 106
skin abscess, recurrent 9–12
  family history 11
  history 10
  investigation 11
  management 11–12
  referral letter 9–10
skin rash *36*
skin testing 88
skin-prick testing 16, *83*
spinal claudication 30
spinal cord compression 55–6
splenomegaly *74*
splinter haemorrhage 36
Staphylococcus spp. 10, **10**, 11, **77**
Staphylococcus aureus 11, **59**
steroids *see* corticosteroids
Stevens-Johnson syndrome 101
Still's disease, adult onset **39**, 119–20
Streptococcus pneumoniae 6, **59**
Streptococcus suis **59**
subacute cutaneous lupus erythematosus
    20, *21*
subarachnoid space, external connection
    6, *6*
sulfasalazine **93**
swallowing difficulties 23–5, 54–5
swan-neck deformity 47, 50
synovial fluid 41, 96
syphilitic aortitis **118**
systemic lupus erythematosus 5, *20*, 34,
    64–6, 103–5
  aetiology/immunopathogenesis 103
  American College of Rheumatology
    criteria 23
  anti-double-stranded DNA antibodies
    125
  cardiovascular manifestations 104
  clinical presentation 103
  epidemiology 103
  haematological abnormalities 104
  kidney disease 104
  musculoskeletal manifestations 103, *104*
  nervous system 104
  overlap syndromes 104–5, *104*
  pulmonary manifestations 104
  skin and mucous membranes 103–4
  treatment 105

systemic rheumatoid vasculitis 35–8,
    38
  history 36–7
  nail-fold infarcts *36*
systemic sclerosis 23, 24, 49, 54–5,
    106–9
  aetiology/immunopathogenesis 106–7
  clinical presentation **107**
  diffuse cutaneous 107, *107*, **107**
  epidemiology 107
  investigations 108–9, *109*
  limited cutaneous 107–8, **107**, *108*
  prognosis 109
  treatment 109
  visceral involvement 108, *108*
  without scleroderma 108
systemic Still's disease 119–20

T

T-lymphocyte defect 126–7, **127**, 128
Takayasu's arteritis 117–19
  aetiology/pathology 117
  aortic arch angiography 117, *118*
  clinical features 117
  differential diagnosis 117, **118**
  epidemiology 117
  investigations 117–18
  prognosis 118–19
  serology 117
  treatment 118
telangiectasia 49, *108*
tenosynovitis 46
terminal pathway complement deficiency
    80–1
  aetiology/pathophysiology/pathology
    80
  clinical presentation 80
  complications 80
  differential diagnosis 80
  epidemiology 80
  investigations 80, *80*
  physical signs 80
  prevention 81
  prognosis 80
  treatment 80
thalidomide, teratogenicity 116
thenar eminence wasting 46
thiazide hypersensitivity **87**
thoracic outlet syndrome 23
thyroid medullary carcinoma **13**
thyrotoxicosis **28**
Tinel's test 89
tophaceous gout *45*, 49–50, 100
Toxoplasma spp. 76
Trichinella spiralis **28**
tryptase 82
tuberculosis **39**
tuberculous aortitis **118**
tumour necrosis factor inhibitors 94

U

ultrasound 132
Ureaplasma spp. *73*
uric acid nephropathy 100
urticaria 8, 12–14
  history 13
  investigation 14
  management 14
  referral letter 12–13
urticaria pigmentosa 13, *14*

V

vaccinations in hyposplenia **61**
vasculitides 109–20, *110*
  Behçet's disease 5, 115–17
  cryoglobulinaemic vasculitis 114–15
  giant-cell arteritis and polymyalgia
    rheumatica 109–10
  polyarteritis nodosa 38, **38**, 113–14
  systemic Still's disease 119–20
  Takayasu's arteritis 117–19
  Wegener's granulomatosis **17**, **39**, 111–13
vidarabine 114

W

Wegener's granulomatosis **17**, **39**, 111–13
  aetiology/pathophysiology/pathology
    111
  clinical presentation 111, *111*
  complications 113
  differential diagnosis 112
  epidemiology 111
  investigations 112
  physical signs 112, *112*
  prognosis 113
  treatment 112
widespread pain 42–3, 56–7
  history 42
  investigation 43
  management 43
  red flag symptoms 42
  referral letter 42

X

X-linked agammaglobulinaemia 4, *72*, 73
X-linked hyper-IgM *75*
X-linked lymphoproliferative disease 74
xerostomia 27, 105

Y

Yersinia enterocolitica 94

Z

Z-deformity of thumb 47